Birds of the
British Isles

Birds of the
British Isles

Edited by Jim Flegg

A LITTLE, BROWN BOOK

This edition published 2001
by Little, Brown and Company (UK)

This book is adapted from *Birds of the British Isles*
Material in this book previously appeared in *The Living Countryside*
Copyright © Eaglemoss Publications and Orbis Publishing

ISBN 0-316-85895-1

Production by Omnipress, Eastbourne
Printed in Singapore

Little, Brown and Company (UK) Limited
Brettenham House, Lancaster Place
London WC2E 7EN

Acknowledgements

Contributing authors John H. Barrett ·
John Burton · William Condry ·
Mike Everett · Chris Feare · Jim Flegg ·
Eric Hardy · Roger Lovegrove ·
Nigel Matthews · Chris Mead ·
Robert Morgan · Malcolm Ogilvie ·
Robert Spencer

Contents

Introducing birds

Birds are beautiful and fascinating creatures. Not the least of their appeal is that they are so numerous and widespread, and far easier for most of us to see without difficulty than, say, mammals or even butterflies. Indeed, they are so ubiquitous that they may be difficult to get away from–should we of course wish to do that, since they contribute so much to the enrichment of our lives. Birds can be found in every conceivable habitat–the golden eagle soaring over the mountain top, the curlew on the moor, the yellowhammer on the farm, the jay deep in the wood, the blackbird in the garden and the house sparrow deep in the innermost heart of the grimy city are in each case just examples of the range of birds to be seen.

Thus birdwatching has the great advantage that it can be pursued with whatever degree of vigour one wishes. Should you so desire, then an expedition can be planned to one of the remoter habitats, and even in well-inhabited areas, remote habitats still do exist within reach of 'civilisation'. But to set against the additional pleasures of breaking new ground– pitting your endurance against a hard day's walking in the hills, for example, to see unusual birds–are the many advantages of what might be considered as mundane garden birdwatching. For the housebound, or those willing to use the house as a large hide, the confiding nature of birds allows them to be watched as they go about their daily business. Even viewed from the kitchen sink their squabbles at the bird table or frantic comings and goings to the nestbox can provide hours of enjoyment. Common birds some of them may be, but in close-up their lives reveal many interesting and even surprising facets of animal behaviour.

As the seasons change, so birds change with them. Spring brings back many of the songbirds that delight us in summer wood-lands, while the onset of autumn heralds the arrival of birds from Arctic breeding grounds. Rarely are these good songsters, but often–as with geese, ducks or waders flying in masses over coastal marshes or an estuary–they are visually more spectacular and thrilling.

Watching, marvelling at the beauty of plumage, or listening to the variety of songs, inevitably leads to other things. Like many hobbies, an increasing involvement fires an increasing interest. The starting point of birdwatching is normally just bird identifica-tion–something to do to enliven a long journey or just the daily walk to school or the station. But next, you want to watch them more closely (perhaps 'studied' would be a better term), and with developing knowledge comes the desire to know more about them– how do they run their daily lives? How far does a robin or a rook commute each day? Where do our migrants go, or come from? What structural adaptations–beaks and feet for example–do they have for their way of life? How long do birds live, and what are the major threats they face? How many eggs do they lay, and how many nestlings survive to become the next generation?

The pages which follow provide answers to just these questions–and others equally fascinating–as well as giving details of plumage and other information to help identification. For, following an introductory general section on bird classification, be-haviour and biology, highly readable and comprehensive accounts are given for over 125 popular common, unusual or interesting British species. The species are grouped in four categories–birds of prey, birds of fresh water, birds of coast and estuary, and songbirds and garden birds–which allow the lifestyles of birds with similar habits or habitats to be the better compared and contrasted.

Opposite: A colony of guillemots on Herma Ness, Unst.

Britain's birds classified

Few groups of animals are so immediately recognisable as the birds, but what are the differences which separate one bird order from another?

Modern bird classification is intended not only as a 'filing system' for easy reference–it is an attempt to show the natural relationships between groups of birds. As in all systems of classification, it can be depicted as a family tree. Like all family trees, the lineage of birds can be viewed from above–from the 'twigs' down the 'branches' to the 'trunk'–or from below, starting at the trunk and following its divisions into branches and then twigs. The twigs represent the various species of birds.

Of these two views, the one from the trunk upwards would in many ways be more satisfying. For if we had sufficient information, for example from fossils, we would be able to construct a classification that was perfectly faithful to evolution. Species, genera, families and orders would be purely natural ones and the taxonomist's work would be done for ever.

Unfortunately, the fossil record is far too full of gaps for this to be remotely possible. Thus bird classification has to depend heavily on the view from the top of the tree, arrang-

Above: A fulmar in flight. White sea-birds are not all closely related to gulls: the fulmar is one of the petrels, a primitive order of birds that are distinguished by their 'tube-noses'. The other white sea-bird on British and Irish coasts that is not related to gulls is the gannet, which belongs with the cormorant and shag in the order Pelecaniformes.

Below: This black-tailed godwit, on the other hand, does not look like a gull, but belongs to the same order as the gulls, the Charadriiformes. The 16 British families in this order include the Scolopidae family of long-legged waders, to which godwits belong, and the Laridae–the gulls and terns.

ing species, genera and families for the most part by what can be examined in a specimen today.

Confusing similarities Two important features are common to all birds: feathers and a pair of wings. These structures have resulted in a number of other common features that conform to the needs of an airborne life–such as lightweight bones, a flexible neck and a streamlined body. These adaptations so dominate the appearance of birds that, as a class, they are far more uniform than other well-known classes such as insects, mammals or reptiles. It follows that the features that distinguish one order of birds from another are often relatively minor. (Species, of course, can usually be distinguished most easily by their plumage patterns.)

The problem of classification into orders is increased, however, where, during the course of evolution, widely separate groups have developed, but which show much the same characteristics. This happens when various birds have a particular activity or habitat in common. The hobby, the swift and the swallow, for example, all live by fast flight, and in each species evolution has emphasized long, sickle-shaped wings with long primary feathers to achieve great speed. Other obvious features (beak and claws) quickly remove the hobby from this trio, but it takes an examination of, for example, the feet to place the swift and the swallow into different orders. The swift has all four toes pointing forward, while the swallow has three toes forward, one back. It is this relatively obscure feature that places swallows in the vast order of perching birds, the Passeriformes, while swifts are not even closely related–they belong with the hummingbirds of the New World, in the order Apodiformes.

Besides the sickle-shaped wings, many other examples can be cited of unrelated birds which have evolved to look alike. This is known as parallel evolution. Just as puzzling, on the other hand, can be the specialist species within an otherwise relatively uniform group. A good example of this is the peculiar beak of the crossbill, a pine-cone eater, compared with the pyramid-shaped beaks of the rest of

the finch family.

The key features False clues apart, however, the majority of the features by which birds are told apart are clearly visible to the ordinary birdwatcher. For instance, the differences between the various ducks are clearly signalled – not only by the different plumage patterns but also by the detailed shape of the beak; and the same goes for the many finches. Birds of prey are distinguished from one another by their feet as well as by their colours. Bird ringers use the length and shape of the primary feathers to separate willow warblers from the similar-looking chiffchaffs, and taxonomists make wide use of the wing feathers in classification.

In certain cases taxonomists also use the skeletal anatomy, the nature of the palate, the shape of the syrinx (part of the windpipe), the layout of the intestinal loops in the gut, the length of the caecum (part of the gut) and many other internal features. Behavioural characters are sometimes used, although more attention is given to the details of physiology. In recent years, studies of blood plasma proteins, nucleic acids and egg-white proteins have joined the classical methods. In many cases the results of these exciting techniques support the established order, but in some cases they indicate that previous thinking may have been wrong.

The system unfolds If we look at the classification of birds – the class Aves – starting from the twigs of our tree, we find that there are about 8600 species of birds alive today in the world as a whole, grouped into about 170 families. Some families contain only one, or a few species, while others contain over 300.

The next level in the family tree is the order, which contains (normally) several families. Here the logic of the groupings may be more difficult for the birdwatcher, with his experience of the bird in the field, to understand. Gulls and terns, for example, which form the family Laridae, are placed by taxonomists in the order Charadriiformes. Some parts of the Charadriiformes seem to 'make sense', for its is natural to link the gulls and terns with the various wader families (oystercatchers, plovers, snipes, sandpipers and others) and with

Above: The barn owl is our only member of the family Tytonidae. All our other owls belong to the family Strigidae, placed in the owl order Strigiformes.

Right: A linnet perches beside its nest of young. The very act of perching is a clue to its membership of the vast order Passeriformes, which includes nearly half the bird species of Britain and Ireland. Although the name of this order means 'perching birds', it is easy to think of non-members that also perch – falcons, pigeons, owls and kingfishers – and of a few 'awkward' passerines that rarely perch, such as swallows and skylarks.

Below: The coot is a member of the order Gruiformes. Its fellow members in Britain and Ireland are the moorhen, the water rail and the corncrake. But the order derives its name from a Continental member, the crane (*Grus grus*).

the skuas. But the same order includes the auk family, including our razorbill, guillemot and puffin, which seem superficially to be vastly different. Another, even more unlikely, fellow member is the tropical family of the lily-trotters; these would seem more sensibly located with the other long-toed birds, such as the moorhen and water rail, which are in the order Gruiformes. Nevertheless, the members of each family placed into a particular order have sufficient features in common for taxonomists to have grouped them in this way.

Most orders contain only a handful of families, though the Charadriiformes, as we have seen, is something of an exception with its 16 families. But the greatest exception of all is the last order in the list, the Passeriformes. This is an enormous order containing about half the bird species existing at present. Its gigantic range embraces wrens, birds of paradise, New World and Old World warblers, flycatchers, thrushes, pipits, tits, starlings, crows, finches, buntings and many others – altogether some 67 families.

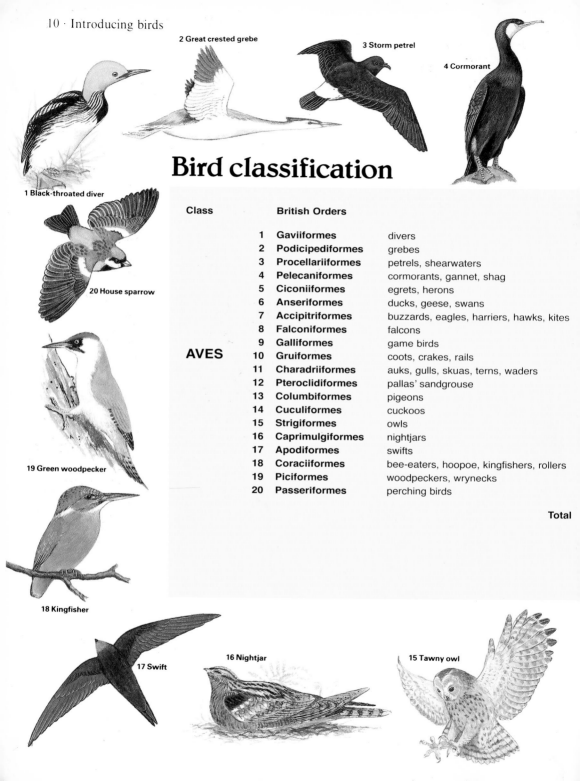

2 Great crested grebe

3 Storm petrel

4 Cormorant

1 Black-throated diver

Bird classification

20 House sparrow

Class		British Orders	
	1	Gaviiformes	divers
	2	Podicipediformes	grebes
	3	Procellariiformes	petrels, shearwaters
	4	Pelecaniformes	cormorants, gannet, shag
	5	Ciconiiformes	egrets, herons
	6	Anseriformes	ducks, geese, swans
	7	Accipitriformes	buzzards, eagles, harriers, hawks, kites
	8	Falconiformes	falcons
	9	Galliformes	game birds
AVES	10	Gruiformes	coots, crakes, rails
	11	Charadriiformes	auks, gulls, skuas, terns, waders
	12	Pteroclidiformes	pallas' sandgrouse
	13	Columbiformes	pigeons
	14	Cuculiformes	cuckoos
	15	Strigiformes	owls
	16	Caprimulgiformes	nightjars
	17	Apodiformes	swifts
	18	Coraciiformes	bee-eaters, hoopoe, kingfishers, rollers
	19	Piciformes	woodpeckers, wrynecks
	20	Passeriformes	perching birds

Total

19 Green woodpecker

18 Kingfisher

17 Swift

16 Nightjar

15 Tawny owl

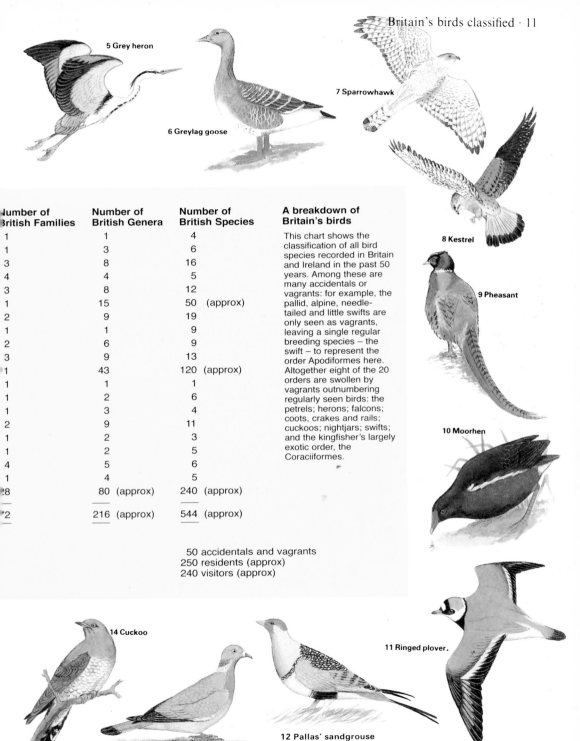

5 Grey heron

6 Greylag goose

7 Sparrowhawk

8 Kestrel

9 Pheasant

10 Moorhen

11 Ringed plover

12 Pallas' sandgrouse

13 Woodpigeon

14 Cuckoo

Number of British Families	Number of British Genera	Number of British Species
1	1	4
1	3	6
3	8	16
4	4	5
3	8	12
1	15	50 (approx)
2	9	19
1	1	9
2	6	9
3	9	13
1	43	120 (approx)
1	1	1
1	2	6
1	3	4
2	9	11
1	2	3
1	2	5
4	5	6
1	4	5
28	80 (approx)	240 (approx)
72	216 (approx)	544 (approx)

A breakdown of Britain's birds

This chart shows the classification of all bird species recorded in Britain and Ireland in the past 50 years. Among these are many accidentals or vagrants: for example, the pallid, alpine, needle-tailed and little swifts are only seen as vagrants, leaving a single regular breeding species – the swift – to represent the order Apodiformes here. Altogether eight of the 20 orders are swollen by vagrants outnumbering regularly seen birds: the petrels; herons; falcons; coots, crakes and rails; cuckoos; nightjars; swifts; and the kingfisher's largely exotic order, the Coraciiformes.

50 accidentals and vagrants
250 residents (approx)
240 visitors (approx)

Bird flight

Birds have perfected their powers of flight over aeons of evolution. The result is a series of brilliant wing designs: some that give high speed, some that allow easy control, and others that provide a useful, all-round range of flying skills.

If numbers of species are a worthwhile guide, birds – with over 8000 species that fly compared with 4000 non-flying mammal species – are arguably the most successful class of vertebrates today. Their success is due in large part to the powers of movement, and thus the wide choice of habitat, that flight allows.

How flight works The mechanical problem concerned with flight is how to lift a weight clear of the ground, keep it airborne for a practical time and propel it forwards at the same time. For this, an upward force (lift) and a forward force (propulsion) are required.

A glance at the wing cross-section of a model aircraft shows the solution to this

because they can do this at a split second's notice, escaping the ever present danger of attacking predators. Taking off requires the maximum output of propelling force (thrust) that the bird is capable of producing.

The smaller species are capable of exerting sufficient effort to lift themselves off the ground with no preliminary 'run'. Heavier birds, on the other hand, have to survive without the ability to respond to danger by an instant take-off. Large waterbirds, such as swans and the great northern diver, attain safety by spending much of their time on the open water, far away from the predators on dry land. Their take-off is so difficult that they often have to 'run' some distance across the water surface, and can only occupy stretches of water large enough to allow space for this long take-off.

To land, birds need to 'spill' the lift that their wings and tails have been providing during flight. One way to lose lift is to raise the tail, thus steering into a descent towards the landing place. To halt their flight, birds rear up in mid-air to an upright posture as

problem. Rounded and thicker at the front than at the slender 'trailing edge', shallowly convex above and concave below, this is called an aerofoil section. Move an aerofoil section forwards through the air, and it causes air to flow in such a way across its surfaces as to produce lift. The discovery of the aerofoil section enabled man to fly: birds have used it for aeons. The inner portion of a bird's wing, which is anatomically equivalent to the human forearm, has a classic aerofoil section.

The next requirement is propulsion. For this, birds rely on the beating of their wings, powered by the breast muscles (the pectorals) which are highly developed. Propulsion is provided by the outer part of the wing, from the angle (where the front edge bends) to the tip. This part is anatomically equivalent to the human hand, from wrist to fingertips. The ten or twelve long, strong feathers at the end of the wing (the flight feathers) are vitally important and merit their technical name 'primaries'.

Variable geometry The vast majority of aircraft have wings and tail securely fixed in position, and only the provision of flaps and ailerons allows their shape to be altered so that the aircraft is manoeuvrable. Some of the most sophisticated modern fighter planes are famed for their 'variable geometry' but this merely allows the wings to swing in and out from the fuselage. It is easy to see, therefore, how much more manoeuvrable birds are than aircraft, with an almost infinite variety of positions, not just of the wings and tail, but of the parts of the wings and often of the individual feathers.

Take-off and landing To complete their manoeuvrability, birds have to be able to take off and land at will. Many survive precisely

Above: Freedom of the air enables these snow geese to choose the best places for feeding and roosting. With advantages like this, birds as a class have evolved twice as many species as mammals.

Opposite: A great tit in flight, showing the outstretched primaries.

Below: A bird the size of a heron needs large wings which it flaps slowly and laboriously.

How an aerofoil works

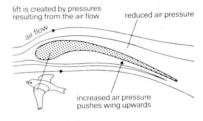

lift is created by pressures resulting from the air flow

air flow

reduced air pressure

increased air pressure pushes wing upwards

Wren 1

Greenfinch 2

Partridge 1

Robin 2

Hobby 3

Swift 3

Gannet 4

Manx
shearwater 4

Raven 5

Buzzard 5

Five types of bird flight
1 High manoeuvrability The wren can fly
neatly among dense undergrowth. The
partridge is an expert at the sudden escape
flight.
2 General purpose Robins, finches and
geese are among the many 'all-rounders'.
3 High performance Long, narrow primaries
give the swift and the hobby maximum power
with the least air resistance.
4 Gliding The gannet and the Manx
shearwater have narrow wings with a long
lift section for sea gliding.
5 Soaring The wings of the raven and the
buzzard are broad with a long lift section,
useful for catching upward air currents.

Above: Brent geese have a
'general purpose' wing
layout, but improve their
flight efficiency by means of
a cunning use of the V
pattern. The bird at the front
creates turbulence in its
wake with the beating of its
wings; this turbulence gives
extra lift to the birds flying
on either flank behind. The
lead bird is usually an old
and powerful female, who
may change places with
another as she becomes
tired. The less powerful
flyers, including youngsters,
stay in the arms of the V.

they approach the selected spot. This tilts the
wings until they are nearly in a vertical plane,
so that they can act as 'brakes', or even beat
against the direction of flight. The tail is
lowered, also acting as a brake against forward movement.

The hard impact of landing is absorbed by
flexible legs and strong muscles, which are
attached to the most rigid part of the bird's
skeleton – the pelvis, which is fused on to the
lower spine for added strength.

Many shapes of wings In the course of
evolution, families of birds have developed
the capability of flight in a number of different
ways to suit the various modes of life they
have adopted.

First, there are naturally many birds without a specialised form of flight and these have
a 'general purpose' wing layout. In this layout,
the lift and power sections of the wing are
roughly of equal length. The wing is twice as
long as it is wide. Garden birds such as the
greenfinch and the robin fit into this category.
So, too, do larger birds like geese.

If the 'general purpose' category is placed
in the middle of a range of flight styles, one
of the extremes on the scale would be 'high
manoeuvrability'. Birds in this category have
wings with lift and power sections of equal
length, but the wing is much rounder in
appearance, rather than long, for it is almost
as broad at its base as it is long from base to
tip. Examples include the game birds, which
need fast and almost vertical take-off to
escape predators, and birds of thick cover,
such as the tiny wren. This wing pattern
provides strong propulsion, but the high
manoeuvrability results from the broad wing
area.

The other extreme consists of the birds
that specialise in extra-efficient flight. Among
these species, flight is developed to the
highest standards of performance. For maximum speed, their wings do not have the same
proportions as those of the other categories
of birds. The power section of the wing (the
primary feathers) is much longer than the
lift section – in some cases by as much as a
factor of four – and the wing is long and thin.

Exploiting wind power

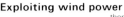

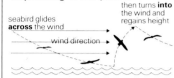

seabird glides **across** the wind

then turns **into** the wind and regains height

wind direction

The seabird takes a shallow downward glide across the wind, then turns into the wind and climbs steeply, until it resumes gliding in its original direction. It thus uses relative wind speeds to power both the climb and control the long, downward glide over the ocean.

air current deflected upwards by hill

Upward air currents are used by ravens, eagles and buzzards. Typical soaring flight is in a slow, circling climb. The birds also exploit thermals, which are upward currents created when the sun's warmth causes air to rise.

Above: The black primaries of the gannet clearly show the proportions of the wing layout: the white lift section is longer, a good gliding characteristic.

Left: A female golden eagle soars effortlessly. The primary feathers are spread out to obtain maximum advantage from rising air currents; they are also specially shaped to reduce turbulence, helping the eagle to gain speed when gliding downwards, after soaring to its peak.

The swift is an excellent example.

Two ways of gliding Gliding (in the case of birds) is flying without flapping wings. Two groups of birds are adapted for this type of flight: those that use wind power to travel over the sea (gliding in the common sense of the word) and those that not only glide but also exploit rising air currents to gain height (soaring).

The 'gliding' birds have extremely long and narrow wings, with a lift section either as long as the power section or longer. Most of them are oceanic birds, best exemplified by the albatrosses of the southern hemisphere but represented in British waters by the fulmar, the gannet and the Manx shearwater.

The 'soaring' birds use upcurrents at a ridge of hills or, in warm conditions, columns of rising air called thermals. In warmer countries these currents are the province of the vultures, but in Britain and Ireland the best examples of soaring flight are given by the raven, the buzzard and the golden eagle.

These birds are quite different in silhouette from the seagoing gliders: they too have a lift section as long as the power section or else even longer, but their wings are much broader. Further, the wingtips, rather than being pointed, have a broadly splayed 'fingered' appearance which helps to reduce turbulence. The birds flap slowly and laboriously into the air in wide circles, but once they catch the rising air they soar effortlessly.

Rowing through the air

1 On the downstroke (above) the wings move forward and then, at the bottom of the stroke, push backwards. The feathers are held firmly together, presenting a flat, blade-like surface.
2 On the upstroke (right) the primary feathers twist, like the vanes of a Venetian blind, and thus open a slight space allowing air through; this reduces air resistance to the upstroke.

Territoriality

Several kinds of territory and territorial behaviour can be observed in the birds of Britain and Ireland, forming an exciting aspect of bird study.

Above: A scene on the Grassholm gannetry, Wales. These are non-breeding birds that do not hold territories, but occupy a small area on the edge of the colony known as a 'club'. They include adults who have failed to secure a territory as well as immature birds such as the mottled sub-adult at the centre.

A territory is a defended area: in discussing territories, the use of the word defence implies that someone will take your territory from you if you do not adequately defend it. Experiments with many species of birds have shown that there is indeed constant pressure on territories: when researchers captured and removed the territory holders, new occupants of the same species quickly replaced them, often in hours rather than days.

Social behaviour in birds contrasts with territoriality, for sociality involves flocking, colonial breeding or the common ownership or use of a particular area. However, sociality and territoriality can be combined in the same species in various ways. For example, in the crow, pairs of breeding birds occupy territories, while non-breeding crows live in a flock nearby, often in an area that is unsuitable for breeding due to a shortage of nest sites. Should a crow territory fall vacant, it is quickly occupied by one of the members of the flock.

Territorial song With such pressure on territory holders, it is essential that they devote as much time as possible to securing their hold on their own plots. However, in many situations it is not possible for a territory holder to see all of his boundary from one vantage point, and he cannot therefore be on hand to see and drive away any marauder. Furthermore, it would take up far too much of his time and energy if he attempted to patrol the boundary with the constancy needed to keep out intruders. In fact, such constant vigilance is rendered unnecessary by a form of communication that works over long distances—song.

Song has several functions, of which mate attraction is perhaps the most obvious. But in an experiment where male great tits were

Below: The nesting colony at Grassholm. The nest sites are densely packed and vigorously defended, making a regular pattern.

removed, their territories were kept free of intruders for some time by playing tape recordings of great tit song over loudspeakers.

In other birds, the posture of the territory owner may be sufficient to signal to a potential settler that an area is already occupied. For example, starlings adopt a characteristic posture while singing, with the wings held slightly away from the body, the feathers of the crown and throat puffed out and the tail directed downwards, giving a 'hunch-backed' appearance. Starlings often adopt this posture while not singing, but while perched on an exposed song post within easy view of any bird looking for a territory.

At first sight, it appears strange that a bird looking for a place to settle should be deterred by a bird that is simply singing or displaying. When this system fails, however, and the intruder does try to stake a claim, the home-owner almost always wins the ensuing contests, whether these consist of threatening displays or physical combat.

It is not entirely clear why a male is usually victorious on his own territory. It may be because of his superior knowledge of the terrain. Whatever the advantage, the presence of a bird advertising that he is the landowner is often sufficient indication to an intruder that if he does attempt to settle, he will use up valuable time and energy in a conflict that he is unlikely to win.

Kinds of territory The kind of territory with

Above: Starlings going to roost at sunset. The birds live in flocks all year round, sometimes joining together in vast communities. The area over which the flock ranges in search of food is known as the home range. Since the birds nest in holes, which are naturally some distance apart, their breeding colonies have to be spread out over a large area. For this reason, starling colonies are not as obvious to view as those of rooks or seabirds.

Left: Part of a rookery, in tall trees by a motorway.

Below: The territorial song of the cock robin can be heard clearly all round his territory. This spares him a lot of the work of patrolling the boundary.

which most people are familiar is that of the garden blackbird. In this type, a breeding pair defends a plot of land of around one fifth of a hectare ($\frac{1}{2}$ acre) against other blackbirds. Within this territory, the pair feed and build their nest.

Breeding pairs of robins also vigorously defend a territory in the breeding season but, unlike blackbirds, robins become aggressively territorial again in the autumn. Now, however, males and females defend separate territories in which each individual feeds, and these autumn territories are smaller than those held by pairs in the spring.

Starlings and rooks, on the other hand, are far more social than robins and blackbirds. They stay in flocks during the breeding season, just as they flock at other times of year. It is readily apparent, from looking at a rookery, that rooks are social while nesting. The same applies to starlings, although their requirement for holes as nest sites leads to a somewhat greater dispersal of nests and their coloniality is less readily visible. Sociality has its limits, however, and around the nest

both species drive off intruders. In these species, the territory is therefore restricted to a small area around the nest. The birds are content to share their feeding grounds, and do not even defend them against birds of their own species from neighbouring colonies.

The area over which the breeding rooks and starlings travel in search of food is thus not a defended territory, and is known as a home range. A tiny nesting territory and an even larger home range, sometimes extending 100km (60 miles) from the nest, is typical of many seabirds, such as the gannet, kittiwake and guillemot. In the case of the guillemot, the defended area is limited to a small length of cliff ledge around the egg or chick, so that each narrow ledge looks from a distance like a line of black and white birds.

Territories with no nests In the breeding territories mentioned so far, the nest site has been a vital component. While this is the case for most British birds, there are exceptions. When shelduck return to their breeding grounds from the moulting areas to which

Above: This scene on a great tit territory illustrates two display postures at the same time. The male (on top of the stump) is displaying to his own mate, but in many species a similar posture is used in defence of a territory. Vanquished males adopt postures rather like the submission posture of his mate, with bowed head and trailing wings.

Below: Robins defend territories in winter as well as spring, as the two photographs clearly show. On the left, a territory holder confronts a stuffed robin that has been placed on his 'patch'. On the right, he triumphs over the intruder, of whom little can be seen but the upturned wooden base.

they migrate in autumn, they spend much of the winter in flocks. In late winter, however, they form pairs. These pairs are territorial and defend feeding sites on the muddy banks of estuaries.

The ownership of a territory is, as in other species, essential for breeding: but shelduck do not breed on their territory. They breed under cover of thick vegetation, or use rabbit burrows in dunes and sea walls, some distance from the feeding territory. During incubation, the feeding territory remains the centre of activity for the non-incubating male, and his mate leaves the nest about four times each day to feed on the territory.

In the case of ruff and black grouse, a small and vigorously defended territory is used neither for nesting nor for feeding, but only for display. Such display territories, or leks, are used by those males that have been able to obtain one in complex ritualised displays which become more and more intense when females are around. The females are attracted to the display territories by the activity of the males, and visit the territories to mate. The lekking area is generally on an open piece of ground, and while 20 or more males hold territories there, the females are attracted to some males more than others. As a result, most copulations are achieved by relatively few of the males. Presumably this polygamous mating system selects the 'best quality' males (a form of natural selection) to father the next generation.

Pied wagtails in winter Like the robin in autumn, some pied wagtails occupy individual territories in winter. These are simply feeding territories, and the occupation of one of these depends both on the individual's status and on how much food is available. Where food is predictably plentiful, high-ranking individual birds hold territories. A juvenile pied wagtail may be allowed to feed within the territory, and when it does it helps in territorial defence. Where food supplies are more transient or scarce, pied wagtails feed in flocks. Should the 'dependable' food supply fail, as when a river bank freezes, then the territory-holders vacate their plots. and join the flocks.

Types of territory

Birds are either solitary or communal nesters. Breeding territories vary from relatively large (eg blackbird) to very small (eg gannet). Similarly birds feed either alone or in flocks. Some solitary feeders (eg shelduck) defend feeding territories, while flocking birds use undefended areas. Pied wagtails are unusual because in winter they feed either in defended territories or in flocks, depending on conditions. The most unusual type is the lek territory (eg ruff): this is used for neither nesting nor feeding, but purely for display and mating.

- ● nest site
- defended breeding territory
- defended feeding territory
- defended display territory
- home range (non-defended area used for feeding)

Blackbird

Robin

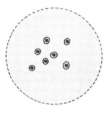

Starling

Rook

river

Shelduck

Ruff

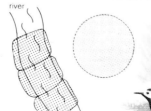river

Pied wagtail in winter

Breeding strategies

Birds have an intriguing variety
of egg colours, laying times,
clutch sizes and nest designs,
arising from the endless search
for ways to ensure survival
of the young.

A long way back in time, perhaps over 140
million years ago, the fossil record shows
that the first truly bird-like creatures developed as an offshoot of the reptiles. Unlike
mammals, birds continue to use the reptiles'
method of reproduction the fertilised ovum
developing inside an egg that is incubated
outside the body of the adult until it is ready
to hatch.

It is not easy to assess whether laying eggs
is a better or worse method of reproduction
than the mammalian system, in which the
young develop inside the mother until birth.
Each method has shown its advantages and
disadvantages, and as the 'egg method' has
endured for over 100 million years, it must

be regarded as a success in evolutionary
terms.

Eggs of all shades One striking feature of
eggs is their intriguing range of colours and
markings. Often it seems easy to attribute
some advantage to the colouring the black-
speckled, sand-coloured eggs of terns or of
the ringed plover, for example, are ideally
camouflaged, for these birds nest on sand,
among fragments of seaweed or on shingle
beaches. The eggs of hole-nesting birds such
as stock doves, woodpeckers and owls, are
generally white: no doubt this helps the incubating bird to locate the eggs in the dark
nest, and so avoid trampling on them. In
addition, it seems natural that eggs so well

Above: An exceptionally
large clutch of mallard eggs—
the normal clutch has seven
to eleven eggs. Large
clutches help to compensate
for losses caused by
predators.

Opposite: A pair of
bullfinches with their young.
Both parents share in the
task of feeding.

Below: A pair of reed
warblers engaged in
courtship feeding: this
builds up the female's body
reserves in preparation for
breeding.

hidden need no colour camouflage. Birds that nest in crowded colonies need to recognise their own eggs, and this may be the explanation for the wide variety of ground shades (the basic colour of the egg) and black squiggles found on the eggs of guillemots in their cliff-ledge colonies.

There are, however, unexplained anomalies. For instance, each egg in every clutch laid by the red-backed shrike is a different colour: this has made them so attractive to egg collectors, from Victorian times to the present day, that the species has been plundered almost to extinction in England. Another anomaly is the dunnock: few birds are so well camouflaged as this species, its colours matching the undergrowth in which its nest is built. But once the sitting bird has flown what could be more glaringly conspicuous than the clutch of bright sky-blue eggs? Quite the opposite of being camouflaged, these must be positively eye-catching to predators such as jays and magpies.

Feeding for fitness For many birds, breeding success must depend heavily on the good physical condition of the pair. The whole breeding cycle must occur during a period when plenty of food is available. Well before the time for laying, the male needs plenty of food to give him the strength to perform his lively song and active display in order to attract a mate. He also needs all his strength to establish and hold a territory against rival claims.

The female must also get into first-class condition for the hardships of the breeding season. Courtship feeding, in which the male fetches caterpillars or other delicacies for his mate, has true practical importance: producing eggs requires a great deal of energy, and the female needs every scrap of food she can get. The female blue tit, for example, stores up so much food in her body that she increases in weight by half as much again during the fortnight before egg laying begins.

Nests of many kinds One advantage of laying eggs is that the mother does not have to carry heavy young within her body. But it gives rise to more problems in turn. First, eggs are fragile and need protection from break-

age. Secondly, they need correctly controlled warmth and insulation from the harshness of the weather. Besides this, the eggs, and in most cases the young, are static and may be vulnerable to a number of specialist or opportunist nest predators. Birds have derived solutions to all these problems from a single feature – the nest.

The simplest 'nests' are merely places where one or more eggs are laid directly on to the ground. The eggs may be protected by their own camouflage or by the sheer inaccessibility of the nest site – a cliff ledge for example. In some waders and many ducks and gulls, the art of nest building is a little more elaborate: nearby vegetation is gathered into a heap to help insulate the eggs and offer some protection against change in the water level. The grebes have a subtle variation of this method: their nests are 'rafts' of vegetation that float on the water, rising and falling with the water level, and moored in place with pliable stems of long foliage.

The cup-shaped nest built by most small and medium-sized birds offers protection in a variety of ways. The eggs naturally cluster

Left: Cuckoos practise a form of parasitism in their unique method of breeding. They do not build nests or look after their young, but lay their eggs into other birds' nests. The young cuckoo hatches first and ejects its potential 'brothers and sisters' from the nest. Here a dunnock is seen looking after a young cuckoo, thinking it is its own offspring. The commonest hosts are meadow pipits, dunnocks and reed warblers.

Opposite: Another unusual breeding method is practised by the short-eared owl: the owl lays its eggs at intervals of two days or more, and starts to incubate as soon as the first egg is laid. The eggs hatch at similar intervals, so that in a clutch of seven there may be a two-week difference in age between the oldest and the youngest chick. There is some flexibility in the size of the owl's brood, although it is achieved in a manner that we find distasteful: should the food supply diminish, the oldest may eat the youngest, and so on, until the family is reduced to a more viable size.

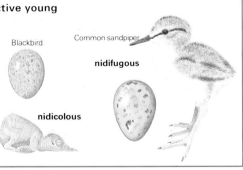

The helpless and the active young

Nidicolous (nest-loving) species of birds hatch naked, blind and helpless: these include most songbirds and some of the larger species, such as eagles.
Nidifugous (nest-fleeing) species hatch with eyes open and a covering of down, and can soon run and feed themselves; these include ducks, gulls and waders.

Blackbird

Common sandpiper

nidifugous

nidicolous

of a particular food supply. This bird has a highly specialised feeding technique, for it lives on the seeds of pine and other cone-bearing trees. These may mature at almost any time of year, and the crossbill is able to adjust its breeding time to coincide with the supply, so it is possible to see crossbills sitting on eggs in winter.

The nesting brood The nestling stage is a time of considerable risk. The young are noisy and inexperienced, and may easily draw the attention of a predator. Parent birds have to spend almost all the daylight hours in ceaseless attempts to keep the young well-fed. In consequence the young are vulnerable to cold weather, heavy rain or hailstorms.

Birds clearly take great pains through spring and summer, and the young have to undergo many hazards before the lucky few that survive fly away and join the adult population. Many eggs and young are lost in the process, so the breeding patterns may seem highly wasteful; but their success can be judged by the variety and the numbers of birds that surround us in their many different habitats.

together in the base of the cup, where they are well insulated from cold and partly hidden from the eyes of predators.

Even better protection from prying eyes is given by domed nests, more complex structures made by small birds such as wrens and long-tailed tits. Tree holes also give good all-round protection, and are used as nesting sites by many species of birds, including owls, woodpeckers and pied flycatchers. Wheatears are well concealed in their nests in cavities among rocks and in walls, as are puffins in their underground burrows.

Timing it right In the course of evolution, a number of patterns of breeding have arisen that specifically take advantage of certain circumstances. The blue tit and great tit populations in Britain are a case in point. The majority of these birds depend on winter moth caterpillars as a supply of food for their young. These caterpillars occur in enormous numbers, but only for a month or so in early summer. To take the best advantage of this annual event, the blue tit or great tit lays its eggs all in one clutch, between 5 and 16 in number. Laying is timed precisely so that the young will hatch and grow to their most demanding size when the caterpillars are fully grown.

In contrast to this, almost a literal case of 'all eggs in one basket', the majority of small and medium-sized garden birds produce two or three clutches, and may even lay more in a good summer. Their clutches are smaller, with only four to six eggs. This method allows them to exploit a moderate food supply throughout the summer, rather than a short-lived glut in June.

The crossbill has a variable breeding time which, like that of the tits, is linked to the time

Above: A ringed plover's nest, superbly camouflaged on the shingle—so well that you may not notice it even when you know it's there! This nest is no more than a place where eggs are laid directly on to the ground, but in some of these 'scrapes' the ringed plover may make a scant lining with a few strands of seaweed or other plants.

Right: The chaffinch conceals its eggs and brood within an elaborately constructed nest. The lichens that it uses to make the outer layers of the nest may also camouflage the nest if it is built on a branch that is also lichen-covered.

Nest sites

A bird's nest can be just a scrape in the ground or an intricately woven cup, but it must protect eggs and shelter young from predators and bad weather.

Nests are the places where birds lay their eggs. But nests are not exclusive to birds: reptiles, fish, various insects, worms and other animals all make structures called nests. All these creatures make a nest for one good reason—to protect its contents. Eggs are fragile and need protection from breakage; they need warmth to develop and must not be exposed to bad weather; the eggs (and the young emerging from them) are particularly vulnerable to predators and must be guarded by the nest's construction and concealment.

Although a bird's nest always contains the eggs, it may not always house the developing young. Most small song birds, and some larger birds such as crows, owls and birds of prey, hatch out naked, blind and helpless and remain in the nest until they are ready to fly. Ducks and waders, on the other hand, hatch with their eyes open, with a covering of down and well-developed legs, and can scamper about or swim as soon as they have dried off.

Early in spring, or even during winter with larger birds, the male establishes his territory. Usually, within that territory there will be a number of suitable nest sites. With some birds, like the wren, the male does the bulk of the construction work on several nests, before the pair finally settles on one and puts the finishing touches to it. In the same way, the male lapwing will make several scrapes (by shuffling his feet and belly to produce a

Above: The eggs of the oystercatcher—perfectly camouflaged against the pebbles on the beach—need no extra protection.

Opposite: The Slavonian grebe builds a floating raft of vegetation on which it lays its eggs—well away from predators.

Below: Nest and eggs of a red grouse; the long grass helps to hide the nest, but the eggs are protected mainly by the camouflage coloration of the hen.

saucer-shaped depression in the soil) before the final site is selected and a dried grass lining added.

With many other birds, it seems that the female plays the major role in selecting the actual site, and subsequently in building the nest. The male, however, does not idly watch his female dash back and forth with beakfuls of nesting material. He still has the vital job of guarding the territory, which demands continual alertness. The biological complexities of the breeding season become apparent: both birds must get themselves into the peak of condition—which means long hours of feeding—but at the same time territory must be secured and patrolled *and* the nest built.

Ground nests The simplest nests are those where the eggs are laid on the ground. Often, in such circumstances, protection from predators comes with the site; for example, guillemots nest on inaccessible sea cliff ledges. For others, such as the oystercatcher or ringed plover, birds which nest on a beach, the camouflage colours of the eggs provide the necessary concealment. Many wader nests look very simple—just scrapes in the ground—but they are in fact structured and in some cases ornamented; one nest contained over 1000 small pebbles, as well as twigs and pieces of shell.

Other waders, ducks and gulls make nests which are a further development of the simple

The basic structure of cup nests is the same, even when the size varies from the few centimeters in diameter of finches' nests to the one metre or more of those made by the heron and golden eagle. An outer framework of stout grasses, small roots, twigs or branches is lodged in a suitable tree fork or similar place. Gradually smaller and more flexible materials are tucked and woven into this structure, until the central cup is ready for lining. This nest is typical of the majority of perching birds – called passerines – which includes most small birds of farm, wood and garden. Where such birds extend their breeding range high up mountains or well to the north where there are few trees, similar nests are built on or close to the ground.

Domed nests are elaborations of the cup nest; additional protection is given by roofing over the structure and making a side entrance. Willow warblers build low-level grass nests of this type, while magpies construct high level, much bulkier versions. The most attractive examples are the long-tailed tits' cobweb-and-lichen, flask-shaped nests which are amazingly flexible to accommodate the

ground type. They gather dead vegetation, flotsam and jetsam into a mound and make a depression at its centre. The structures made by ducks and waders are usually at a low level, but the black-headed gull makes a built-up nest on the flat terrain of estuarine saltmarshes or moorland bogs, where the water level may rise suddenly and inundate low-lying eggs.

Game birds are also ground nesters and lay their eggs in grass-lined hollows. The hen protects her clutch from predators by her own camouflage colouring and will not budge from the nest unless it is absolutely necessary. Game birds do not have a strong scent, so predators like foxes find it hard to detect a red grouse or ptarmigan hen on a nest.

The floating nest is the next logical development. The little grebe's nest, loosely anchored to nearby vegetation, can rise and fall with the floodwaters and naturally survives far better than those of the coot or moorhen, which are fixed firmly in the reeds or on a low-hanging bough. For specialist swimmers like the grebes, which have legs set well back on a torpedo-shaped body, walking is awkward; floating nests are easier to get on and off.

Cup nests The cup is a practical shape for many purposes: the eggs cluster naturally in the bottom safe from disturbance and, if the nest is well constructed, safe too from the eyes of prying predators. Often the cup is lined with dried mud, fine grasses, moss, fur or feathers, which provide excellent insulation for the eggs; this also enables the incubating female to slip off occasionally to eat or drink. This insulation becomes more important when she has to help gather food for the young.

Above: Song thrush with young on nest. The cup shape of the nest stops the eggs rolling out and keeps the chicks safely in.

Right: Up to 12 chicks can be stuffed into the tiny, stifling, dome-shaped nest of the long-tailed tit. The nest is built of moss and cobwebs and is lined with countless feathers.

Nest boxes in the garden

One of the major problems for birdwatchers who wish to observe nesting behaviour is that birds try to make their nests as inconspicuous as possible. A nest box in your own garden gives you the opportunity to watch nesting birds at close quarters and in comfort. You can buy or make suitable boxes, or even put out an old kettle or an oil can.

Position the box high enough up a tree or the side of a house or shed so it is well out of reach of marauding cats (or children), but so that you still have a clear view. Make sure the box is not in direct sunlight or beating rain – you don't want the nestlings to overheat or drown. If you want to put up several boxes, position them at least 18m (60ft) apart, so different families do not disturb each other.

Once the box is in position, watch carefully to see which species of birds take an interest in it, and what nesting materials they use. The birds do not usually object if you want to look inside the box to check progress, but don't disturb a female sitting on eggs; watch for her to leave, then look but don't touch.

growing brood, and the better known dried leaf constructions of the wren. The male wren may build in any sort of crevice, from a tangle of ivy to an old jacket pocket in the garden shed.

Cavity nests Several birds, notably the owls, jackdaw and stock dove, nest in natural or man-made cavities such as hollow trees and church belfries. The house sparrow is a notable exploiter of cavities in buildings (although fully capable of building an untidy, domed nest outdoors). You might think these nests would be safer than other types, but this is not the case. The tit family are cavity nesters, but are vulnerable to attack from mice, woodpeckers and weasels.

Right: Suspended securely between reeds, the nest of the reed warbler is well hidden from predators and is so shaped that the eggs will not fall out even though the reeds sway in the wind.

Below: The great spotted woodpecker uses its strong beak like a hammer and chisel to excavate a nest hole high up the trunk of a tree where few predators will venture.

Other species, such as the woodpeckers, kingfisher and sand martin, excavate their own cavities in wood or the soil. Woodpeckers, which make a speciality of hammering and chiselling out nest cavities in tree trunks, are equipped with an extra pad of cartilage tissue situated just between the end of the beak and the nasal bone that acts as a shock-absorber, preventing the birds from developing a splitting headache.

Soil excavation is done with the feet and (sometimes) the beak. In sandy soils, some species produce metre-long tunnels ending in a nest chamber. The Manx shearwater and puffin – both seabirds – are also tunnel nesters. Both use natural rock crevices or oust rabbits from burrows in the cliff-top turf.

Suspended nests Perhaps the most sophisticated nests of all are the suspended ones. In the British Isles, the best examples are the woven mossy hammock nest of the tiny goldcrest and the basketwork nest of the reed warbler which incorporates supporting reed stems. This structure must withstand not only the movement of the reeds in high winds, but also (as the reed warbler is a common foster parent) the massive weight of a young cuckoo.

Exceptions to the rule In general terms it is possible to group nest types and relate them broadly to groups of birds and their habitats; but there are always exceptions. One example is the woodcock, which is a wader and would therefore be expected to nest on the seashore or in swampy moors and marshes; in fact it scrapes its nest on the ground in deep woodland. Another exception is the goldeneye – a duck, and therefore likely to nest on the ground beside water – which actually nests in holes in trees, often high above the ground.

Types of eggs

Eggs come in a splendid variety of shapes, sizes, colours, markings and clutch numbers—each adapted to meet specific survival needs. Egg-laying and incubation are equally varied.

Over the years collectors have stored the shells of eggs in cabinets for their marvellously varied colours. For some years now this activity has been illegal for almost all species. Despite this, undercover egg-collecting still continues, which is all the more tragic when you consider the fascination that the live egg offers.

Development of the shell During the egg's time in the female's oviduct a watery jelly egg-white (albumen) is deposited around the yolk. The albumen is itself surrounded by two soft, but relatively strong membranes, and finally by successive thin layers of a chalky (calcareous) deposit. These harden to form the protective shell. The two membranes both lie very close to the shell except at its broadest end where an air pocket, from which the hatching chick will eventually draw its first breaths, separates them.

The hard, porous shell is designed to protect the egg's contents from injury; the pores allow the passage of air for the developing embryo, but prevent the intrusion of water and other liquids, as well as the evaporation of the egg's liquid contents.

Egg-laying intervals Unevenly shaped eggs are often laid broad-end first, however painful that may seem; but evidence suggests that some birds lay theirs pointed-end first. Birds of many species lay eggs at daily intervals, usually early in the morning, until the final complement of eggs in the nest (clutch) is complete. In these cases incubation of the eggs by the parent begins when all, or almost all the eggs are laid. The result is that the nestlings are roughly the same size when they hatch, and are able to compete on equal terms with each other for the food brought by their parents, which is normally in plentiful supply.

However, some birds at the top of food pyramids, such as the tawny owl (see page 52), the kestrel (see page 50) and the heron lay their eggs at two day intervals, or even longer, and may begin incubation as soon as the first or second egg is laid. So, when all the young have hatched they are of unequal age and size. The apparent reason for this is that the birds have adapted their egg-laying to a variable and uncertain food supply.

In breeding seasons when there is a food shortage, only the oldest nestlings are strong enough to secure a sufficient share of the available food to fledge successfully, and the youngest die. If they were all the same size in times of food scarcity, then all would be in danger either of starving, or fledging in too weak a condition to survive the hazardous first few months of life on their own. In seasons when food is abundant, all the nestlings may fledge successfully. Conversely, if there is a dramatic drop in the food supply the parent bird may not breed at all.

How birds incubate The female, together with the male in some species, incubates the eggs by sitting on them and warming them with its body heat. This stimulates the embryo to grow. Many species have a feather-free area under their bodies, known as a brood patch. This patch allows the eggs direct contact with bare skin through which the incubating bird transfers heat from well-developed blood vessels. In those birds where incubation is shared by the sexes, such as the avocet (see page 124), the males may also have brood patches. Other species, including the gannet, use their fleshy feet to incubate eggs and therefore lack brood patches.

Incubation periods vary considerably according to the species. It takes 10 to 14 days for the eggs of most perching birds (passerines) to hatch, but rooks and other crows, for instance, take up to 19 days. Herons, ducks,

Many waders, such as the avocet and the lapwing (above), lay relatively large, pear-shaped eggs which do not roll away from the nest on the ground when left unattended. Usually four eggs are laid. The incubating parent arranges them so that the pointed ends are turned to the middle of the nest; this makes it easier to sit on them, and even less likely that they will roll away. Notice the 'egg-tooth' on the chick: this is a small extension on the upper bill which the developing bird uses to break out of the egg. It falls off shortly afterwards.

Opposite: A black-headed gull incubating its clutch of eggs.

auks and some birds of prey take 25 days, while gannets take 40 days, and petrels, including the fulmar and Manx shearwater, incubate for as long as 50 days.

You can sometimes spot an incubating bird turning the eggs: such behaviour is believed to ensure that the eggs receive an even amount of warmth; they are also positioned to make it easy for the young birds to hatch.

On the whole, those young birds which are most developed on hatching belong to species which have fairly long incubation periods. Thus newly hatched ducklings are active, covered in down and able to feed themselves right away; while passerine nestlings, which hatch after relatively short periods of incubation, are naked, blind, utterly helpless and entirely dependent upon their parents for food.

Emergence from the egg Whether the chicks inside the egg are downy or naked, they escape from the egg-shell either by chipping out a small hole or a line of weakness in it (depending upon the species) with an 'egg-tooth' – a small protruberance on the upper mandible which falls off afterwards. The break-out is completed by a series of convulsive stretching movements. The broken egg-shells, which could attract the unwelcome attention of predators, are then usually removed by the parents and dropped at a safe distance.

Clutch-sizes It is difficult to discover precisely what factors determine the characteristic clutch-sizes of different species. In those species whose young are hatched in a helpless condition and have to be fed by the parents, not only to the point of fledging but for some time afterwards, it seems obvious that the time and energy available for collecting sufficient food is crucial. Thus within these limits the parents rear the largest number of young for which they can provide adequate food, and the clutch-size has become adjusted accordingly. This is borne out by the fact that within particular species clutch-size tends to increase the further north the birds are because there are more daylight hours for the birds to collect food.

In some species with helpless young, such as tits and short-eared owls, the clutch-size

Above: The large, elongated pear-shaped egg of the guillemot would be easily blown off the bare cliff ledge on which it is laid – were it not for its shape, which causes it to roll round in a tight circle on its axis.
Right: Grebes often cover their white eggs with decaying waterweed and this, together with the mud, stains them brown. So on shallow flats, where the eggs are exposed to view in the open nest, some camouflage is achieved.

Development within the egg

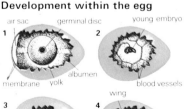

air sac · germinal disc · young embryo
1 · 2
membrane · yolk · albumen · blood vessels
wing
3 · 4
eye · developing chick · well-developed chick · leg

When freshly laid (1) the fertilised egg of a grey partridge (left) has already begun to develop. By the third day (2) the main blood vessels are visible. A week later the network of blood vessels is advanced (3) and the chick's eyes and legs are evident. Close to hatching (4) the chick begins to twist round. Right: The little tern is conspicuous against its open sandy nest, so it leaves its well-camouflaged eggs to avoid the gaze of predators.

can nevertheless vary from year to year, or location to location, according to fluctuations in their chief sources of food. Birds such as ducks and game-birds, whose offspring are more or less capable of fending for themselves on hatching, often lay very large clutches because the parents do not have to collect food for them. Of course, the ability of a sitting bird to cover the eggs in its nest comfortably is, in itself, an additional limiting factor, and probably influences egg-size too. It could also have something to do with the bird knowing when it has laid enough eggs; though precisely how it knows when to stop is not yet understood. Certainly more eggs are produced within the female's ovary than are required, but they are re-absorbed once the requisite clutch has been laid.

Eggs that suit the nest Birds' eggs vary in shape between the species as well as in size. The egg-shape is generally related to the type of nest or nest-site. The guillemot's eggs are pear shaped, an adaptation which prevents them falling off their precarious cliff ledge and smashing hundreds of feet below. The pear-shaped eggs of waders, and other birds which nest in a scrape in the ground, helps prevent them rolling away if left unguarded. The eggs of those birds which build cup-shaped nests, such as many song birds, or nest in holes or similar secure places, such as puffins, are often oval or spherical in shape as they are in no danger of rolling away.

Colours, spots and blotches The first birds' eggs were white like those of their distant reptilian ancestors, and many birds today still lay white eggs – the petrels, ducks, owls and woodpeckers in particular. In those species which nest in holes or burrows the white eggs are more easily seen in the darkness by the incubating bird and thus less likely to be broken.

Coloration (pigmentation) appears to have evolved in response to a need to protect the eggs from the prying eyes of predators. The pigments are deposited during the later stages of the formation of the shell in the oviduct. While basically similar, tints and markings show a good deal of individual variation both within the species and between eggs laid by the same female.

The eggs of species which lay in open nests or scrapes on the ground are marvellously and effectively camouflaged. Sometimes, as in the little tern for instance, they are almost indistinguishable from their surroundings. It may be difficult to understand what protection is achieved by the brightly coloured and conspicuously marked eggs of some song-birds, such as the song thrush or yellowhammer; but here it seems that the effect is disruptive: breaking up the outline of the eggs sufficiently, especially in the constantly moving, dappled sunshine and shadow thrown by the adjacent vegetation, to deceive the eyes of a less perceptive intruder. Such patterns also help birds in colonies recognise their own eggs.

Left: The tufted duck lays its dozen or so greenish-grey eggs in a depression in a grass tussock, hidden from any predator's view. Ducks' eggs are normally oval, but they cannot roll out of their nests which are cup-shaped. After the chicks have hatched the broken egg-shells are left in the nest. This is unusual, as most birds hide them to avoid predators.

Above: The chaffinch's eggs are bluish-white with red wine-coloured blotches. Four to five is the normal clutch. These eggs are well concealed and protected by the cup-shaped nest of lichens, moss and spiders' webs.
Right: The clutch of a song thrush's bright blue eggs, spotted with black, and nestled in a smooth mud cup of the compactly constructed nest, seem surprisingly poorly camouflaged against the mottled green and browns of the foliage.

Migration

Single migrations of over 6000 miles seem to us to be beyond the capabilities of such small birds as swallows and willow warblers. But billions of these birds make vast trips each year.

Those birds which migrate, rather than remain at home, do so for one simple reason – to find food. Birds which breed in the far north in summer come to spend winter in Britain because there is no food available in their Arctic breeding grounds. (In the Arctic tundra in summer there is a short-lived flush of insect life which, together with other

sources of food, sustains the birds while they mate and raise young.) In the same way, there is not enough food in Britain in winter to supply most of our insect-eating birds. Such aerial species as swallows (see page 138), swifts (see page 140) and martins have almost no chance of finding flying insects to feed on during the winter. Similarly, the warblers and flycatchers that depend on arthropods which are plentiful during the warmer months, cannot rely on them being available during the winter. These birds therefore move south to winter in the tropics.

Perhaps the most interesting question is why do they ever return from their winter home – where there is plenty of food and nesting space? The answer is that there is a wide variety of local birds – including several species of swallow, for instance – that are specially adapted to a year-round existence in the tropics. There is no chance of a vast number of northern birds being able to breed and compete successfully for food in such a network of tropical species.

Above: Arctic terns are the longest distance migrants of all birds. Those that breed north of the Arctic circle spend winter close to the Antarctic pack ice and so experience continuous daylight for up to eight months of the year. Several Arctic terns from Europe have been reported from as far away as Australia.

Above: The observatory at Fair Isle in the Shetlands which sees an astonishingly large percentage of rare migratory birds from as far afield as North America and the Far East.

Left: A Heligoland trap at the Fair Isle Observatory. Such traps are derived from the traditional bird-catching methods in the remote island of Heligoland, and they have been used for the last 30 years. This trap is built in a gully, others may be located over areas with bushes where migrating birds gather naturally. Most Heligolands are about 3.5m (10ft) high and up to 17m (55ft) wide at the entrance.

Summer migrants
(birds that come to
Britain in summer.)
Swallows winter furthest
south in Africa. Route
northwards in spring just
east of southern route in
autumn.
Swifts in Britain only in
May, June and July.
Winter in Malawi.
Lesser whitethroats
winter in east Africa.
Intermediate fattening
area in northern Italy,
also call in on Nile Delta.
Whitethroats migrate
south-south-westerwards.
Autumn fattening area in
N-W Spain; winter in
Sahel region of W Africa.

Seabird and wader routes
(not illustrated).
Knots reach Britain from
Greenland and Canada.
Manx shearwaters
winter off Brazil.
Gannets migrate further
as juveniles than adults,
to tropics and
Mediterranean.
Ruffs from E Siberia to
Britain, winter in W
Africa, return via Italy.

To feed or fly away During the winter months, British birds have two options: sit it out or move southwards. If they remain they must either exploit a new food source, or a specialised feeding style which allows them to feed in the same way. In the first case, species like the blue and great tits feed during the winter on dormant insects and their eggs that are hidden in the bark of trees, or on different foods like the tor. of peanuts fed to them by bird-lovers. In the second case, birds such as wrens and dunnocks remain here, feeding largely on the arthropods which they prize out from shelters in thick cover.

Network of routes The journeys that bird migrants make vary enormously. Many people think of bird migration as something which just concerns swallows from Europe reaching southern Africa; but this is only a minute part of the web of migration woven round the British Isles. Not only do our summer birds leave here to winter in warmer areas, but our islands also play host to millions of birds spending their winters with us. The geographical position of the British Isles on the western flank of Eurasia, with the warming influence of the Atlantic and the subtropical water brought north-east to our shores by the Gulf Stream, makes them a welcome refuge for many species of waterfowl which spend their summers in Siberia.

The distinction between migratory and sedentary species, is not clear-cut because there are continental populations of many resident British birds which are themselves migratory–some of them, like starlings and blackbirds, reaching Britain as winter visitors in large numbers.

Timetables of flights The timing of migration is crucial; in spring returning birds cannot afford to arrive too early. They would starve on arrival if their food supply was not available. On the other hand the individuals which arrive first, and manage to survive, are able to occupy the best territories.

In most bird species the males arrive first so that they can mark out territories and then attract the females to them. On the other hand some species, particularly ducks and geese, pair off in the winter quarters and migrate to the breeding grounds together. Sometimes the ducks which pair in the winter originate from very different areas but, once joined together, one will follow the other to unfamiliar territory. This phenomenon–called abmigration–accounts for some puzzling recoveries of ringed British-bred ducks in central Russia during the breeding season.

The main activity for most birds, which starts immediately they come to Britain in summer, is breeding. But for many birds this is followed by another crucial period–the annual moult–when they renew all their feathers. The timing of the autumn migration is also crucial: for the adult birds, the moult follows the busy breeding period, and for the young birds the autumn pre-migration period determines whether they will be able to build up their strength and survive.

Daylight trips Those birds that make their journey in daylight are called diurnal migrants. Generally the diurnal migrants make their trips in rather short bursts of a hundred or so miles at a time. Often their routes are greatly influenced by the local landscape, the birds funnelling through mountain passes or across short stretches of sea. In the British Isles the autumn flights of finches, meadow pipits and skylarks down the east coast, and the flights of geese up the mountain passes of Scotland, are an unforgettable sight.

These concentrations of diurnal migrants are responsible for the enormous congestion of soaring birds at the Straits of Gibraltar and the Bosphorus each autumn. Hundreds of thousands of white storks and birds of prey congregate at these places each year. Falsterbo, in southern Sweden, provides another concentration point for migrants moving southwards from Scandinavia. Britain is not endowed with such spectacular sites, but you may see high numbers of diurnal migrants at many south and east coast headlands during the autumn–Portland Bill and Selsey Bill, Beachy Head, Dungeness, Gibraltar Point and Spurn Head are all good vantage sites.

Night-flights Those bird migrants that travel at night–nocturnal migrants–are not always as easy to see when they migrate; but you can infer their movements by watching

Winter migrations

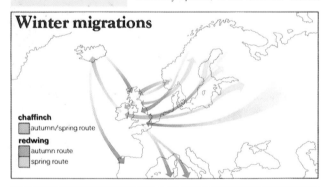

chaffinch
☐ autumn/spring route

redwing
☐ autumn route
☐ spring route

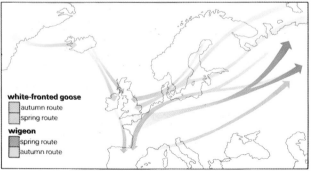

white-fronted goose
☐ autumn route
☐ spring route

wigeon
☐ spring route
☐ autumn route

Summer migrations

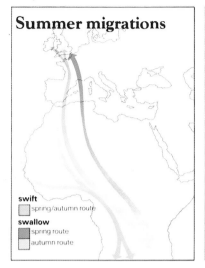

swift
  spring/autumn route
swallow
  spring route
  autumn route

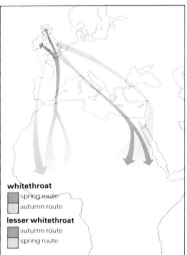

whitethroat
  spring route
  autumn route
lesser whitethroat
  autumn route
  spring route

Winter visitors (to the British Isles).
Wigeons wintering here breed across Scandinavia into Siberia.
White-fronted goose in Ireland and west Britain come from Greenland; those in south and east England (also Slimbridge) are from northern Russia.
Redwings, common birds in Britain in winter, come from Iceland (where there is a distinctive species *colurni*), and from Scandinavia and Russia. Many travel even further south to Spain, Italy and as far as Greece and Turkey.
Chaffinches resident here have brick-red underparts.

any suitable area and recording the fluctuating numbers. This is particularly easy on offshore islands or coastal headlands where migrants that would never normally be seen in such barren areas may appear in large numbers. Bird observatories dotted around the country, have been operating for up to 30 years and carefully record the birds which pass through. Their records show what the common birds do each year as well as the activities of rare visitors.

In contrast to the short steps generally made by the diurnal species, nocturnal migrants may fly non-stop for more than three days—in some cases regularly for 80 or even 100 hours. With an air speed of about 25 miles per hour this means that many can fly 2500 miles in one stretch. The birds which do this, such as sedge warblers, store fat under their skin (subcutaneously) to use as fuel on their flight. They may well double their weight before migrating. Sedge warblers take off from southern England in the autumn weighing about 22g (¾oz), fly for four days and land in Senegal, south of the Sahara, four days later weighing about 10g (¼oz). Other species, like the closely related reed warbler, do not make such long single trips, but stop off on the west coast of Portugal to refuel.

How do they navigate? Such long journeys are not without their hazards. Even if the bird has fuelled up adequately it must still be able to find its way properly. Birds navigate by referring to the sun, stars (which implies some sort of in-built timing mechanism) as well as to the earth's magnetic field. They also rely on an inbuilt homing device to give an indication of direction. They have evolved their migratory routes simply because these routes work. It is certain that the newly hatched warbler, for instance, has within its genetic make-up

the information it needs to accomplish its migration.

Perhaps the one aspect that makes bird migration such a fascinating part of ornithology is the tremendously varied habitats that one individual bird visits and lives in during its year. For example, the Black-headed gulls which take bread from the tourists on Westminster embankment include individuals bred on marshes in Poland, Czechoslovakia and Scandinavia. The swallow nesting in your garage may have been feeding among the debris of a South African gold-mine last winter, and will have passed over the vast expanse of the Sahara during March.

Above: House martins congregate on telegraph wires, before migrating on the long trip to their wintering quarters in Africa. Our best known migrants, the swallows, also do this; and both species, which find ample supplies of insects to catch on the wing in summer, migrate in winter rather than attempt to exploit different food sources.

Birds of prey

The birds of prey have long had a special fascination for man. The owls, for example, are often associated with the supernatural—no doubt on account of the strange hoots and shrieks of the tawny and barn owls, their nocturnal habits, and their ghostly silent flight, often near churchyards. More often, they are synonymous with wisdom. This stems from ancient Athens, where the little owl was the city's symbol. *Athene*, the generic name of the little owl, has an obvious derivation from the goddess of Wisdom.

Other birds of prey, like the golden eagle, are renowned for their majestic size and power as hunters, and even today there remains much speculation and occasional fierce debate on the lifting power of a golden eagle: some arguing that it has the power to carry off prey the size of a red deer calf—an animal it could certainly kill even if it could not lift it. Hunting prowess also makes the peregrine falcon a well-known bird, despite the fact that it is really a scarce bird, and one from habitats rarely visited by most people. The very skills that the peregrine falcon displays in the speed and control of its hunting power-dive or stoop may be a major threat to its existence, since it is so popular for falconry.

Perhaps the birds of prey are held in rather inflated esteem: most of them (like all predators) are lazy, and many often feed on carrion rather than on prey secured after a hot-blooded hunting foray. And most, even birds as large as a buzzard, often feed on prey as mundane as an easily captured earthworm or beetle!

The owls dominate the night-time hunting scene, with ultra-acute sight and hearing, coupled with feathers adapted to silence their flight. Among the daytime birds of prey, the hunting techniques are varied and usually well suited to the habitat of the particular species. The golden eagle and the buzzard are soaring birds, watching and waiting on high, as is the peregrine falcon, cast in the role of the modern fighter-interceptor aircraft. At lower levels are the slower-moving harriers, quartering their rather featureless marsh or moor hunting grounds and dropping suddenly, from a few feet up, on to prey taken unawares. In woodland the long wings and associated speed of the falcons are useless, and so this is the habitat of the agile and manoeuvrable sparrowhawk, which is far better adapted to chases through the trees due to its rounded wing geometry. Wetlands are exploited by the osprey, one of the most cosmopolitan of birds, its feet and talons well adapted to hold the slippery fish for which it plunge-dives.

Even the kestrel, commonest and most widespread of the European birds of prey, and one that (like the tawny owl) has adapted well to urban life, must give the birdwatcher cause to marvel. Hovering, even into a stiff wind, it can keep its head rock-steady, stable enough to allow its supremely acute eyes to spot even a beetle moving several hundred feet below. As a group, the birds of prey show enormously detailed and varied adaptations to their ways of life, which are not only the secret of their success, but also the basis of their fascination to birdwatchers.

Opposite: This goshawk shows the all-seeing eye and powerful hooked beak typical of the birds of prey.

Golden eagle

For the birdwatcher there is no more magnificent
sight than that of a golden eagle soaring in the
sky, yet centuries of ignorance and persecution
have brought this bird close to extinction.

Golden eagles were once widely distributed throughout the mountainous regions of the British Isles, but over many years their numbers have steadily dwindled. Now they are essentially birds of the Scottish highlands and islands, with a few pairs nesting in the uplands of south-west Scotland and two pairs recently re-established in the Lake District.

The most reliable estimates put the size of our golden eagle population at 250 to 300 pairs. Their numbers were thought to be fairly stable, but recent evidence suggests that they may be declining slightly. Certainly there are suitable tracts of country where eagles are either scarce or absent altogether, and other areas where breeding success is poor. On the other hand, some areas have thriving local populations.

Despite its lack of numbers, the golden eagle is the most widespread large eagle in the world. It is found in all the main mountainous areas of Europe, from arctic Norway and Russia down to Spain. It has outposts in North Africa and occurs right across Asia, apart from the Indian sub-continent and south-east Asia. It is also found in the New World from Canada down to Mexico.

In all these areas it is primarily a mountain eagle or a bird of wide desolate upland plains, but in some areas it also occurs on rocky sea-cliffs, particularly in north-west Scotland and the Hebrides.

Golden nape Adult golden eagles are mostly brown, although there is a lot of variation between individuals, some birds looking quite dark while others are much paler. All adults have the rear crown and nape a pale straw-yellow—hence its English name. This feature may be difficult to see in the field, but on some birds it can be conspicuous and, in bright sunlight, may appear almost white. Another feature possessed by most adults is paler feathering on the shoulders and wing coverts (where the wing joins the body).

An immature eagle is usually much darker than an adult and has characteristic white patches on its wings. The tail is white with a black band at the end. These white markings disappear as the bird matures, and have virtually gone by the time it reaches the age of five, although breeding adults show traces of it for some time.

Look-alikes In this country the bird most likely to be confused with a golden eagle is the common buzzard. If the bird is not too far away then you can tell the two species apart by size: the golden eagle is much bigger. Otherwise, compare the underparts. Those of the buzzard have characteristic white and dark markings, whereas an adult golden eagle is plain brown and the young brown with white patches.

In poor light or from far away, shape is an important aid to identification. The golden eagle is longer in the wing, with a much more prominent head and tail. When soaring it holds its wings flatter—buzzards hold their wings up to form a 'V' shape.

Hunting techniques Golden eagles are superb fliers, able to hunt in the wildest terrain and in all but the most ferocious of weather. They rarely rely on sheer speed or manoeuvrability when hunting. For these birds it is a much more painstaking business. The eagle flies low over the ground, patiently going back and forth, contouring along hill sides and across valleys, until it locates its prey, then killing with a swift pounce or a brief chase. The kill is achieved by means of its powerful feet and huge curved talons. The bill may be used to kill prey but is really designed for feeding with afterwards.

Quite often, a golden eagle hunts from a vantage point on a rock or some other look-out in the manner of many other birds of prey. It may even chase down and kill a flying bird, but this is rare. Without some height advantage to give it impetus a golden eagle is not at its best and a fit grouse can usually outfly it over a short distance.

Take-away food Eagles much prefer to carry their food away rather than eat it at the scene of the kill. This limits the size of the prey they attack. Golden eagles are immensely powerful birds, but there is still a lot of nonsense talked about their lifting powers. Much depends on the lift they can get from the wind and whether the ground slopes.

Common buzzard

mottled brown and white underparts

mature

white patches on wings and tail

plain brown underparts

Golden eagle

immature

Above: The only species likely to be confused with the golden eagle is the buzzard. Close up, size alone separates the two birds, the golden eagle being half as big again. Further away, look for the contrasting light and dark markings on the underside of the buzzard. A mature golden eagle is plain brown beneath, whereas the immature bird has white markings on the wing and tail.

Opposite: A young golden eagle. Older birds develop the characteristic straw-yellow plumage on the nape. Notice the heavily feathered legs and powerful talons for killing.

Golden eagle (*Aquila chrysaetos*). Resident bird of prey, now confined mostly to the Scottish highlands and islands. The male is 75-90cm (30-35in) long; the female usually about 7.5cm (3in) longer.

Common, rough-legged and honey buzzards

Buzzards, usually seen wheeling and soaring, gained an early reputation for laziness, although patient waiting is part of their efficient hunting strategy. They are not agile, relying mainly on a silent planing approach to catch their varied prey.

Three buzzards occur regularly in Britain, the common buzzard, the much scarcer rough-legged buzzard and the unrelated, but equally scarce, honey buzzard which is a similar sized bird to the other two but belongs to an entirely separate family.

The common buzzard (pictured left) is a familiar bird of prey in Wales, south-west England, the Lake District and Scotland, although it is absent from much of lowland England. It is the British bird which, perhaps, comes nearest to the familiar conception of what a bird of prey really looks like. One of the most obliging features, for the bird watcher, is that this bird is so conspicuous. Perched, it has a slightly hunched attitude, and its compact, robust features are clear; in flight, its broad wings, short tail and soaring habit, often with wings rigid and upturned, immediately proclaim it as a bird of prey. In sunny weather it spends much time in the air, wheeling and circling above woodland or open hillside, often calling loudly with a plaintive and characteristic mewing.

Although it is predominantly a brown plumaged bird, relieved only by the bright yellow of its feet, legs and cere (the fleshy covering at the base of the bill), individuals are very variable. The wings can be the whole range of colours from blackish brown through all shades of blotching and streaking to almost white in some birds.

In population terms the buzzard qualifies as a successful bird in the British Isles. There are 20-30,000 individuals, although they are by no means universally distributed. In upland areas where the buzzard is now concentrated numbers may be prodigious. Although buzzards are numerous in the south-west, slightly less so in the Lakes and Scotland, they are nowhere more numerous than in Wales. Here on a sunny day in April you may see up to 100 individuals in a day's travelling, with pairs breeding at intervals of half a mile or so. The densest buzzard population yet recorded was on Skomer Island where up to eight pairs have been noted on the 722 acres.

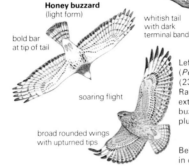

Rough-legged buzzard

Right: **Rough-legged buzzard** (*Buteo lagopus*), 55cm (22in) from beak to tail. Breeds in Scandinavia where it is at the mercy of fluctuating populations of small mammals for food.

legs feathered to toes

dark belly patch

whitish tail with dark terminal band

Honey buzzard (light form)

bold bar at tip of tail

soaring flight

broad rounded wings with upturned tips

Common buzzard

Left: **Honey buzzard** (*Pernis apivorus*), 58cm (23in) from beak to tail. Rare summer visitor in the extreme south. (Common buzzard also shown for plumage comparison).

Below: Some buzzards nest in crags or cliffs; pairs move to a new site annually.

Osprey

The osprey has suffered from a history of ruthless
persecution by egg collectors and gamekeepers,
causing it to be absent from Britain for over 40 years.
Since the return of the first breeding pair in 1959,
numbers have been gradually increasing.

Throughout the long history of their evolution, many different birds of prey have emerged, taking advantage of an immense variety of potential foods, and belying the popular impression that they all live on a diet of small mammals, birds or carrion. From the bat falcons of Central America and the insect-hunting falconets of eastern Asia to the monkey-hunting and even deer-hunting eagles, the range of predatory birds is truly wide, and few potential victims escape the attention of one or another of them. It is hardly surprising, therefore, that among birds of prey some highly expert fishers have evolved. The osprey is supreme among these: it is a large predator that hunts and breeds successfully in many parts of the globe, perfectly equipped to find all its food in water.

Plunging for prey The bird has a striking appearance: the white undersides of its body and wings contrast sharply with its rich brown upper plumage; and its length of 60cm (2ft) is dwarfed by enormous angular wings which, when fully spread, measure 145cm (5ft). It is capable of catching and carrying away fishes of several pounds in weight, but it rarely seizes the larger ones: most frequently it takes fishes between ½lb and 1lb (230-450g).

The osprey's plunge-dive is an awe-inspiring sight. It searches slowly over the water for suitable prey and when it has found a likely victim it banks, circles and hovers. Basking or surface-swimming fishes of many species, such as pike, perch, trout or carp, are all taken by the osprey. Quickly it enters a graceful plunge, at the end of which it takes its selected victim in its talons. Often the dive is fairly gradual, but sometimes it is almost vertical; and often the osprey plunges from heights of 16m (50ft) or more.

As the bird strikes the water, it thrusts its talons forward to take the fish (at the same time they help to absorb the impact of hitting the water). The osprey holds its wings high as it enters the water. It is thought that the bird seldom dives deeper than 1m (3ft), and usually goes a far shorter distance below the surface. Almost immediately it rises from the water again for, provided that the dive has been performed well, the bird has little difficulty in regaining the air.

Terrible talons The feet of the osprey are specially adapted to assist it in seizing and retaining such slippery prey as fishes. The feet and legs are particularly large and powerful; the claws are strongly curved, and the undersides of the feet are equipped with spiny scales that grip the body of the fish. Perhaps most remarkable of all is that one of the four toes is completely reversible—the osprey can turn it either backwards or forwards. With this toe pointing back, alongside the true hind toe, the osprey can hold a fish securely by two claws in front and two behind. Once it has risen from the water, the osprey turns the fish so as to hold it in a fore-and-aft position and carries it away to eat at leisure. Ospreys

Osprey (*Pandion haliaetus*). Rare summer visitor, 23 pairs recorded in 1981, numbers slowly increasing. Breeding in the Highlands of Scotland. Two or three eggs, richly marked in reddish brown or chocolate colour. Length 60cm (2ft), wingspan 1.4m (5ft).

distinctive white underside of body and wings

fish carried head-first in flight

soaring in search of prey

Opposite: The large nest is made of sticks and a typical site is in the top branches of a Scots pine or other tree. Ospreys have been known to build nests on tall buildings or high cliffs. The two birds seen in this nest are juveniles.

plunge-dive may be nearly vertical

wings raised and talons lowered as bird nears water

hind toe

reversible toe

sharp spiny scales help grip slippery prey

digest even the bones of fishes without difficulty.

From the edge of extinction In 1981, as many as 23 pairs of ospreys were known to be breeding in Britain, all of them in the Scottish Highlands. For over 40 years in the first half of this century, this splendid bird was extinct as a breeding species—a result of ruthless persecution, mainly by egg collectors. The eggs were considered a great prize by enthusiasts, whose determination to build up their collections led to the disappearance of the species from Britain.

Another major cause of the decline of the osprey in Britain over the past 200 years was the fact that it depends on fishes for its living. Gamekeepers and water bailiffs assumed that this made the osprey a serious competitor with man for the fishes in Britain's rivers and lakes. The latter part of the 19th century was a particularly ruthless period of game preservation and unbridled destruction.

Sparrowhawk and goshawk

The sparrowhawk and goshawk are the supreme
predators of our woodlands. Swift, silent and deadly
in the hunt, they are ideally adapted to the low-level
pursuit of small birds, and specialise in the techniques
of close encounter and surprise attack.

The sparrowhawk is well distributed throughout our more heavily wooded counties and is reasonably familiar to many people. But the goshawk is still a rare bird in the British Isles and its present status is poorly recorded and subject to much local secrecy.

The sparrowhawk and goshawk are extremely difficult to tell apart, although relative size can help. The female goshawk (as large as a buzzard at 50cm [20cm] in length) is about twice the size of a male sparrowhawk, while a large female sparrowhawk approaches the size of a male goshawk. (Like most hawks, the females are much larger than the males.) Both hawks are powerful fliers and, although difficult to tame, can be trained by falconers to take a wide variety of prey.

A hawk or kestrel? Because these two hawks are so similar in appearance, identifying and separating them in the field depends on spotting them at close quarters. What is surprising, and makes for further complications, is the considerable public confusion between the sparrowhawk and the more familiar and conspicuous kestrel (see page 90).

People say they have seen a sparrowhawk hovering over a roadside verge, when this is the kestrel's main hunting method, and something which sparrowhawks never do. Unlike the kestrel (which is a member of the falcon family), the sparrowhawk or broad winged hawk (an accipiter), is a shy, inconspicuous bird and the goshawk even more so. This is because both are predominantly woodland birds, and spend most of their time in the cover of trees.

Apart from a period in late winter and early spring when their high circling displays make them more visible, you are most likely to encounter a sparrowhawk as it sweeps low over gardens, along a country lane or hedgerow, or as it crosses at grass-top level from one wood to another. It sometimes makes a series of 'kek-kek-kek' calls, and also has a short cry 'pew'.

Territory and display The annual cycle of establishing a territory, advertising it to likely mates and courtship, begins much earlier than the usual breeding season of other birds. Sparrowhawks begin to soar and spiral above the nesting woods from late February onwards, especially on clear and breezy days. Females are usually more active than males, and the intensity of their high circling displays reaches its peak as nest building begins in the second half of March.

At this time of year the display also frequently includes a series of exciting, bounding undulations above the nesting wood. These are often so vigorous that the bird seems to 'bounce' upwards from the base of each steep descent. This is the one time of year when the birds are regularly in evidence, and you can expect to look for them with some degree of success.

Goshawks stake out their territories even

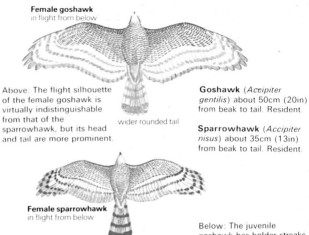

Female goshawk in flight from below

Above: The flight silhouette of the female goshawk is virtually indistinguishable from that of the sparrowhawk, but its head and tail are more prominent.

wider rounded tail

Goshawk (*Accipiter gentilis*) about 50cm (20in) from beak to tail. Resident.

Sparrowhawk (*Accipiter nisus*) about 35cm (13in) from beak to tail. Resident.

Female sparrowhawk in flight from below

Below: The juvenile goshawk has bolder streaks on its underparts and is more amber in colour than the adult.

Juvenile goshawk

bold streaks on underparts

earlier in the year than sparrowhawks. The female can become vocal soon after the new year. She is notably noisy early in the morning – when you may hear a harsh chattering cry ringing through the breeding woodlands even before dawn.

Females call the tune Part of the reason for the louder, more noticeable female display is due to the dominant role that the much larger, more robust females play in each season's pairing. The females also tend to stay in or near their nesting territories throughout the year; this makes them sitting tenants when the new year comes. The females make the first moves in attracting a mate into the territory that they have kept exclusively as their own for the past three or four months.

The hawks probably seek new mates each year, since they go their separate ways at the end of the breeding season. Both the male and female usually remain solitary throughout the autumn and winter, each with its own hunting territory. The female stays in her nest and the male drifts away, or even sometimes migrates south.

The goshawk lays her eggs from early April onwards, and the sparrowhawk some three weeks later. Clutch sizes are surprisingly large; five to six is normal for the sparrowhawk, and three to four for the goshawk. The female is almost exclusively responsible for incubating the eggs while the male does all the hunting – calling the female off the nest to feed her once or twice each day.

Woodland cover Before the sixteenth century, when the British Isles were still heavily wooded, sparrowhawks and goshawks were abundant. Nowadays their presence and distribution are strongly influenced by the number of suitable woodlands still remaining.

The sparrowhawk survives just as well in a pattern of small woods and open fields as it does in extensive woods.

Below and opposite: The adult goshawk has a narrow white tail covert with a darker coloured crown and ear coverts. With its flame-coloured iris the bird looks fierce and alert.

Adult goshawk

pronounced white supercilium

Marsh, hen and Montagu's harriers

Harriers are large, broad-winged birds of prey. In
Britain only three species occur – the hen, marsh and
Montagu's harriers – out of a world total of about
nine or ten; and all three are now rare and very
restricted in their distribution here.

The shape, size and silhouette of harriers are all distinctive and unlikely to cause confusion with other birds of prey. They are broad-winged, slender-bodied birds with long narrow tails. When seen in flight they are very distinctive, flying buoyantly and gracefully, usually low over the ground, with dexterous turns and changes of direction as they quarter for food or make a half-pass at likely prey.

As with most other birds of prey, female harriers are noticeably larger than the males, in this case by some 5cm (2in) or so. They are also less brightly coloured.

When three apparently similar species occur in the same area, there is usually a clear ecological separation between them, often in their use of different types of habitat. This is amply demonstrated by the three British harriers. The hen harrier is a moorland specialist, and the marsh harrier a reed bed and marshland bird, while Montagu's harrier – a rare summer migrant – has a strong preference for lowland heaths and arable fields. This latter species is a little more catholic in its choice of habitat than the other two although, being confined in Britain to land below 76m (250ft) or so, it no longer overlaps with the hen harrier.

Distinguishing our harriers There are few more exciting sights for bird-watchers in Britain than a dove-grey male hen harrier sweeping buoyantly over the dark, rolling expanses of a heather moor. The males are uniformly pale grey above, relieved only by broad black wing tips and a white band at the base of the tail. At a distance the males can appear so pale that they often resemble a large gull. The females are much darker, being brown birds with a white rump patch that stands out clearly. Hen harriers are confined to heather moors.

Above: A female hen harrier drops down to her nest with prey for the young.

Identifying harriers

dark wingtips

pale grey plumage

4-fingered wingtip

brown plumage

Hen harrier

♀

white rump

barred tail

Hen harrier (*Circus cyaneus*). Resident in northern heather moors or lower ground in winter. Length 43-51cm (17-20in).

3-fingered wingtip

Marsh harrier

black wing bar

pale crown

smaller and more slender in build than female hen harrier

♂

brown streaks on belly

chestnut-streaked belly

grey tail

chocolate-brown plumage

Montagu's harrier

Montagu's harrier (*Circus pygargus*). Very rare summer visitor to Devon, Cornwall and Norfolk. Smallest harrier at 41-46cm (16-18in).

Marsh harrier (*Circus aeruginosus*). Very rare summer visitor to parts of East Anglia. Largest harrier at 48-56cm (19-22in).

♀

♀

barred tail

Peregrine

Among all the birds there is none to rival the
peregrine falcon in its powers of flight and its
devastating speed. Even when perched in upright
stance on cliff top or mountain ledge, it seems to
embody the essence of nobility and freedom.

Stooping to conquer

the quarry has been sighted

view from above

view from beneath

going into the stoop—wings held in sickle shape and tail open

the tight stoop—tail and wings closed and flight starting to level off

Everything about the peregrine falcon conveys strength and power. It has powerful shoulders, a short neck, broad chest, large eyes, immensely strong legs and disproportionately large feet armed with formidable talons. The dark eyes, framed in a bright yellow orbital ring, are of enormous size, occupying a large part of the skull, and give the peregrine visual acuity at least four times as sharp as that of humans. The slate grey upperparts of the adults, and the bold black moustachial stripe, contrast with the pale, finely barred underparts.

It is on the wing, however, that the full majesty and speed of the peregrine has to be seen to be fully appreciated. In silhouette from below, as you would normally see it, it is sickle-shaped and heavily built, with a short tail and neck. In level flight it has the rapid wing-beat shared by other falcons such as kestrels and merlins, but it also soars and glides high above the hillsides and sea cliffs where it lives.

In its famous 'stooping' dive, in which the peregrine attacks its quarry (principally other birds), it has been estimated that the bird may reach speeds of between 150 and 200mph, depending on the angle of descent. In level flight the peregrine can attain 60mph or more, with short bursts of speed up to 80mph. But whatever the hunting method it employs—whether it is the stoop or a strike upwards from below—the passing silhouette of the predatory peregrine casts a feared shadow on the ground. It can induce panic in flocks of wildfowl or waders, occasionally putting them into the air to fly at great heights, sometimes for hours on end, and on the ground, nesting grouse, plover and lapwing crouch motionless as the lethal sickle shadow passes over.

Above: The peregrine feeds almost exclusively on other birds up to the size of a grouse or pigeon, catching them on the wing by sheer force and speed. The most dramatic technique is the stoop, in which the peregrine, having gained height above the quarry, closes its wings and accelerates at breathtaking speed in a stooping dive of several hundred feet or more to hit the unfortunate prey with its talons in a bone-shaking flurry of feathers.

Peregrine falcon (*Falco peregrinus*): resident bird of prey haunting cliffs and mountains. Male 38cm (15in), female 46cm (18in).

Below: An immature female peregrine; it lacks the adults' black 'moustache' and slate grey underparts.

the catch and lift-off—the quarry is killed with a blow from the hind toe

Kestrel

The kestrel's old folk name–the windhover–catches the essence of this bird whose most characteristic posture is its skilful, seemingly effortless hovering. If you see a bird with wings winnowing, tail fanned out and head down it's probably a kestrel after prey.

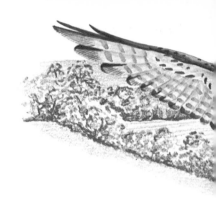

A pair of kestrels at their woodland nest; as with many birds of prey, the male (left) is smaller than the female (right). The nest was not built by this pair; it is an old one made by another bird (possibly a carrion crow) and taken over by the kestrels. When the eggs–up to five in number–are laid, the female does most of the incubating while the male hunts, periodically bringing his mate food–such as the vole she is holding in her beak.

The kestrel is our most common and widespread bird of prey. It is also unique in the way it has come to terms with man and become an independent and resourceful city dweller. Its urban takeover bid has been very successful; in a special survey carried out in 1977 no fewer than 337 breeding pairs were reported in London, at least seven of them right in the heart of the city. The kestrel has also learned to exploit the thousands of miles of infrequently mown grassy motorway verges which harbour the small rodents that make up its principal food. In fact, a stretch of country motorway is one of the best places to see these slim, long-tailed members of the falcon family. Male and female do not look alike. The striking blue-grey head and tail and light chestnu back spotted with black identify the male kestrel, while the female's plumage is barred and streaked in brown and reddish-brown colours. Both sexes have a conspicuous black band on the end of the tail which is clearly visible when the birds are hovering, and both have creamy underparts streaked with black or dark brown.

Varied feeder Towns and motorways are not, of course, the only haunts of the kestrel. It frequents downs, heaths, moors, mountains, parkland, farmland and cliffs–almost every land habitat barring the middle of thick woods where there is not enough room for its particular style of hunting. (In these woods

The kestrel's hunting technique

Left: The hunting kestrel holds its position in the air with continuous small corrective movements of outstretched wings and tail while at the same time keeping its down-pointed head (and eyes) perfectly steady.

the kestrel's place is taken by the sparrow-hawk).

One secret of the kestrel's success is its ability to adapt to a very varied diet. In country areas small rodents such as mice and voles form nearly two thirds of the kestrel's food – making the bird a distinct benefit to the farmer. The next most important items of diet are insects, particularly grasshoppers and beetles, and some small birds such as finches. Some enterprising individuals have been known to take turtle doves and lapwings – birds almost as large as themselves.

In towns where small outdoor mammals are in short supply, the kestrel preys principally on small birds such as house sparrows and starlings. Distance is no serious obstacle if the kestrel knows that a good supply of food awaits it at the end of a journey; for instance, one pair of outer London kestrels flew five miles regularly to hunt at a sewage works frequented by starlings.

Skilled hunter The kestrel is an exceptionally keen sighted bird – as it has to be since it often hunts from heights of up to 60m (200ft). As it hovers, the kestrel keeps its head absolutely still – eyes fixed on the prey far below – while maintaining its position in the air with constant small adjustments of wings.

Right: To catch its prey the kestrel must be fast and accurate. When its keen eyes have picked out the movements of a mouse or vole on the ground below, the kestrel swoops down on it in a series of stepped descents. The kill is made with the strong, fearsomely sharp talons which clutch the victim in a deadly grip. Open ground is essential for this type of hunting – in dense woodland with tangled undergrowth the kestrel could severely damage its long, pointed wings.

Below: After the kill, the kestrel sometimes 'mantles' its prey, with its wings outspread and its tail forming an almost circular cover. It is thought this is done to screen the prey while the bird recovers from the flurry of the hunt.

Left: Although the kestrel will sometimes eat its prey on the ground, it prefers to carry it to a secluded perch. The feet grip the prey firmly while the strong hooked beak tears off flesh.

Tawny owl

The tawny owl is most in evidence during the hours of
darkness when its exceptional hearing and sensitive
vision–through 360°–make it a particularly
effective hunter. You are more likely to hear its call
or pick up its outline as it flies past the lights of your
car than to see it perched in a tree.

Tawny owls are highly specialised nocturnal hunters. Although the head may seem disproportionately big, inside the skull are two large, asymmetrical ears so sensitive that they can pick up the rustling and high-pitched squeaks of nearby prey after dark. They can pinpoint a moving target like a mouse with such accuracy that a miss is rare. In addition owls have unusually large eyes. These are forward-facing—like human eyes and binoculars—for three dimensional vision, which enables owls to judge distance accurately. (Most birds have eyes on the sides of their heads.) The retina of each eye is extremely sensitive to light and so designed to enable the owl to see in very poor light.

The owl can turn its head both left and right (like a radar scanner) to inspect a full 360°, so the bird can search for and locate its prey while keeping its body still. The 'facial disc' of rather stiff, bristly feathers serves as a reflector, collecting sounds and focusing them on the ears.

Silent hunter The essence of effective nocturnal hunting is the silent approach—and again, in the tawny owl, evolution has come up with the necessary adaptations. The outer surfaces of the feathers have a velvety finish to deaden noise, and the feathers of the leading edge of the wing have a special comb-like fringe to silence the wing as it cuts the air.

Tawny owls will usually sit motionless on a branch, waiting for some unwitting meal to pass below. The owl then drops silently on to its victim, seizing it in the fierce grip of large, sharp talons. If this does not kill the prey instantly, the death blow may be administered by a sharp bite at the base of the skull.

In flight, tawny owls seem dumpy and top-heavy with broad, rounded wings and rather moth-like, fluttering wingbeats. They often appear misleadingly pale in car headlight beams but, when seen in daylight, the blacks, browns, buffs and chestnuts of their streaky plumage provide excellent camouflage against a tree trunk. This so-called 'cryptic' plumage has its values: if the tawny owl were not well concealed, its daytime resting period would be rudely shattered by tormenting groups of mobbing birds, trying to drive it away.

Food supply Although the tawny owl is primarily a rodent killer (voles, mice and rats are all acceptable), shrews and small birds have good reason to be concerned by its presence, as their remains regularly feature in pellets. Owls often swallow their prey whole and the regurgitated pellets are made up of the indigestible remains of its prey such as bones, fur and feathers. These left-overs can provide valuable clues to its diet. In the case of the tawny owl, rodents and birds occur prominently, but the wide variety of its diet (and thus the adaptability of the species) can be gauged by the regular presence of fish, amphibian and reptile remains.

Opposite: A tawny owl lands whilst hunting.

Right: A dark triangle on the crown is a distinctive marking of the tawny owl.

Above: Primary and secondary feathers are soft to deaden the noise of the owl's descent—giving it the element of surprise and enabling its sensitive ears to do their job without disturbance.

Holes in trees provide a safe nest for the round white eggs which fit compactly in a small area.

Tawny owl (*Strix aluco*) Also called brown or wood owl; 38cm (15in) from beak to tip of tail; 40-45cm (16-18in) high; distribution widespread but absent from Ireland and some Scottish islands.

upper left ear

lower right ear

Below: The tawny owl uses its disproportionately large feet to good purpose when hunting. The formidable talons often penetrate a vital spot to administer an immediate death blow and, because they are widely spread and can grip effectively, they enable the owl to carry even small rabbits.

Top: Asymmetric ears enable the owl to locate its prey.
Above: Ear holes are so large that a human finger can fit inside.

Barn owl

The barn owl, sometimes called the white owl,
is–apart from the rare snowy owl–the palest of the
six species of owl nesting in the British Isles.
Although lacking the camouflage of its relatives, it is
well adapted to a nocturnal predatory life.

The barn owl, probably the best known and most widely distributed owl in the world, is primarily a tropical species. Most live between the latitudes of 40°S and 40°N of the equator, and in Scotland barn owls are at the northernmost part of their range. They seem to benefit from Britain's relatively mild maritime climate, the winters in other countries further from the sea being, by comparison, too harsh. However, even in the British Isles, barn owl numbers are severely reduced in cold winters, and they tend to avoid mountainous areas.

Most owl species are well camouflaged so they can rest in trees during the day without being constantly mobbed by other birds. The barn owl, with its white face and underparts, has no such camouflage, so it hides away in holes and old buildings by day to avoid being noticed. Females are larger than males and tend to be greyer above and slightly spotted below. On the continent, and occasionally in south-east England, you may see very grey-looking barn owls with buff-coloured breasts.

Barn or tawny? Barn owls are smaller than tawny owls (see page 52) and have even been killed by them. However, they usually avoid competition for food and nesting sites by staying outside the tawny owl's woodland habitat. Also, the barn owls' wings are relatively longer than the tawny owls' and therefore more suitable for flight over open ground than among trees. Barn owls prefer to hunt over rough grassy areas, farmland, marshes and bogs, scrub and young forestry plantations.

Unlike tawny owls, barn owls do not call. They mark out their territory with a wild shriek, often made while flying.

Above: A clutch of seven young chicks peer out from their hay-loft nest.

Below: The female owl, in a crouching, defensive posture, shelters her young behind her spread wings.

Opposite: The male barn owl has a white face and underparts. The upper parts are orange-buff, delicately spotted with grey, brown and white, while the tail has four greyish bars.

Right: The female barn owl, larger than the male, is greyer above and slightly spotted below.

Little owl

Owls are usually regarded as birds of the night, but not all of them fit into this stereotype. The little owl (above) is active during the day and can often be seen perching in some prominent place, although it does most of its hunting at dawn and dusk.

Little owl (*Athene noctua*). Resident bird of prey; at 23cm (9in) long, the smallest British owl. Its habitat ranges from open farmland and wasteland to urban areas, but it avoids woodland.

Owls are well known for their extraordinarily keen eyesight that enables them to hunt at night. Yet they can see just as well during the day, though few owls take advantage of this to hunt while the light is still good. The reason for this is that their victims – mice, voles, worms and insects – are mostly nocturn-al creatures.

A few species of owl, however, prefer to be active throughout the day. One of these is the little owl, which does most of its hunting at dawn and dusk. In this way, it can hunt both daytime and nocturnal creatures.

Where to see little owls The ideal habitat for little owls is open farmland with old trees and buildings to provide nesting sites. Other favourite haunts include old orchards, quarries and wasteground, and it is not un-usual to find them near the coast among sand dunes or around cliffs and islands. Some have even adapted to an urban environment and nest in city centres. The only habitat they seem to avoid is woodland, probably because this is the domain of the much larger tawny owl, which is known to eat little owls.

The best way to see a little owl is to scan its favourite perching places: telegraph poles, fence posts, stone walls, the roofs of buildings and prominent rocks and branches of trees. Seen from a distance the little owl is easily overlooked because its greyish colour and

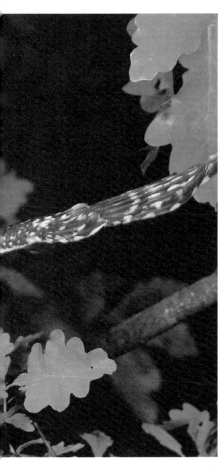

bright yellow
eyes with
dark pupils

heavily barred
underwings

Little owl

Tawny owl 38cm (15in)

Right: Little owls can be
distinguished from other
owls by their much smaller
size. For example, they are
about half as big as a
tawny owl. Both male and
female owls have the
same plumage and are about
the same size as each other.

Below: A little owl
perching outside its nest.
Its relatively large feet
and sharp talons are made
for pouncing on prey and
killing it.

Little owl 22cm (8½in)

squat rounded shape blend well into the
background.

The little owl's flight and call are useful aids
to identification. Its flight is deeply undulating and resembles that of a woodpecker. The
two most distinctive calls are a shrill barking
'werro' and a more plaintive mewing 'kiew',
noises that can often be heard when two little
owls call to each other. Little owls also make
a high-pitched penetrating 'ooo', repeated
every few seconds, and they have an alarm
call–a loud 'kip-kip-kip'–used by adults to
warn their brood of danger.

Distinctive markings At close quarters the
little owl is easily identified by its beautiful
and distinctive markings. Both the male and
the female have grey-brown upperparts with
white bars and spots. The underparts are
whitish with dark brown streaks. Their eyes
are a distinctive bright yellow with large
black pupils.

Snowy owl

Owls are an almost universally successful group of birds. Few of the world's terrestrial habitats have not been exploited by this adaptable family, and one owl species, the snowy owl, even lives in the Arctic wastes. This species has also bred in Shetland.

Below: A captive female snowy owl poses for the camera. High quality insulation is provided by the dense plumage, the heavily feathered legs and feet, and the long feathers of the facial disc, which partly conceal the strong black bill.

Snowy owls are very rare birds in Britain, although they have long occurred in small numbers during winter, usually as part of the post-breeding season dispersal of some of the population in northern Scandinavia and other Arctic regions. The Shetland Islands, far to the north of mainland Scotland, are the nearest part of Britain to the snowy owl's regular breeding grounds, and it is here

that individual vagrant birds, normally males, have been seen with comparative regularity since the early 1960s.

Large, white owl The male is much the whiter of the two adult birds, often with no markings other than a few dark flecks on the wings and back. The female, noticeably larger, with a wingspan of up to 1.5m (5ft), is more heavily barred on the upperparts and slightly less so on the underparts. This barring, which acts as camouflage for the female when incubating on the nest, tends to become less marked as summer advances because of wear and tear. The chicks, thickly insulated with grey down, resemble the adults by the end of their first summer. It barely needs saying that body insulation needs to be of the highest order for a bird which spends so much of its life in a devastatingly cold and hostile climate. This requirement is amply met by the bird's thick and fluffy plumage at all ages.

The Arctic habitat The true home of the snowy owl is on the inhospitable tundra, frozen solid and buried in a blanket of snow for more than half the year. The tundra is a flat, empty expanse of land, but in the brief Arctic summer it is far from being a barren desert, for once the days lengthen and the strengthening sun thaws the snow and ice, this landscape pulses with life. Migrant birds and mammals return to breed in the bounty of plant, insect and aquatic life, and with them come the inevitable predators, which sustain themselves at the expense of others - arctic fox, gyr falcon, skuas, glaucous gull and snowy owl.

Breeding on the tundra Snowy owls have a circumpolar breeding distribution, nesting on the tundras around the coasts of the Arctic Ocean, as well as on most of the archipelagoes. In a few areas, they breed further south, for example in Iceland and the mountainous snow-covered spine of Scandinavia. Wherever they are, however, the breeding grounds of the snowy owl are among the most inaccessible and desolate places in which any birds choose to nest. Observations suggest that these remarkable birds stay in the same range through the icy cold of the Arctic winter as well.

A diet of lemmings In its Arctic and sub-Arctic home in summer, the snowy owl feeds mainly on lemmings, and to a considerable degree the cycles of both brown and collared lemming populations determine the abundance or scarcity of the owls themselves. The number of lemmings normally rises to a peak every four years; at peak times the owls thrive, rearing large broods. After the peak summers, as the supply of lemmings wanes, numbers of snowy owls tend to move south, and in winter these 'emigrants' are seen in areas where the species is not normally encountered. This is the background of all the sightings in Shetland.

If lemmings form the bulk of the diet, however, they are by no means the only prey of the snowy owl. Willow grouse and arctic hares are taken, and in summer a variety of smaller birds – waders (especially their chicks), snow buntings and occasionally young wildfowl. In winter the main birds taken are ptarmigan and seabirds.

Shetland discovery In the spring of 1967 the RSPB's Shetlands Officer, Bobby Tulloch, observed a female snowy owl several times on the island of Fetlar, and on 7th June he

Snowy owl (*Nyctea scandiaca*). Arctic species of owl visiting Scotland as a vagrant, mainly in Shetlands. Length: males 53cm (21in), females 60cm (24in). Wingspan of female 1.5m (5ft).

Below left: A snowy owl chick on the typical low vegetation of its habitat.

gliding, buzzard-like flight

♀

numerous streaks on wings and back

defence posture

a few dark flecks on wings and back

intruder – raven looking for eggs

Above: A female snowy owl roosting on a limestone outcrop. Her plumage is richly barred with brown, especially on the back and wings. This is good camouflage at breeding time in the Arctic, when the background often consists of broken patches of snow.

Right: The long feathers of the facial disc of a male snowy owl. He lacks the mottled crown of the female. The eyes of both sexes are a liquid golden yellow.

came across a nest with three eggs on the hill of Stakkaberg on the northern slopes of the island. This was the first time on record that the snowy owl had come to nest in Britain. The nest scrape, in a grassy patch on rocky ground, was on the slopes of this windswept hill, where low vegetation all round was reminiscent of the prostrate plant cover typical of the bird's Arctic breeding grounds.

In Shetland, the low hill on Stakkaberg gave a wide view of the surrounding area, giving some warning of any approaching danger. Although lemmings do not occur on the Shetlands, there are rabbits in plenty, and these formed the major part of the food of the birds that lived there, and later their young. Other birds breeding in this part of the island were also taken – arctic skuas, oystercatchers and other waders. In 1967 the Shetland pair produced seven eggs, and eventually in August five young successfully flew.

Fetlar is much visited by birdwatchers, and from the outset in 1967 it was clear that the secret could not be kept.

In 1968, to the delight of the many birdwatchers among whom word had gone round about this exciting phenomenon, the original pair of snowy owls were still on Fetlar and reappeared on the breeding site. During the seven years from 1968-75, these two parents raised a further 11 young. In some years a second female was seen to have laid eggs, but these did not result in new families. Eventually, the old male snowy owl disappeared and, having previously driven off all the young males, left the females without a partner. The short, exciting phase of snowy owl breeding in Britain had ended, for since then only a few individual birds have lingered on, and none has paired or bred.

Short-eared owl

Food is first in the short-eared owl's life—a life totally governed by the availability of field voles, its main prey. Not only is the size of its brood influenced but also its territory, lack of voles often forcing the owl into a nomadic existence.

The short-eared owl is one of the most wide-spread of the world's 133 owl species. Found throughout most of Europe and North America, the northern half of Asia and the southern half of South America, it has even made its way to a dozen remote oceanic islands, such as the Galapagos Islands, 965km (700 miles) west of Ecuador, and Hawaii in the very centre of the Pacific.

Despite this enormous range, the short-eared owl is not a common bird in Britain—barn, little, tawny and long-eared owls all have much larger populations. Although it has been breeding in Scotland, Wales and northern England for many years, it has only recently colonized the coastal marshes of East Anglia and Kent. Nevertheless, since it is primarily a day-time hunter, and since the population is augmented by migrants from the Continent in winter, it is not difficult to find. You may come across several of them together, roosting on the ground, or floating like giant moths over the wild and treeless terrain they tend to favour.

Bouncy flight Extensive tracts of moor, bog, heath, rough grass, dunes and coastal marsh are ideal habitats for the short-eared owl, quite unlike those of its relative, the long-eared owl which is a rarely seen, highly nocturnal forest dweller. Gliding just a couple of feet above the grass, with slightly raised, extraordinarily long, outstretched wings, you might well mistake one for a harrier, were it not for the large, round head which could only belong to an owl. Compared to the weight of the body, the wing area is very large and the resultant buoyant, rather bouncy, flight is characteristic.

When seen flying close-to, the striking appearance of this owl becomes obvious. The black-centred, pale yellow eyes are each high-lighted by a ring of smoky black feathers which merge into the pale buffs and greys of the facial discs. Almost hidden among these feathers, like a secret weapon, is the cruelly hooked, razor-sharp beak.

The back is mottled and streaked with buff and brown, while the wings are a similar colour but with white spots. In contrast the underparts are pale, boldly streaked with brown on the breast but fading to fine, rather delicate streaks on the belly. Like other owls, the thick and muscular legs and feet are covered with tiny white feathers right down to the long, curved, needle-sharp claws. In flight the wings and tail are noticeably barred and there is a dark patch at the angle of the wing the carpal patch.

Cunning hunters Short-eared owls use a 'glide, surprise and grab' hunting technique which makes them proficient hunters, each one able to catch several thousand voles a year. Using eddies and upcurrents in the wind, they often glide for considerable distances without a single flap, their soft, well-padded plumage ensuring totally noiseless flight, so

Above: In flight the short-eared owl is identified by its long wings which have a dark 'carpal patch' at the angle of the wing.

Opposite: This species is not often seen in trees, preferring to perch on posts or even on the ground.

Below: The owl's short 'ears', which can be raised or lowered at will, have nothing to do with hearing, but are thought to convey its mood—fear, excitement and so on—to other owls.

Round-up of British owls

The tawny owl is found among trees and the long-eared in fir woods; the short-eared owl favours open country, and the barn owl old buildings and farms. The little owl has a more general habitat, unlike the snowy owl which is limited to the Shetland Isles.

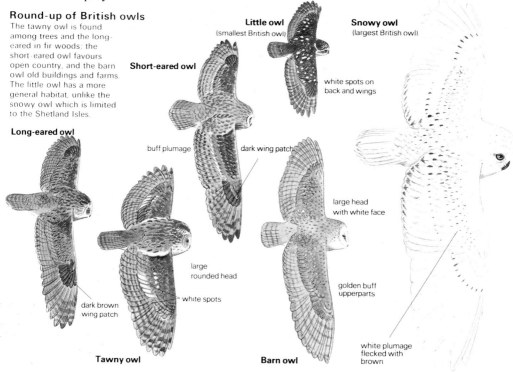

Little owl
(smallest British owl)

Snowy owl
(largest British owl)

Short-eared owl

white spots on back and wings

Long-eared owl

buff plumage

dark wing patch

large head with white face

large rounded head

golden buff upperparts

dark brown wing patch

white spots

white plumage flecked with brown

Tawny owl

Barn owl

Below: Young short-eared owls are a comical sight, covered in white and later grey down, quite unlike their parents. Fledging takes 20 to 30 days but they do not stay in the nest all this time. After only a fortnight they venture out and hide in the surrounding vegetation, even though they cannot yet fly. This behaviour makes it more difficult for predators to find them.

that the unsuspecting vole gets no warning.

Their prey-detection equipment is no less ingenious. The forward-facing eyes give superb binocular vision for accurate judgement of distances, while the discs of feathers surrounding each eye focus the slightest rustle on to enormous, highly sensitive ears, so that even in the gloom of dusk, when owls (and voles) are most active, they can pinpoint the position of their prey with ease.

Nomadic existence It is often thought that predators control the numbers of their prey. This is not true – the opposite usually applies, as is the case with the short-eared owl, whose own life is dominated by the field vole which forms most of its diet. Since vole populations are far from stable, the fortunes of the owl and the strategies it adopts vary dramatically from month to month and from year to year.

Apart from hiding among long grass, the voles' only defence against short-eared owls is prolific breeding. During the summer they produce litters at the rate of five young every seven weeks. As the youngsters can themselves breed when about six weeks old, vole populations often reach plague proportions (on average about once every four or five years).

Evidently short-eared owls thrive during these vole plagues, especially since the voles become noisy and may eat much of the grass that would otherwise conceal them. This has two main effects: first, owls from many miles around flock, as if by magic, to the bountiful food supply, and secondly, the owls capitalise on the easy pickings by 'breeding like voles' – laying 10 or more eggs (14 is on record) and sometimes having two broods in a season. The glut is usually short-lived. In such crowded conditions voles stop breeding and this, combined with the heavy predation, results in a population crash. Consequently, in the year following a vole plague, any owls that have not moved on find the larder seriously diminished and may not breed.

Birds and their feathers

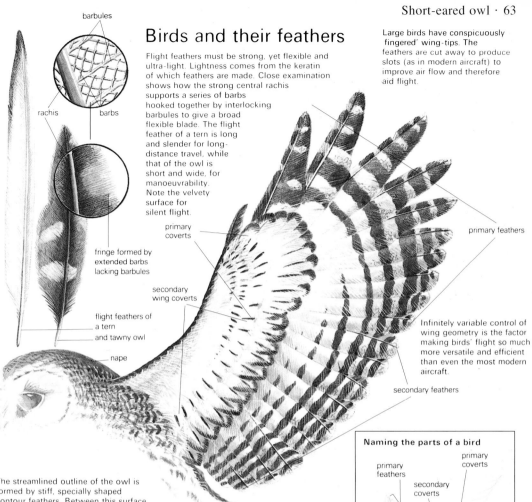

barbules

rachis   barbs

Flight feathers must be strong, yet flexible and ultra-light. Lightness comes from the keratin of which feathers are made. Close examination shows how the strong central rachis supports a series of barbs hooked together by interlocking barbules to give a broad flexible blade. The flight feather of a tern is long and slender for long-distance travel, while that of the owl is short and wide, for manoeuvrability. Note the velvety surface for silent flight.

Large birds have conspicuously 'fingered' wing-tips. The feathers are cut away to produce slots (as in modern aircraft) to improve air flow and therefore aid flight.

primary coverts

primary feathers

fringe formed by extended barbs lacking barbules

secondary wing coverts

flight feathers of a tern and tawny owl

nape

Infinitely variable control of wing geometry is the factor making birds' flight so much more versatile and efficient than even the most modern aircraft.

secondary feathers

The streamlined outline of the owl is formed by stiff, specially shaped contour feathers. Between this surface layer and the body is a layer of down feathers—the bird's 'thermal underwear' —very necessary for survival through cold winter nights. This insulation may be provided by an aftershaft attached to the contour feather or by special down feathers.

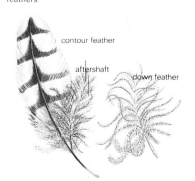

contour feather

aftershaft

down feather

Feathers are vital to a bird's survival. They power flight and supply warmth, and the colours and patterns used in courtship, aggression or camouflage are all in the feathers. Thus their maintenance is of utmost importance. Disarranged barbs must quickly be put straight to maintain flight efficiency, and this is the purpose of preening, which seems to occupy so much of a bird's time. Preen oil is applied by wiping the beak across a gland above the tail and then passing each feather through the beak, when rapid nibblings re-adjust any displaced barbules.

Naming the parts of a bird

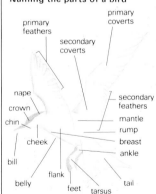

primary feathers

primary coverts

secondary coverts

nape

crown

chin

cheek

bill

belly

flank

feet   tarsus

secondary feathers

mantle

rump

breast

ankle

tail

Whether you want to describe a bulky bird like an owl or a slim tern, the same words apply to both. The parts vary in colour and shape, providing a means of identifying each species. To help identify an unfamiliar species, it is worth keeping a note book and making a rough sketch, labelling the colour of each part.

Birds of fresh water

Freshwater birds are, perhaps not unnaturally, as wide-ranging as their habitat, which embraces waterways and their immediate surrounds from their source in the hills down to the sea. Included are streams and rivers, as well as the ponds, pools and lakes into which they run: these are long-established components of the countryside, and many of them are natural features, like the moorland lochs that provide breeding sites for the diver family. But man has influenced the course of streams and created, usually many years ago, many of the lowland ponds and lakes that today have a natural, rather than an artificial, appearance. There are also more recent man-made additions to the landscape, and bird populations have been quick to adopt them as habitats. Some are now of considerable ecological importance, particularly to grebes and to the various species of diving ducks which congregate on them in winter. These 'newcomers' to the scenery include reservoirs and sewage works (the latter being particularly popular with snipe) and, most recent and most important, flooded mineral workings. These may be sand pits or clay and ballast workings, are usually to be found on the flood plains of river valleys, and are all valuable replacements for wetland lost to drainage schemes.

The wetland system begins with streams. Upland streams often flow over stony beds, and they are fast-running and clear, particularly so on higher ground. This is the typical habitat of the dipper. In contrast, on lower ground with deep soils streams are few and far between, and the rivers that they feed are often cloudy and meander sluggishly through a flat countryside. These slow-moving waters are the haunts of the kingfisher, heron and moorhen, and are often adjoined by extensive swamps, reedbeds, or marshland.

If one could design the ideal marshland habitat for birds it would be an extensive low-lying area, fringed with an almost impenetrable stunted woodland of alder and willow, intersected with ditches. At the heart would be an open expanse of water, deep in the centre but shallowing rapidly to give a band of exposed damp mud, out in the open, on which snipe would feed, before a thick belt of that most typical of marshland plants, the common reed (*Phragmites*), home of reed and sedge warblers during the summer.

Any birdwatcher who has visited freshwater wetlands during the warm days of summer will be able to testify to the potential richness of the food supply: some midges are content to perform their mating dances in smoke-like clouds, but other insects such as mosquitoes seek warm-blooded mammals for a meal! Thus, in summer, there is abundant food for the warblers, and for visiting swifts, swallows and martins. The larvae of these insect hordes are aquatic, and ensure that fish are in plentiful supply—hence the popularity of such sites with fish-catching birds ranging from kingfishers and grebes to herons and ospreys. But these are habitats for all seasons, except when all the water freezes over. Once the summer migrants have gone, it is the wintering ducks, grebes and coot that predominate. Never is this a dull habitat.

Opposite: Bewick swans flight into the Wildfowl Trust reserve at Slimbridge, Gloucestershire.

Great crested and red-necked grebes

The great crested grebe, the largest member of its family in Britain, is a resident but the species often mistaken for it–the red-necked grebe–is a winter visitor here.

The great crested grebe has a slender body that sits rather low on the water, and a long thin neck that is generally held upright. In the breeding season this handsome water bird is readily identified by its black crest and prominent chestnut and black frills, usually called 'tippets', on either side of its head. The bill is dagger-like and brown, strongly tinged with red, in colour. The upperparts are grey-brown, while the face, neck and underparts are gleaming white. The tippets are shed in the autumn and the great crested grebe in winter is then an altogether duller bird, with a white face, dark crown and a thin white stripe over the eye. In this winter plumage it can sometimes be mistaken for our other large grebe species, the winter-visiting red-necked grebe.

Sad story with a happy ending The great crested grebe is a common breeding bird throughout the lowland areas of Britain and much of Ireland, being found on shallow lakes, reservoirs and gravel pits. It also breeds on some stretches of river. At the time of the last countrywide census in 1975, there were some 6500 pairs nesting in Britain.

This is very different from the bird's breeding status about 100 years ago, when the species was brought to the brink of extinction in this country. Up until about the middle of the last century, great crested grebes bred freely, though in comparatively small numbers, in some 13 counties of southern and central England. At about that time, however, the skins of grebes, with their thick layers of down feathers, became highly fashionable as articles of decorative wear. It is thought that as a result of being hunted for their skins there may have been as few as 32 pairs of great crested grebes left in the whole country.

Many efforts were made to protect the species, and gradually matters improved, with laws passed in the 1870s and 1880s to stop the exploitation. The number of pairs slowly increased, probably helped by immigration from the Continent. In 1931 a census taken throughout Britain revealed a total of just over 1200 pairs, nearly all of them in England

Above: A family party of great crested grebes. The adult male and female are very much alike in plumage, although the male is larger, with a heavier bill and larger crest and tippets.

Great crested grebe (*Podiceps cristatus*). A resident bird on shallow lakes, reservoirs and gravel pits throughout lowland Britain and much of Ireland. Lays 3-4 blotchy white eggs any time from April-July. Length 48cm (19in) – our largest member of the grebe family. Winters on estuaries and on the sea, like the red-necked grebe.

Grebe distribution

☐ great crested (breeding)
■ red-necked (winter)

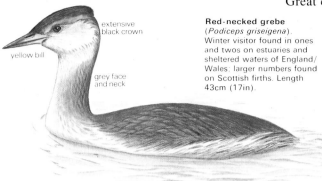

extensive
black crown

yellow bill

grey face
and neck

Red-necked grebe
(*Podiceps griseigena*).
Winter visitor found in ones
and twos on estuaries and
sheltered waters of England/
Wales; larger numbers found
on Scottish firths. Length
43cm (17in).

predators. Once the attractive, striped young
have hatched, the parents take them straight
on to the water. The brood often rides on the
back of one parent while the other dives for
food to bring them.

The young are fed on small insects at first,
graduating to smaller and then larger fishes
as they grow. After about four weeks, the
brood may be split between the two parents,
each adult taking some of the chicks to
different areas of the nesting lake. After about
two and a half months, the young fledge and
become independent of their parents.

Elaborate courtship The displays of the
great crested grebe, as in other birds, are a
form of communication between the male and
female. They are used first to establish a
strong bond between them, forming a pair that
can breed successfully and then be maintained
through to copulation and egg-laying. Most
of the courtship takes place on the water.

There are four different displays in the
great crested grebe's courtship ritual: the
'head-shaking' ceremony, the 'discovery'
ceremony, the 'retreat' ceremony and the
'weed' ceremony.

The commonest of the four displays is the
head-shaking one. It is performed by both
male and female birds, one starting off and
the other soon joining in. The crest is raised
into two shaggy ear-tufts rising from the back
of the head, while the tippets are fanned out
to the sides.

and Wales. In the next few decades the number increased, the grebes at the same time
spreading north into Scotland and westwards into Ireland.

Nesting and breeding The nests made by
great crested grebes are huge floating platforms of waterweed, anchored to stands of
reeds or rushes, or even an overhanging willow branch trailing in the water. The nest
often projects only a couple of inches above
the surface, although there is usually a much
more substantial pile of waterweed lying
underneath.

Great crested grebes usually lay three or
four whitish eggs. When the incubating bird
leaves the nest it flicks a few pieces of weed
over the eggs to conceal them from passing

Above: In winter plumage
the red-necked grebe, a
winter visitor to Britain,
lacks the white eye stripe
of the great crested grebe,
and has grey areas (not
white) on the face and neck,
a more extensive black
crown, and a yellow (not
red) tinged bill. In summer
plumage the red-necked
grebe's rich chestnut colour
on the neck contrasts
strongly with a white face
and black crown. Very small
ear tufts also develop, but
are not nearly as obvious as
the great crested grebe's crest.

Ceremonies of courtship

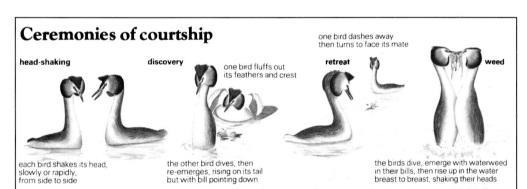

one bird dashes away
then turns to face its mate

head-shaking **discovery** one bird fluffs out its feathers and crest **retreat** **weed**

each bird shakes its head, slowly or rapidly, from side to side

the other bird dives, then re-emerges, rising on its tail but with bill pointing down

the birds dive, emerge with waterweed in their bills, then rise up in the water breast to breast, shaking their heads

The great crested grebe has one of the
most elaborate and distinctive courtship
displays of any British breeding bird.
When displaying, the pair are extremely
intent on each other. At first the displays
may appear to have little pattern, but close
watching reveals that they occur in four
parts or phases: the 'head-shaking'
ceremony (**1**); the 'discovery' ceremony
(**2**); the 'retreat' ceremony (**3**); and the
'weed' ceremony (**4**). In the picture (right)
a display has been interrupted by an
aggressive intruding male.

Red-throated, black-throated and great northern divers

A rare and thrilling sight on remote lochs and islands, divers–hardy, Arctic birds–are experts at diving and underwater swimming. At breeding time their wild, shrieking calls ring out by day and night.

Below: A black-throated diver walks ashore to its nest. Divers sometimes build a substantial heap of waterweed and grass, but the simple type shown here –a grass-lined hollow–is more usual for all species.

All four of the world's species of divers are to be seen in Britain and Ireland, although one, the white-billed diver (which breeds in Arctic North America), occurs very infrequently, usually only one or two individuals being seen during a year. The two smaller species, the red-throated and black-throated divers, breed in the north and west, but travel south to spend the winter at sea around all our coasts, so that they can be found somewhere in Britain and Ireland at any time of the year.

The great northern The huge and spectacular great northern diver was made famous for many in Arthur Ransome's book for children, *Great Northern.* In most years, some adults spend the summer on remote lochs in northern Scotland, and once every few years a pair attempts to breed. Only once in recent decades, in 1970, has breeding proved successful and resulted in a couple of youngsters.

Most great northern divers breed in northern North America, Greenland and Iceland. On the other side of the Atlantic they are called 'loons', a name which is often thought to derive from their song. Of all bird calls, that of the great northern diver must count as one of the most thrilling. Its weird cry, like a whooping, lunatic laugh, echoes wildly across the lochs between the mountains and forests of their breeding grounds.

Divers in summer plumage

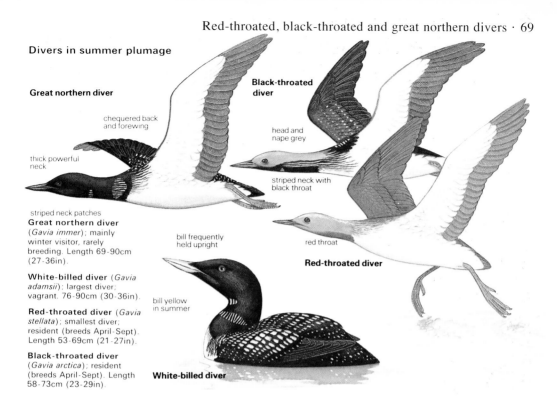

Great northern diver

chequered back
and forewing

Black-throated diver

head and
nape grey

thick powerful
neck

striped neck with
black throat

striped neck patches

Great northern diver
(*Gavia immer*); mainly
winter visitor, rarely
breeding. Length 69-90cm
(27-36in).

bill frequently
held upright

red throat

Red-throated diver

White-billed diver (*Gavia
adamsii*); largest diver;
vagrant. 76-90cm (30-36in).

bill yellow
in summer

Red-throated diver (*Gavia
stellata*); smallest diver;
resident (breeds April-Sept).
Length 53-69cm (21-27in).

Black-throated diver
(*Gavia arctica*); resident
(breeds April-Sept). Length
58-73cm (23-29in).

White-billed diver

In full summer plumage, the bird is as spectacular as its song. Great northern divers are goose-sized, but with a short, thick neck and a powerful, dagger-like beak. The head is black with a greenish metallic sheen, and the back is black, but chequered with many brilliant white squares. On the side of the neck is a small black and white striped patch. In winter the plumage is much drabber: dark grey-brown above, shading to greyish white below.

Black-throated diver In summer, this bird could be mistaken for the great northern, as its plumage colours are an equally crisp combination of black and white. However, the black-throated diver is considerably smaller and slimmer, and has a less powerful looking neck and beak. The underparts are white and the back is black, with a chequerboard pattern of white blocks similar to that of its larger relative, but the head and nape of the neck are a plain dove-grey, while the throat, as the name suggests, carries a large, pure black 'bib'.

In winter, although the basic colours are similar, the dividing lines between dark upper parts and pale underparts are far more precisely defined than the smudged margins of the great northern, and head and beak sizes remain a good identification feature.

Red-throated diver This is the smallest of the family, though only slightly smaller than the black-throated. In summer it is easily recognisable because the upperparts are clearly brown, not black, and quite uniform rather than spotted. The head and neck are a finely streaked grey, and the 'bib' is a rich deep chestnut red, though at long range this may look black. An excellent identification feature at all times is the beak, which is slender and always seems to be tilted upwards.

In winter, the beak remains the best distinguishing feature separating red-throated from black-throated divers, but in addition the red-throated diver's back is brownish-grey and densely speckled with small white spots – a useful guide at close range.

Divers in flight The divers have a very characteristic flight silhouette, which helps (particularly in winter) to separate them from cormorants, shags, ducks, geese and grebes. The body is pencil slim, the wings slender and set well back, and the flight is straight and fast with powerful wingbeats. In the case of the black-throated, the wingbeats are conspicuously (and surprisingly) shallow. There are no interruptions for spells of gliding, as in the gannet or cormorant, for example. The tail and feet often seem to be held slightly depressed, and in the two smaller species the head and neck also droop a little, giving a hump-backed appearance.

Breeding areas of Britain's divers

black-throated diver

red-throated diver

Grey heron

The grey heron is the top bird predator of the freshwater food pyramid–a status which affords it a wide range of diet, but also makes it most vulnerable to the build-up of toxic chemicals in the water. Despite this and other threats, the number of British heron pairs remains at a stable 4000–5000.

Above: A magnificent bird with a wide wingspan of 175-195cm (68-76in), the grey heron has a white head with a dagger-like beak, and a broad black streak running from the eye to the tip of the crest.

The large, stately and distinctive-looking grey heron is generally found beside or in fresh water. You may also spot it flying with its long neck tucked in against its body and its legs stretching far beyond the tip of its tail. The harsh, honking 'fraank' call of the heron is a familiar sound on the marshes, instantly recognisable to birdwatchers and the many anglers who come across herons while they themselves are fishing.

Colonies Herons breed in colonies, preferring huge nests in trees; but sometimes they nest on cliffs, or at ground level on islands in lakes and lochs, especially in Scotland. A very few colonies, including the one at Tring in Hertfordshire, have nests in reed-beds–

sites more commonly favoured by the purple heron on the continent. Most colonies contain 10-30 nests, but a few colonies in England exceed 100 pairs.

Herons at a colony refurbish their old nests in January, or even December, ready for the early breeding season. Most colonies have traditional 'club' areas close by, where the 'off-duty' herons stand around. These gatherings are called 'sieges' and provide the sites where the birds begin their courtship display.

The male choses a site and then advertises himself and his site to the females. When one of the latter shows interest, both sexes display together; this leads to mutual preening and the start of nest-building. The male generally

Grey heron (*Ardea cinerea*), total length about 95cm (36in), body length about 43cm (16in). Distribution beside almost any freshwater margin, especially marshes. Resident.

collects sticks, twigs, leaves, grass and other nest material and the female arranges them – in most cases using the base of the original nest. The birds mate on the nest or in the immediate vicinity.

From February right through to May, and even June, the female lays her eggs, which both parents incubate; two broods are rare.

Migration Herons often fly long distances to find new sources of food during cold spells, and are good at locating springs, sewage farms and other open water. In severe weather they also forage on the shore, as the salt in the sea prevents the water from freezing.

Herons from Scandinavia arrive in Britain for the winter as they are not able to survive this season in the colder parts of Europe. A few British herons leave for France, Spain or Portugal, but the majority remain within 100 miles of their native heronry.

Predator and pest Herons forage for a mixed diet of fish, eels, frogs, small mammals (quite often voles) and sometimes large

drin, accumulate in animals from the bottom of the heron's food pyramid upwards, and concentrations of these poisons increase until they reach the heron, which is the top bird predator of this pyramid. Analysis shows that the build-up of chemicals in the heron's body causes its egg shells to thin – to the point where in some cases they collapse or are broken by the weight of the brooding parents.

Population The effects of toxic chemicals and the gun put severe pressure on the heron population. In 1954 protection was granted against shooting, though it was sometimes difficult to enforce, and numbers returned to previous levels (as they also do after a fall in heron numbers caused by a hard winter). The most recent census figure for Britain stands at just over 4000 pairs – rising to 5400 in a really good year. This makes a maximum population at the start of the breeding season of 12,000 birds. These census figures, which have been kept for over 50 years, are only possible because herons breed in colonies.

Below: The heron flies to a nearby field to beat its prey to death or swallow it.

Below: The heron spots its prey and stands motionless, with neck outstretched and head near the water ready to strike.

Left: The heron stabs its victim (in this case an eel) with a very fast, accurate blow. Just before the strike the heron often re-adjusts the position of its head, to make sure the final stab tells.

Below: All herons, including the purple heron (*Ardea purpurea*), can keep the head still, while swivelling the eyes downwards.

insects such as grasshoppers and emerging dragonflies. In the past, water bailiffs persecuted herons for their fish-eating habits, and trout farm owners today find individual herons persistent and expensive pests. Herons also welcome the source of food provided by suburban fish-ponds – goldfish are particularly easy to see.

With such a varied and abundant source of food, it is perhaps not surprising that herons have long lifespans. The record is held by a German bird that survived for 24 years; the two oldest British herons lived for 18 years.

Mortality Life can be hard for herons. All sorts of hazards may cause death – choking on large fish, being shot, becoming entangled in barbed wire, being killed by foxes, and (8% of all ringed recoveries) flying into overhead wires. The British Trust for Ornithology's sample census of heronries, which is the longest running survey of bird numbers in Britain, also shows how devastating the effects of severe winters can be.

Toxic chemicals, such as DDT and diel-

Mute swan (*Cygnus olor*)
Length (bill-tip to tail-tip)
152cm (5ft); weight—cob
(male) 12-20kg (26-44lb),
pen (female) slightly less;
distribution: on most slow-
flowing waters.

Mute swan

The mute swan that once graced the tables of medieval banquets is now protected from this fate. It is, however, vulnerable to the modern hazards of overhead power cables and lead weights in fishing tackle. Despite its name, the mute swan will snort and hiss noisily if it feels threatened.

Below: Downy cygnets take to the water early and are guarded carefully by their parents, who pull up underwater vegetation for them. It has been suggested that the adults also paddle vigorously to bring food to the surface for the young.

You will find mute swans wherever there are sizeable expanses of relatively still water. These majestic birds are at home on slow-flowing rivers, lakes, gravel pits, large ponds —even in heavily built up areas such as London, where they add a touch of serenity to stretches of the Thames. Their haunts are not, however, restricted to freshwater, since they also frequent harbours and estuaries and have been sighted as far offshore as the Solent on the south coast of England.

Striking appearance The mute swan is one of the most easily identifiable of British birds. The adult's plumage is pure white and the thickly feathered neck is long and curves in a graceful 'S' shape. The head is small with a

down-pointed, orange-red beak tipped with a black nail, and there is a black knob over the nostrils at the base of the bill; this knob is more pronounced on the male than the female —and most obvious in spring. The webbed feet are black. The young swan has a greyish plumage which begins to turn white during the first winter and becomes pure white by the third spring, while the beak takes two years to assume its bright orange-red colour.

The swan uses its long neck to feed on underwater plants; pondweed and semi-aquatic plants make up the bulk of its diet. It also eats algae and shore plants and occasionally will take worms, insects and fish; it swallows grit and fine gravel for

Taking to the air

An adult swan is too heavy to take off from a standing position. To gain momentum it runs along (on land or on the surface of the water) with its neck outstretched and its wings thrashing violently. In a strong wind, it may have to run as far as 100m (300ft) before taking off. In flight the wing beats make a loud rhythmic noise. In order to land, the swan slows itself down by spreading out its wings and using its feet as brakes.

roughage. In deep water, where its neck is not long enough to reach certain food, it upends like a duck.

Its calls are quite out of character with its name and appearance, since it will snort, grunt and hiss threateningly when provoked; it also gives a shrill, trumpet-like call—particularly to the young who reply to the adult in a high-pitched tone.

Mating breeding and nesting Mute swans pair up, often in the autumn, when they are between two and four years old. Paired swans are not gregarious, preferring to nest isolated in their own aggressively defended territory. Non-breeding individuals and those of pre-breeding age may congregate together in areas where there is plenty of food and space. In spring, when their courtship and mating rituals reach a peak, you can see a pair of swans facing each other, swaying their heads sideways or dipping their heads in the water, extending their necks and bills vertically and even upending. Once the pair has been established, the cob (male) and pen (female) return annually to the same territory to breed again. Swans seldom change their mate, unless they fail to breed.

The cob selects a nest site close to the water's edge and well away from other nests. Building the nest is mainly the pen's task, although the cob helps by gathering vegetation, often from previous nests, and passing it to her. The pair makes little attempt to camouflage the nest, which is a huge pile of reeds and sticks lined with a thin layer of down.

The pen lays her chalky, round-ended eggs every other day for up to 12 days; this occurs any time from April to July. The pen does most of the incubating, although the cob will take his turn and keep guard over the nest.

The eggs hatch after 36 days and the pen carries the broken shells to the water's edge. The young, which are born with their eyes open, are covered with soft, fur-like grey down; this is replaced by woolly feathers which change slowly to a drab brown colour. At five days they are independent enough to leave the nest during the daytime, although for up to a month they may continue to gather

in the nest at night. Cygnets will walk long distances to water, marching along in single file behind their parents. If you are lucky, you may see one riding on its parent's back between the arched wings. They fly at four months and are usually driven away from the nest area in the following spring, when their plumage has changed from grey and when territories are redefined and their parents begin to prepare for the next brood. After leaving the nest the young join the summer flocks of non-breeders until they are ready to mate.

Less than half the swans in the British Isles are breeding stock. You can easily identify the non-breeders, which are immature birds or those which have yet to form a nesting pairs, since they have pale pink bills and small nostril-lobes.

mature

immature

This mute swan is in aggressive mood as it protects its eggs (which lie in the large platform nest of reeds and sticks) from intruders. The wingspan can reach 2m (7ft).

Brent, barnacle and Canada geese

Brent and barnacle geese visit various coastal sites of the British Isles in winter, after breeding in separate areas in the Arctic Circle. Canada geese (below) are mainly resident here, though they were originally introduced from America 200 years ago.

The Brent Goose, the smallest goose species, is not much bigger than a large duck. It has a circumpolar distribution and breeds on coastal tundra and small islands in the high Arctic. Over thousands of years, separate populations have evolved plumage differences – with underparts ranging from dark grey to silvery white – sufficient for them to be described as sub-species.

Breeding and migration The dark-bellied Brent Geese have dark grey underparts and breed in northern Siberia. These birds migrate to north-west Europe for the winter, living in estuaries in eastern and southern England, the Netherlands and France.

There are also three separate populations

of light-bellied Brent Geese, which have silvery-grey underparts. The largest, numbering about 100,000, breeds in eastern Arctic Canada and winters on the east coast of the United States. A second population of about 9000 birds, breeds in the very north-east of Arctic Canada and northern Greenland, and winters in Ireland. The smallest population, of under 3000 birds, breeds in Spitsbergen and winters in Denmark.

Arctic breeders Brent Geese breed in the far north, almost all of them well north of the Arctic Circle. Here the brief summer is only just long enough for them to complete the breeding cycle. Indeed, in order that the young are on the wing before the cold of winter returns in September, the eggs are often laid while the snow still lies on the ground, in late May. The nest sites, on low ridges and hummocks, are free of snow, but the flat, marshy tundra around them is still covered. Until the snow melts there is no food for the geese, which graze on marsh plants in the summer, and they have to live on their fat reserves built up before the spring migration.

With timing so critical, any delay in the start of the breeding can be disastrous. If the spring is late and the snow is deeper than usual, or takes longer to thaw from the marshy ground, then either the birds are unable to lay their eggs at all, or if they do, then continued bad weather may force them to abandon their nests. Heavy rain or snow in the period when the eggs are hatching, or the young are still very small, can cause severe mortality.

The effects of weather Bad summers occur quite regularly, but clearly, since the birds do breed in the far north, there are also sufficient good summers. When the geese arrive in the autumn on their wintering

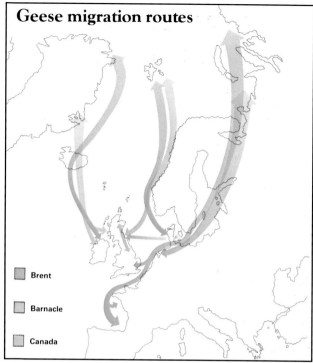

Geese migration routes

- Brent
- Barnacle
- Canada

Below: The male and female Brent goose are similar: the upperparts, head, neck and chest are completely black, the only relief being a small white patch on either side of the neck. Underparts vary from dark grey to silvery white.

grounds in north-west Europe, it is possible to ascertain how well they have bred that summer. The young birds show pale barring on the wings, but lack the white neck marks, and by scanning through the flocks with a telescope the number of young can be assessed. A flock can consist of as many as 50% young birds in a very good breeding year, to none at all in a bad one.

These enormous variations in breeding success naturally have a considerable effect on the overall size of the population and the way it changes. For example the dark-bellied Brent goose experienced rather more good years than bad through the late 1960s and early 1970s, and this coincided with increased protection as first France, and then Denmark, banned the shooting of them. Britain and the Netherlands, the other two main wintering countries, had protected the Brent in the 1950s. The population rose sharply from about 25,000 in 1964 to 120,000 in 1975, and has gone on rising, though more slowly, to its present level of 150,000.

Greylag goose

The greylag goose is the ancestor of the familiar white goose of farmyards and fairy tales. Semi-domestic greylags are widespread, but wild birds are confined to the north.

The greylag goose is one of several species of so-called 'grey' geese found in Britain. The others are the pink-footed, bean and white-fronted geese; all have predominantly grey plumage which distinguishes them from the Canada, Brent and barnacle geese, which are brown or black.

The greylag goose is the heaviest of the grey geese–an adult weighs about 2-3kg (4½-6½lb) and differs from the others in its combination of large round head, stout orange-pink bill and pink legs. No other grey goose has all these features. In flight the bold pale grey forewings of the greylag show up clearly and also help to distinguish it from other geese.

Visitors from Iceland Although Britain supports a small but growing population of breeding greylags, the great majority found in this country are winter visitors from their breeding grounds in Iceland. Most of these birds can be seen in lowland areas of Scotland, particularly Aberdeen, Perth, Kinross, the Lothians and the Solway Firth.

These winter visitors arrive during the second half of October and head immediately for the stubbled fields of harvested barley and wheat, where they feed off spilt grain. Soon afterwards, the potato harvest is gathered and the greylags perform a useful service to the farmers by eating all the broken and small

Above: Many greylags are semi-domestic.

Opposite: Greylags and other wildfowl at Slimbridge, Gloucestershire.

Below: Greylag distribution.

flocks fly
in V-formation

orange bill

pink legs

pale grey
forewings

white rump

Greylag goose (*Anser anser*). At 75-90cm (30-35in) long, the largest of the grey geese found in Britain. Apart from size, it is distinguished from other species of grey goose by its paler plumage, pink legs and orange bill – though some birds in eastern Britain have pink bills.

eastern race
has pink bill

Below: A typical brood consists of between four and six chicks. Both parents help to look after the chicks, and the family stays together into the winter.

tubers left behind. Without this 'mopping up', these tubers would sprout again the following year as 'rogue' potatoes.

These food sources are soon exhausted, however, and from late November through to the spring the geese turn to feeding on grass, so becoming the farmer's enemy rather than his friend. At first the problem is not serious since, in winter, sheep and cattle are usually brought in and fed with hay and other foodstuffs. But as soon as the animals are turned out to graze on the spring grass they and the geese come into direct competition.

Numbers increasing The conflict between the migrant greylag geese and Scottish farmers has intensified in recent years because of the steadily increasing population of winter visiting greylags. Since 1960 their numbers have more than doubled to their present total of about 90,000.

This increase is due partly to better protection, with reserves being set up to prevent the birds being shot. The other major factor is the change in Scottish agriculture in recent years. Much more barley and potatoes are being planted now, and more pastures are being improved and fertilised. So, as the farmers grow more and improved crops, they provide better feeding for greylag geese. Farmers now use scaring devices to keep the geese away from certain fields, but only with partial success.

Return to Iceland In late April the winter migrant greylags return to their breeding grounds in Iceland. Their favourite sites for breeding are lowland river valleys, and marshy areas beside rivers and shallow lakes. The nest is usually a simple scrape, hidden among thick vegetation. The eggs, usually between four and six, are incubated by the female alone while the male stands guard; the process takes 28 days.

The family stays together throughout the autumn migration and following winter, so that the young learn directly from their parents the best migration routes and where to feed and roost over winter.

Resident greylags Not all our winter population of greylags depart for Iceland in the spring. A few wild greylags are resident in Britain, mainly in the north-west of Scotland and the Outer Hebrides. These are the remnants, no more than 2000-3000 individuals, of a population that once bred widely in England and Scotland. As recently as the 17th century greylag geese bred commonly in the fenlands of East Anglia. But gradually man's activities have reduced their numbers to their present level, both by direct persecution and by draining the bird's marshland habitat.

Fortunately, the tiny Scottish population is now increasing. Greylag geese have begun breeding on uninhabited offshore islands and on islands in large lochs. One of our largest breeding colonies is on Loch Druidibeg in South Uist, where there are many small islands covered with bracken and scrub – ideal habitat for greylags. The Loch is now a part of the National Nature Reserve.

Semi-domestic greylags All the greylags described so far can be seen only in Scotland and the far north of England. Yet greylags appear in many different parts of the British Isles. These birds are neither the winter migrants from Iceland nor the indigenous wild greylags of Scotland. They are semi-domestic and have been introduced to their present breeding grounds. Over the years, landowners, people with private collections of wildfowl and wildfowlers themselves have all established free-flying flocks of greylags.

Mallard

The mallard is a popular bird because it takes to many man-made surroundings, and tamely accepts food from the hand. In summer it moults its feathers and cannot fly.

The mallard is the most common, widespread and best-known duck in the British Isles. Although it is a water bird, the mallard has followed the example of other successful species – for instance starlings, pigeons and house sparrows – by adapting to man-made habitats.

Many water-birds have declined because pollution and the drainage of marshes have destroyed their natural environment. But the mallard has managed to outweigh such losses by colonizing the artificial lakes and ponds in many town and city centres, as well as taking to the smallest farm ponds. Even in the centre of London, you'll find mallard on the ponds in all the major parks. It is also invariably a mallard which features in press photographs of a policeman holding up the traffic to allow mother and brood to cross the road safely.

Courting You can see the courtship behaviour of the mallard on any mild winter's day, as the birds begin to form pairs ready for the summer breeding season. Ducks form a new pair in winter or spring, and then break up again after the breeding season. The female is actively courted by the males (drakes), often several at a time. From a group of displaying males the female eventually chooses her mate. She presumably selects the one which is displaying with greatest vigour, showing him-

Above: The dappled brown female mallard leads her downy nestlings to the water, almost as soon as they are hatched. They feed themselves without any parental help.

Right: The traditional mallard nest site in the wild is in thick vegetation – nettles, brambles, bracken and heather. Unusual sites, more associated with Man, include water tanks, flower boxes and bridge supports. The female builds her nest using plant debris, grasses, and down feathers plucked from her own chest. She usually lays 7-11 pale bluish-green eggs, which she alone incubates. The young become independent at the same time they fledge – about six weeks after hatching.

Duck displays

There are a number of behavioural gestures, mostly associated with courting, which the male performs.

1 Grunt whistle is the most common display. The male tucks his head down to his chest, and lifts the front half of his body right out of the water. He then just flicks the surface with the tip of his bill, sending a little spray of water droplets up into the air. At the same time he lets out a low grunt, followed immediately by a clear whistle.

2 Head-up, tail-up involves both chest and tail coming up off the water. This emphasises the colouring of the male's neck and breast, as well as the black and white pattern on the tail.

3 Raised wing is another action where the male tucks his head behind the raised wing, as if to preen. This really serves to expose a blue-green bar (speculum) edged with white, along the rear of the wing.

Though not actually involved in the courtship rituals, this male **(4)** is alerted to the proceedings and quacks in response. When there is a surplus of males, they continue to court females already paired.

self off to be the brightest and largest bird present, and therefore the most suitable to fertilise her eggs.

Choice of nest site Mallards tend to choose nest sites on the ground, where they will be concealed in marshy vegetation; but they also adapt to all kinds of artificial situations–including nest boxes and holes in, and even under, buildings. They may nest a trifle precariously in the crowns of pollarded willows, and even on broad branches many metres off the ground. One much-publicised site was in a window box of the house next-door to the Iranian Embassy in London, facing on to Hyde Park. The duck sat through the trauma of the 1980 siege and rescue, apparently without budging from her nest.

Nest construction When nesting off the ground, the female mallard uses little or no nest material because she cannot carry things in her bill. On the ground, however, the duck constructs a shallow cup of such vegetation as it can reach from the nest, pulling and pushing stems and leaves into a circular rim.

As the mother begins to lay the clutch of seven to eleven eggs, she also begins to pluck down from her breast. This process starts slowly with a few bits at a time, but by the end of the egg-laying–she usually manages one egg per day–there is a thick layer of pale greyish down under and around the eggs. The down serves two functions: first it insulates the eggs from the cold, and often damp, ground; secondly, when the female leaves the eggs for her twice daily feed and bathe, she pulls the down and some of the nest material over the eggs, concealing them completely from any passing predator.

Incubating the eggs The drake takes no part in the incubation, and rarely has any contact with the female once she finishes laying and begins to sit on the eggs all day. He waits nearby to meet her when she comes off the nest. He also keeps watch while she has a hasty feed, but only does this for a week or so. In fact this is just as well: the female's mottled brown plumage is perfect camouflage, and fits in with the nest surroundings, but the contrasting green, purple and white plumage of the male could catch the eye of a fox or crow, and lead such predators to the nest with its precious clutch of eggs.

Brooding the chicks The female incubates the eggs for 26-28 days. The young hatch out over a short period–all within 24 hours. Depending on the time of day and the weather, the female will brood them in the nest for

2 head-up tail-up

female

3 raised wing

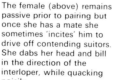

4 alert, quacking

1 grunt whistle

The female (above) remains passive prior to pairing but once she has a mate she sometimes 'incites' him to drive off contending suitors. She dabs her head and bill in the direction of the interloper, while quacking noisily.

several hours, during which their down dries, and they become fluffy and active. Then she leads them off the nest, and takes them to the nearest stretch of suitable water where they can find food. Most nests are within a hundred metres of water, but some ducks may have to trek double that distance, and even cross roads to get there.

The young can run and swim as soon as they leave the nest, and also feed themselves, pecking instinctively at any small object. They quicly learn to distinguish between small seeds and insects which are good to eat, and surface debris, which is of no value to them.

Tufted duck and pochard

Two of our most attractive diving ducks, the pochard and its close relative the tufted duck, are becoming increasingly common on Britain's lakes and reservoirs. Many are now breeding here, but most are winter visitors from northern Europe.

Above: A male tufted duck. The female has a much less pronounced tuft.

Tufted duck (*Aythya fuligula*). Resident duck, breeding next to lakes, gravel pits and reservoirs throughout much of lowland Britain. Length 43cm (17in).

Pochard (*Aythya ferina*). Resident duck, but far less common in the breeding season than the tufted duck and confined mostly to natural lakes. Length 46cm (18in).

As with so many species of duck, male pochard and tufted duck are strikingly coloured birds. The females, on the other hand, are dull by comparison since they need to be well camouflaged when they incubate their eggs and raise the young.

The male tufted duck has black upperparts set off by brilliant white sides and belly. It gets its name from the tuft on the back of its head, although this feature is not always conspicuous. The female tufted duck has only a rudimentary tuft and is brown with slightly paler sides. Sometimes, she has a pale patch at the base of her bill. In flight, both sexes show a long white bar on the upper side of each wing.

The pochard is larger and more heavily built than the tufted duck. The male is unmistakable, his pale grey body contrasting sharply with a black chest and dark chestnut neck and head. From a distance, the male seems to have a uniformly dark head, neck and breast, and a pale body. The female resembles a larger version of the female tufted duck, but she has a paler back and buff markings around the bill and eye. In flight, the pochard shows pale grey wing-bars, the only species of duck with this feature.

Winter visitors The numbers of tufted ducks and pochards breeding in Britain has increased considerably during the last hundred years – in the case of the tufted duck the increase has been spectacular – yet most of the birds seen in Britain are still winter visitors from other parts of Europe. It is estimated that there are between 40,000 and 50,000 of each species wintering in Britain, compared to the summer breeding figures of about 5000 pairs of tufted duck and only 300 pairs of pochard. It is, therefore, not surprising that they are our commonest diving ducks to be seen on lakes, reservoirs and gravel pits during winter.

Many tufted duck wintering in Britain arrive here from Iceland, the rest coming from northern Scandinavia and northern and arctic Russia. The former population winters mostly in Scotland, western England and Ireland; the latter usually settles in southern and eastern England. Flocks of several thousand may gather, particularly on large areas of water such as the reservoirs around London.

Our wintering pochard come to us from Russia, though further south than the tufted duck's breeding grounds. Like the tufted duck, pochard form huge flocks numbering several thousand. A notable gathering point is a tiny pool, called Duddington Loch, lying within the city limits of Edinburgh, which used to hold a staggering 8000 pochard crowded together, though their numbers are now declining. The London reservoirs and gravel pits in the Thames Valley also support large winter populations of pochard.

Favourite foods During winter, large numbers of both pochard and tufted duck happily coexist on the same lake or reservoir–happily, because they are not in direct competition with each other since they have different food preferences. Generally, the tufted duck is carnivorous and the pochard is herbivorous. However, both species feed on the other's food if it is abundant. The main food source for the pochard is the stoneworts and pondweeds; the tufted duck feeds mainly on insects and shellfish.

Both species feed by diving, usually beginning with a slight upward jump to give them impetus to dive deeper. Once under water they swim with their feet alone, keeping their wings tightly closed. The dives last for about

With its striking black and white plumage and tuft, the male tufted duck is far more distinguished than its dull brown and white female. After mating, the male adopts a characteristic 'bill-down' posture.

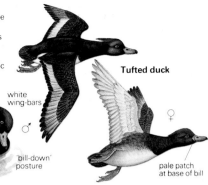

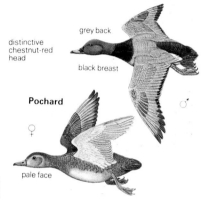
Tufted duck

Right: The characteristic chestnut brown head of a male pochard contrasts sharply with its black chest and pale grey wings and back. The female pochard is dull brown.

Below: Pochards and tufted ducks share the same habitat but rarely compete with each other for food since they have different preferences. Tufted ducks generally feed on animals, whereas pochards concentrate more on plants.

15-20 seconds and the birds emerge close to where they submerged.

Segregated flocks In both species, the winter flocks consist predominantly of one sex or the other, rather than being evenly mixed. The reason for this is that the males leave the breeding grounds well before the females and so arrive at their wintering grounds much earlier. By the time the females arrive the more northerly wintering sites (the ones nearest to the breeding grounds) may already be full of males, so the females have to move on further south.

Even if a flock comprises males and females it is noticeable how often the sexes remain separated. The males tend to feed in deeper water further from the shore. Being larger, they can dive deeper and stay submerged for longer, up to 20 seconds compared to the females' 15 seconds. By feeding in deeper water the males reduce the competition for food by exploiting a different source.

Resident tufted ducks Most pochards and tufted ducks migrate in spring back to their summer breeding grounds, but increasing numbers are now breeding in Britain. The earliest recorded instance of tufted ducks breeding in Britain was as recent as 1849, when a pair bred in Yorkshire.

Pintail and shoveler

The pintail is easy to recognise with its long, fine tail, as is the squat shoveler with its remarkably large bill. Both breed in Britain and Ireland, although breeding pintail are rare; and both populations are outnumbered in winter by visitors from northern USSR, coming in their thousands.

Above: A male shoveler in breeding plumage. When swimming, shovelers have a distinctive appearance, lying noticeably low in the water. The stoutness of the neck is emphasized by the large head, ending in the great spatulate bill, held pointing slightly downwards as if a little too heavy for the bird.

Below: Both species breed in lowland areas with marshes and flood meadows.

Of the 20 species of wild duck seen regularly at some time of the year in Britain and Ireland, seven belong to the genus *Anas*. These are mallard, teal, garganey, wigeon, gadwall, pintail and shoveler. Here we look at two of these, the pintail and the shoveler.

Measured from bill to tail tip, the pintail is the second longest of the group (after the mallard) at 56cm (22in), while the shoveler shares third place with the gadwall at 51cm (20in). As a breeding species the pintail is the rarest of the group, while the shoveler has the third largest population after the mallard and teal. Apart from the garganey, which is a summer visitor, the breeding populations of these ducks are reinforced by large numbers of birds migrating to Britain and Ireland from more northerly breeding grounds.

Pintail The slender body of the pintail is enhanced by its long thin neck and greatly elongated central tail feathers. The latter make up one fifth of its total length. The dark chocolate-brown colouring of the male's head continues down the back of the neck to the mantle (lower back). The front and sides of the neck are a bright and contrasting white which continues as a narrow streak up each side of the head. The underparts are also white, while the back and flanks are finely vermiculated (marked with tiny wavy stripes) in grey.

The squat, heavy-headed silhouette of the

Distribution

■ pintail
□ shoveler

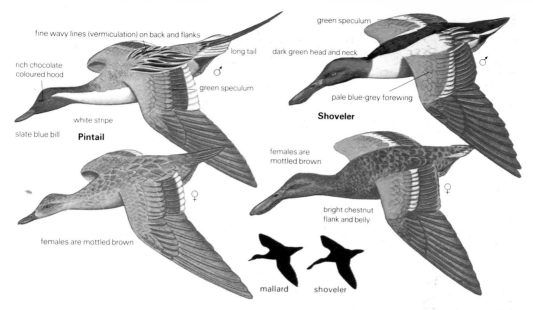

fine wavy lines (vermiculation) on back and flanks

green speculum

rich chocolate coloured hood

long tail

dark green head and neck

♂

green speculum

♂

pale blue-grey forewing

white stripe

Shoveler

slate blue bill **Pintail**

females are mottled brown

♀

bright chestnut flank and belly

females are mottled brown

♀

mallard   shoveler

shoveler is in direct contrast to the graceful pintail, though the male is not unattractive, having colourful plumage. The male is visible from a great distance thanks to its gleaming white chest. The head and neck are dark green, appearing almost black, while the flanks are a bright chestnut, further set off by a white patch between them and the black undertail coverts. The back is black but has two white stripes running from front to rear, one on each side. Female shoveler are a mottled brown all over, their bill and squat shape serving to identify them.

Breeding grounds The pintail and shoveler both breed in Britain, but the pintail is comparatively scarce, with probably no more than 50 pairs, while the shoveler, following a period of increase in recent years, is now estimated to total about 1000 pairs. The pintail has been found breeding in scattered small groups of one or two pairs, quite widely over northern England and Scotland; but many of the sites are only used once or twice in several years. Some of the more regular breeding places are to be found in East Anglia and north Kent. Here they nest in wet pastures, concealing their eggs under overhanging tussocks of grass, and never very far from shallow areas of fresh water.

Similar habitats are chosen by the shoveler, one of the major breeding sites for the species in Britain being on the Ouse Washes on the Norfolk/Cambridgeshire border. Here there has been a considerable increase in pairs, also reflected elsewhere in the country. In the 1950s there were probably no more than 50 pairs, but this had increased to about 100 by the 1960s, reaching a peak of over 300 in 1975, or perhaps a third of the total for Britain. Elsewhere there are few concentrations, but the species is widespread in all but the more upland areas of the country.

Winter numbers In winter the relative status of the two species is reversed. The pintail is much more common, with a regular peak of about 25,000 and perhaps occasionally as many as 30,000. The shoveler, on the other hand, rarely numbers much above 5000-7000, with an absolute peak of perhaps 10,000. A few years ago a peak of 5000 would have been unusual, but the increase recorded in breeding birds has been reflected by an increase in wintering numbers, at least during the early part of the winter.

Pintail migration The great majority of the pintail wintering in north-west Europe breed in the northern part of the USSR. But this is only a small part of the total number of pintail migrating out of this area each autumn. Perhaps 75,000 winter in north-west Europe, compared to some 300,000 in the Mediterranean and Black Sea areas. Some of these even cross the Sahara to winter in Senegal and Niger, West Africa.

Above: Recognition features of the birds in flight. The silhouettes show how different a shoveler looks from a mallard—chiefly because of the bill. Also, the shoveler looks as if its wings are set further back because the bill extends so far forward. The pintail has a slim body with a long tail. It also has a green, shiny area (a speculum) behind the forewing. The shoveler, on opening its wings, reveals a pale blue-grey forewing and behind it a green, white-edged speculum.

Below: A male pintail preens his back feathers, of which the remarkably long scapulars are clearly seen pointing outwards across the front of the wing.

Coot and moorhen

Coots and moorhens are freshwater birds but, unlike the ducks, they spend much of their time feeding on land, running about on their disproportionately long feet. In the breeding season both species become very aggressive in defence of their territories.

Below: A moorhen among the grasses at the edge of a pond. The bright red beak 'shield' and the white area under the tail distinguish it from the coot. Another characteristic is its habit of jerking its head back and forth as it swims.

The coot and the moorhen, close relatives belonging to the rail family, are common and widely distributed throughout the British Isles. The coot is all black, with a white 'shield' above its white bill, and a faint whitish wing bar (as it does not fly very much, however, this last feature is rarely seen). Its legs are greenish in colour. The moorhen is brown-black in colour, tending to grey on the sides and underparts. Its shield, smaller than that of the coot, is bright red, as is its bill. There is a whitish bar down the flanks, and the area under the tail is also pure white. Its legs are green.

Both coots and moorhens can become totally accustomed to man. Moorhens, especially, breed beside the smallest farm or village pond, and also appear throughout the year on lakes in city and town centre parks. At a distance, both species can be confused with ducks. The moorhen, however, is smaller than most ducks, raises its tail well out of the water, and jerks its head backwards and forwards as it swims. The coot has a rounded, dumpy outline–very different from the straight-backed appearance of most ducks. Once you see the short, pointed bill you can easily distinguish both birds from the broad-billed ducks.

Territory, nests and chicks During the breeding season coots and moorhens defend territories against others of their own species. The area of the territories varies greatly, but

Like ducks, coots swim well and dive for food. Instead of having duck-like webbed feet, however, the coot has broad lobes on each toe (see below) which help to propel the bird through the water. (The moorhen is less aquatic in habits than the coot and has no lobes on its long toes.)

lobe

the coot usually defends a much larger one (up to an acre or more) than the moorhen. Some moorhen territories may be less than 100 square metres (123 sq yards) in size. The territories provide all that the pair needs in the way of food and nest sites.

The nests of coots and moorhens are built of dead leaves and the stems of rushes and other water plants. They are often placed in shallow water among concealing vegetation, sometimes anchored to the bottom, but often just floating on the water. Moorhens, more than coots, also build on dry land, occasionally a little way off the ground in thick bushes. A shallow cup at the top of the nest is lined with green leaves and finer material. Both species lay between six and nine pale buff eggs that are liberally spotted with brown.

Young coots and moorhens are able to walk and swim within a few hours of hatch-

ing; moorhen chicks tend to stay close to the nest for the first few days at least, returning to it to be brooded by the parents at night or in cold, wet weather. Around the time of hatching the adult male coot builds one or two 'platforms' within the breeding territory. These are similar to the nest but flatter on top and are provided with one or more ramps leading up from the water. The young coots are brought to these platforms and brooded there rather than in the nest.

The young of both species are blackish in colour, with reddish heads. In the case of the coot this colouring comes from the tips of the down plumules, but the moorhen's head is bare—it is the skin that is red. This colour also extends to the bills and tiny shields of the young of both species. The bright colour in the middle of the reddish head shows as a central 'target' area for the parents who are feeding the chick. It is noticeable that as the young grow and begin to feed themselves, the reddish colour fades.

Above: Coots just taking off for flight from a lake. The lobed toes on the feet assist the bird in its laborious take-off from the water surface. To gain the necessary speed and impetus the coot has to patter over the water for several metres. It always looks rather laboured in flight.

Coot (*Fulica atra*); 38cm (15in) from beak to tail; distribution widespread, on lakes and meres. Resident.

Moorhen (*Gallinula chloropus*); 33cm (13in) from beak to tail; distribution widespread, on ponds, marshes, lakes and rivers. Resident

Moorhen

red shield

yellow tip

white undertail area

white flash on flanks

red head

chick (second brood)

juvenile (first brood)

white shield

floating nest

Coot

red head

chick

Lapwing

The lapwing is one of the easier birds to spot in our countryside, with its distinctive crest and dark green plumage with white wing patches. It can be seen at all times of year, breeding on hillsides, marshes and farmland, or wintering near ploughed fields.

Peewit, green plover and lapwing are just three of a multitude of colloquial names for this particular bird, an indication of how diverse and confusing local names can be. Nevertheless, each name has a meaning: 'pee-wit' clearly comes from the plaintive rasping cry so familiar over meadows and marshes. 'Green plover', too, is a more appropriate name than would, at first, seem. Take a close look at this apparently black-and-white bird on a sunny day: the 'black' back is really deep bottle-green, shot with iridescent purple. Often you see lapwings in the air, when their floppy, clumsy looking wingbeats give a clear indication of how this, their most widely accepted name, was derived.

Lapwings are medium-sized waders, about as large as a pigeon but with the horizontal body posture and long legs of a wader. Besides their pied plumage, they have other useful identification features, such as the short beak and the slender, upturned crest, which is rather longer in the male than in the female lapwing. It is well worth seeking a closer look (using a car as a hide is an excellent idea) to appreciate the beauty of the crest and the sheen of the back feathers.

When they hatch, the young chicks are superbly camouflaged: the basic coloration of the down is a sandy fawn, with copious black or dark brown markings. There is a conspicuous white patch on the back of the head, easily seen when the chick is upright and running about, and doubtless an aid to its parents in keeping track of its whereabouts. When the chick squats, this prominent mark vanishes. As they grow, the chicks begin to resemble their parents, but with much reduced crests and with fawn fringes to the greenish-black back feathers, giving them a markedly scaly appearance.

Many habitats Lapwings are classed among the wading birds, but unlike the majority of these their prime habitat is not the shore. Their short, typically plover-like beaks are ideal for catching small ground insects and other invertebrates. They often feed well away from the water, and in Africa many of their close relatives are birds of arid grassland.

In winter, most lapwings are found on

Above: A male lapwing incubating the eggs. Even a small tuft of rushes is sufficient cover for the lapwing's nest.

Left: The lapwing's nest is relatively elaborate for a wader, but the eggs are typical: irregularly blotched, and laid with their pointed ends inwards.

Right: When the parent bird gives an alarm call, the chicks squat down to hide in the grass.

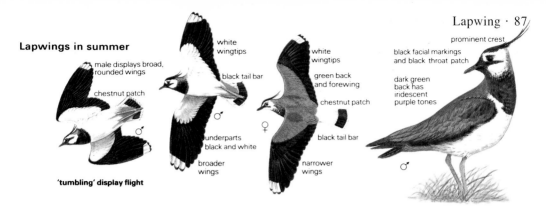

Lapwings in summer

male displays broad, rounded wings

chestnut patch

♂

'tumbling' display flight

white wingtips

black tail bar

♂

underparts black and white

broader wings

white wingtips

green back and forewing

chestnut patch

black tail bar

♀

narrower wings

prominent crest

black facial markings and black throat patch

dark green back has iridescent purple tones

dark green back has iridescent purple tones

♂

damp grassland or ploughed fields, with relatively few on the moors. They occasionally visit the shore, but usually only when snow or hard frost has made feeding difficult inland. On farmland, it is amazing to see how a flock of such conspicuously black and white birds can apparently vanish into the ground when they land. Their food at this time includes a great many worms and insect larvae driven out of the soil by the shallow flooding associated with winter rainfall. Often, lapwings congregate in flocks, sometimes hundreds of birds strong, but towards the end of winter these flocks begin to fragment as migrants return to their breeding areas overseas and as local birds begin to take up their territories.

Lapwings breed in a considerable range of habitats, but these do have a common feature: the territories always have patches of short vegetation or bare ground nearby, suitable for feeding. In some areas, most breeding birds are found on waste or marginal land, such as that surrounding gravel pits, chalk quarries, refuse tips or sewage farms. Elsewhere, they are farmland birds, breeding on permanent pasture or on freshly ploughed land sown with winter or spring corn. In upland areas, lapwings tend to congregate in the more sheltered situations, rather than on the moors. They usually set up their territories in the valleys, where any arable farming also tends to be concentrated, so improving the range of feeding habitats available.

Defending the home Territories are easily recognised as the air overhead in spring is full of tumbling, calling birds performing their aerobatic displays. Besides the calls, the wingbeats themselves are audible: the rounded, 'fingered' wings of the lapwing produce a unique 'whooshing' noise. Interestingly, male and female can be told apart at this time by the width of the wings: with the major role to play in display, it is natural that the male's wing is noticeably broader and thus noisier. Wing noise is not just used for display, but also as a terror weapon to repel invaders of the pair's territory.

Ground-nesting birds are vulnerable to attacks from predators – magpies, crows and

Above: The breeding plumage of the lapwing. The pied plumage proves, on closer inspection, to be a combination of black on the outer part of the wings, white mainly on the undersides and bottle-green with iridescent purple tones on the back. The winter plumage is similar to the summer plumage, but looks mottled, for many of the feathers have buff edges.

Lapwing (*Vanellus vanellus*). Wader adapted to inland habitats including farmland and upland meadows. Resident, with additional wintering population from Europe. Length 30cm (12in).

Below: A small flock of lapwings over a ploughed field in winter.

foxes – and any marauders, even humans, are instantly attacked by both birds as they cross the territorial boundary. The swooping, screeching lapwings, with these thumping wingbeats, are usually enough to put off any intending predators and thus increase the chances of the eggs being unharmed and the young surviving. It need not be the threat of losing in combat that deters the predator, for if there are other good hunting grounds nearby that are free from the distracting noise and behaviour of lapwings, the predator simply takes the easier option and hunts elsewhere. It is the aggressive appearance of the lapwing, rather than its fighting capability, that keeps danger away.

Often quite innocent parties become involved, and the sight of a pair of partridges straying accidentally into a lapwing territory while feeding, and then attempting to withdraw and maintain some dignity under such an onslaught, can be extremely amusing to watch.

Snipe and jack snipe

Snipe, noticeable for their long, straight bills, are small wading birds most often seen in inland marshy areas, damp meadows and river valleys.

The two species of snipe regularly seen in the British Isles are both birds of rank vegetation in damp, fresh-water areas. Both birds have richly mottled and striped brown body plumage, with characteristic creamy stripes along each side of the back. The jack snipe is known only as a winter visitor and is the smaller of the two species, with a shorter beak. The common snipe is a widespread breeding species, and its numbers are augmented during winter by an influx of larger birds from the rest of Europe; it has a very long bill.

Common snipe breed in damp meadows, river valleys, coastal fresh-water marshes, bogs, and over damp moorland throughout the British Isles. They are thinly scattered in the more populated areas of south-eastern England but become increasingly common in western and northern Britain. There are particularly large breeding populations in the boglands of central Ireland, over much of the Highlands of Scotland and on many Scottish islands, especially the remote St Kilda group. The birds are quite small–roughly the size of a starling, but look much longer as they have 6cm (2½in) long bills.

'Drumming' flight It is easy to discover that common snipe are holding territory, as the birds have a conspicuous aerial display called 'drumming'. The displaying bird flies above its territory, periodically swooping down with its outer tail feathers pushed out into the passing airstream. The feathers are strengthened and stiff so that they whirr as the air passes them, causing the 'drumming' sound. In fact, to most people the sound is not so much a drumming noise as a bleat, sounding rather like a goat. Such displaying birds also utter a 'chippering' note.

These noisy displays may take place at any time of day but are most usual early in the morning or during the evening; some birds display at night as well if there is a bright moon. There is another territorial call, generally given from an elevated perch such as a fence post or tree stump, and this is a sharp, loud 'tock'.

Territorial displays may take place as early as February in southern England–at

The jack snipe is a winter visitor that breeds in the north-eastern parts of Europe and western Siberia. It is smaller than the common snipe but less shy; if approached it does not fly away until the last possible moment.

Jack snipe
(*Lymnocryptes minimus*), 19cm (7½in) from beak to tail. Shorter bill and rounder wings than common snipe and no white on tail. Sept-April visitor.

Common snipe
(*Gallinago gallinago*), 27cm (10½in) from beak to tail. Very long bill. Resident.

Above: Common snipe feeding in marshland – their typical habitat. You usually see them in groups, probing with their exceptionally long bills for worms and other food. They also take insects from the surface.

least two months earlier than the displays of birds in northern Scotland.

The chicks are most attractive, with striking markings. They are able to fly after 18-20 days but, like all waders, they leave their nest within a few hours of hatching. In some areas two broods may be reared, but most pairs are thought to be single brooded.

Long sensitive bills The common snipe's long bill is used to obtain food from deep in the ground. It is a precise and sensitive tool and a bird can insert the whole length of the bill into soft ground and still open the tip to take worms or other food. Snipe take food items from the surface as well.

When the marshy areas where snipe normally feed freeze rock hard, they are adept at finding areas which have not frozen, such as where a spring has kept the ground open. Here they may congregate in large numbers. Flocks of snipe, known as wisps, flushed out from the marshes by shooting parties, usually number fewer than 10 birds, but in freezing weather favoured areas might provide flocks of 50-100 birds. If frosts persist native birds may be forced to move to Ireland, where it is generally warmer in winter, or southward to France or Iberia.

Worldwide distribution The common snipe is a widespread species away from the British Isles. The main population breeds right across northern Europe and northern Asia, and another group occupies most of South America; there are even common snipe breeding over much of East Africa. Some of the island populations, such as those on St Kilda and other outlying Scottish islands, are slightly bigger and darker than the general run of British and European birds. The birds in the Faeroes and Iceland are certainly big and dark, and it is probably the influence of the island's isolation which causes these differences in colour and size.

The jack snipe is much rarer than the common snipe and is a native breeding species of the north-easternmost parts of Europe and western Siberia. The wintering birds reach the British Isles in October and leave again in March or early April. The birds are superficially similar to common snipe, but their bills are shorter and they are, overall, about two-thirds the size of the common snipe.

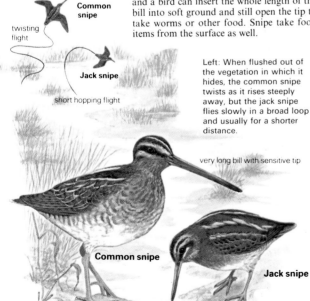

Common snipe

twisting flight

Jack snipe

short hopping flight

very long bill with sensitive tip

Common snipe

Jack snipe

Left: When flushed out of the vegetation in which it hides, the common snipe twists as it rises steeply away, but the jack snipe flies slowly in a broad loop and usually for a shorter distance.

Dipper

Dippers (above) nest beside fast-flowing streams and flit low over the water, alighting on favoured stones and boulders. They stand bobbing and bowing for a while, and then plunge into the rushing water to hunt aquatic creatures–they even walk beneath the surface, gripping the stream bed with their powerful claws.

Dipper (*Cinclus cinclus*) seen mainly beside fast, stony streams in upland areas; solitary dweller. Resident. Sexes look alike. Length 18cm (7in).

Below: The dipper is found in areas between 320 and 640m (1000-2000ft) above sea level; but in the north, in places where hills descend steeply to the sea, dippers nest close to the shore as well.

With its bold plumage and strong association with rivers and streams, the dipper is normally an easy bird to identify. Perhaps best likened to a 'thrush-sized wren', it has a jaunty, tail-cocked posture, and as it stands on some stone or boulder it frequently bobs up and down. Its legs are strong and look similar to those of a starling, while its beak is like that of a thrush in both colour and size. The upperparts are a rich, plain-chocolate brown, and the wings and tail look short in proportion to the distinctly plump body. By far the most conspicuous feature is the large, strikingly white 'bib' extending across the throat and breast, and down on to the belly.

In the case of English and most Scottish-breeding birds, this white bib has a broad chestnut margin which merges gradually into the near-black of the flanks and belly. Irish-breeding dippers (and also those in the Hebrides) have considerably less chestnut, and birds of the Continental race (which sometime stray to east and south-east England in spring and autumn) have almost no chestnut at all. The Continental race of dipper is in fact known as the black-bellied dipper.

Stony stream dwellers Just as characteristic as the plumage is the habitat of the dipper. Apart from stray migrants, which are sometimes seen on the coast or on slow-moving

Dipper distribution

The British and Irish dippers

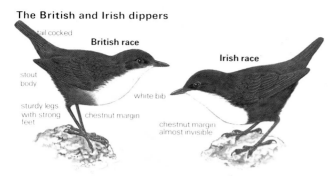

tail cocked

British race

Irish race

stout
body

white bib

sturdy legs
with strong
feet

chestnut margin

chestnut margin
almost invisible

often in mid-stream, and the dipper stands on them, bobbing up and down continuously. Against the background of broken white water, the clear white bib offers surprisingly good camouflage. As the dipper bobs and dips its tail, it also blinks, using its so-called 'third eye lid' or nictitating membrane, which travels fore-and-aft, rather than up and down, to wipe the eye surface clean. In the dipper, the nictitating membrane is conspicuously white. Under water, this membrane is thought to protect the dipper's eye from gritty particles; when submerged it becomes transparent and does not hamper the bird's underwater vision.

Underwater hunter From the boulders in

streams in the lowlands, dippers are typically birds of fast-flowing streams and the shallow rocky shores of lochs and tarns in hilly or mountainous country. In Britain, only those dippers that inhabit the south-eastern edge of the breeding range (roughly along a line from Swanage in Dorset to Flamborough Head in Humberside) frequent slower-moving lowland rivers or streams. These birds usually favour stretches near weirs or sluices, where the water flow is broken.

Most dippers are sedentary birds, establishing a territory on a suitable stream or river and rarely straying far from it. Those in the far north, or at higher altitudes, do descend to lower waters during the winter, but in general, severe winters (especially those with a sudden, rapid-freezing onset) are fatal for many dippers.

Dippers are usually to be seen singly or in pairs (except when they have newly fledged young), and most pairs maintain their territories through the winter months. They are reluctant to cross the 'border' with adjacent territories, and double back when reaching this invisible line. Usually their flight is low and fast, with frequent, penetrating 'zit . . . zit . . . zit' calls, generally over their home reach of water; occasionally, if alarmed, they fly overland.

Not only do they have a 'home reach' of water, but also a number of favoured boulders within this, from which they hunt. These are

Above: The dipper's nest is dome-shaped and built of grasses and mosses. Many dippers nest behind waterfalls, and nowadays in man-made sites such as mills, weirs or under bridges.

Below: In lowland territories, two broods a year are usual, the first eggs being laid in early March. In the Scottish Highlands, laying is up to a fortnight later, and often only one brood is raised.

its stream, the dipper hunts, often beneath the surface but occasionally just 'up to its waist' in the shallows. To submerge, the dipper may jump straight into deep water, or gradually walk into the stream until lost from sight. Once beneath the surface, it hunts on foot, and this is where the disproportionately stout legs and powerful, sharp-clawed feet serve a vital purpose in holding the bird's buoyant body down on the stream bed. Under water, the wings are used like the fins of a fish, both for propulsion and to maintain balance in strong currents – sometimes dippers swim for considerable distances.

Most small underwater animals form part of the dipper's diet at some stage, but favourite items include caddisfly larvae (in their 'portable homes' of tiny fragments of shell, stone and vegetation) and water-beetle larvae; worms and small shellfish; freshwater shrimps; the occasional small fish; and, in season, tadpoles.

The breeding season This begins early in the year. The tunefully sweet, if slightly disjointed, warbling song can be heard in the territories from October onwards through the winter, until towards the end of the nesting period in the subsequent June. Both sexes indulge in song with equal enthusiasm: yet another colourful feature of this attractive waterside bird.

Reed, marsh and sedge warblers

Three small songbirds that live in our waterside habitats
in summer are the reed, marsh and sedge warblers, welcome
visitors which come to breed here each year.

Warblers are a large, world-wide family of insect-eating birds, most of which migrate south to Africa in autumn, returning in spring to breed. During their few months in this country, most British warblers are inconspicuous, tending to stay hidden within trees and bushes—one reason why many people are not familiar with them. There are three main groups in this country—'leaf', 'bush' and 'reed-bed' warblers; the reed, marsh and sedge warblers belong to the last of these groups.

The 'reed-bed' warblers have a characteristic shape and appear to be pointed at both ends. At one end the fine, relatively long bill merges smoothly with the head. At the other, the graduated tail with shorter outer feathers is supported by unusually long tail coverts (the small feathers that lie above and below the tail). In colour the birds are generally sandy brown above and creamy white below.

Broadly speaking, the group contains streaked and unstreaked species. Sedge warblers, with contrasting colours on the head, back and wings, are streaked. Reed and marsh warblers are typical of the unstreaked category, although both have a pale, indistinct stripe above the eye. These two species are so similar that they can only be safely distinguished by the colour of their plumage if a very good view is obtained.

Adult marsh warblers have more olive upper parts, while reed warblers tend to be more rusty in colour. Ornithologists have to catch the young birds before they can positively identify them, and even then some are indistinguishable.

Habitat Reed-bed warblers tend to stay within thick cover. When they fly they rarely cover much distance, although their wings flap rapidly, before diving back into the vegetation. Consequently even sedge warblers may not be easy to identify. Often the habitat is of little help since there is considerable overlap and all three species may nest together.

Perhaps reed warblers are the most aptly named, since they are frequently found among stands of common reeds, close to water. Their ability to cling to vertical reed stems is obvious as they slide up and down, one foot always higher than the other. Sedge warblers are less dependent on water and inhabit overgrown hedges and marshy ground with bushes and ditches, as well as reed-beds. Marsh warblers require vigorous undergrowth of plants such as nettle, willowherb and meadowsweet, although they will also inhabit reedy places with bushes. All three are found in colonies in a suitable habitat; the edges of lakes and flooded gravel pits are favoured.

Opposite: The sedge warbler can be identified by the creamy stripe with a dark outline above the eye; its wing feathers have pale edges. The nest is cup-shaped and rather bulky, and is attached to supporting reed stems.

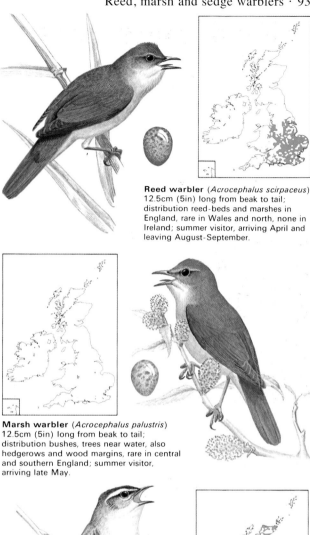

Reed warbler (*Acrocephalus scirpaceus*) 12.5cm (5in) long from beak to tail; distribution reed-beds and marshes in England, rare in Wales and north, none in Ireland; summer visitor, arriving April and leaving August-September.

Marsh warbler (*Acrocephalus palustris*) 12.5cm (5in) long from beak to tail; distribution bushes, trees near water, also hedgerows and wood margins, rare in central and southern England; summer visitor, arriving late May.

Sedge warbler (*Acrocephalus schoenobaenus*) 13cm (5¼in) long from beak to tail; distribution widespread in waterside habitats, bushes, hedgerows and crop fields throughout British Isles; summer visitor, arriving early April.

Kingfisher

The kingfisher is one of our most brilliantly coloured birds but its small size and rapid flight can make it difficult to spot. However, once seen it is seldom forgotten.

In flight the kingfisher looks like a flash of bright blue light as it skims fast and low over the water. It is one of Britain's most beautiful birds, with upper parts of an iridescent cobalt blue – or emerald green depending on the angle at which the light catches them – and a very noticeable paler blue streak stretching from nape to tail. The underparts and cheeks are a warm chestnut colour, which is most obvious when the bird is perching, and there's a patch of white on the throat and sides of the neck. And as if all this colour were not enough for one bird, the legs are a bright sealing-wax red. Juveniles generally have a duller plumage, shorter bills with a white tip and dark legs.

Opposite: Chalk streams such as the River Itchen in Hampshire are favoured haunts of the kingfisher. Inset: A stickleback meal helps to show the size of a kingfisher.

Below: Apart from its distinctive colouring, the kingfisher can be easily identified by its stumpy body, large head, short tail and long, dagger-shaped beak.

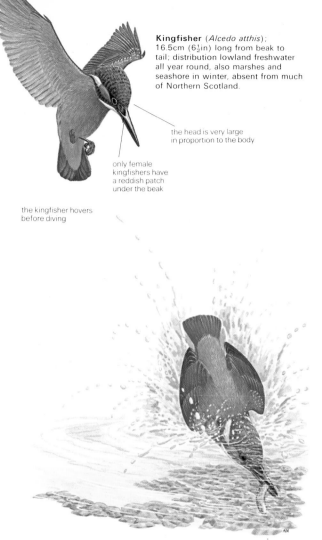

Kingfisher (*Alcedo atthis*); 16.5cm (6½in) long from beak to tail; distribution lowland freshwater all year round, also marshes and seashore in winter, absent from much of Northern Scotland.

the head is very large in proportion to the body

only female kingfishers have a reddish patch under the beak

the kingfisher hovers before diving

the kingfisher's diet; but it will eat insects such as caddis fly larvae and dragonflies, as well as tadpoles, small molluscs and crustaceans such as crayfish.

As its name implies, the kingfisher is an expert fisher. It normally perches on a post or branch over the water, watching intently for fish; if a suitable perch is not available, it hovers over the water. The instant a fish is spotted the kingfisher dives headlong straight into the water and grabs its prey with its open, dagger-like beak; the complete action, from leaving the perch to returning to it, is over in a matter of seconds. Minnows may be immediately swallowed head first, but spiny fish such as sticklebacks are beaten against the kingfisher's perch until they are dead and their spines flat enough for the bird to swallow them comfortably. You might see the kingfisher juggling the fish in its beak to get it the right way up to swallow. On average, adults catch a fish once every two or three dives, while juveniles only catch one every eight or ten dives until they gain expertise. In learning the art, some young birds drown because they dive too often and their feathers become waterlogged.

Pairing and nest-building Throughout autumn and much of the winter individual kingfishers keep to their own territory, male and female using separate areas of water; but in January or February the pair bond is established or renewed. The birds chase each other, often at considerable heights, in a swooping, diving aerobatic display, or they perch on a branch bobbing and bowing to each other. The attentive male will even fetch fish to feed to his partner.

From mid-February to mid-April you may hear the infrequent song of the kingfisher—a rapid, high-pitched succession of varied whistles. The bird's normal and very distinctive call is a loud, shrill 'chee' or 'chikee'.

As the weather warms up the pair look for a nesting site, usually in an exposed bank of a stream or lake. Once a suitable location is found they excavate a tunnel, which they start by flying at the bank and driving in their strong bills; they then build a chamber at the end of it. The tunnel, anything from 15-100cm (6-40in) long depending on how hard the soil is, slopes gently upwards. If a suitable waterside bank is not to be had, the kingfisher will nest among the roots of a fallen tree or in a sandpit, sometimes as much as 300m (330yd) from the nearest water. If you spot a kingfisher flying through woodland, the chances are it will be fetching food to take to an inland nest.

You can recognize the nest by the circular entrance hole to the tunnel, positioned near the top of the bank. Later in the season, disgorged fish offal round the opening will provide evidence of a nest, as will the dark slime trickling from the hole—the excrement of the young which is directed into the tunnel from the nest chamber.

It would be surprising if such a colourful bird had escaped mention in myth and legend; the most attractive story comes from the ancient Greeks who said the bird–which they called 'halcyon'–bred in a floating nest at sea at the time of the winter solstice, calming high winds and stormy waves. Today 'halcyon' has come to mean any calm, peaceful and happy time.

Expert angler The place to spot the elusive kingfisher is near fresh, rather slow-flowing rivers, canals, lakes, ponds, streams, flooded gravel pits and even tiny streams in towns– almost wherever a ready supply of small fish such as minnows, bullheads and sticklebacks is to be had. These fish make up the bulk of

Birds of coast and estuary

Western Europe has a tremendously varied coastline, and nowhere is this more so than Britain. Much of it is low-lying, giving rise to wide, sandy and shallow bays so attractive to holidaymakers, and to sheltered and equally shallow estuaries. Here rivers bring some of the richness of the land to mingle with the richness of the sea in a warm environment, the mixture producing areas of mud and water, aesthetically pleasing to some people and unsightly to others, but undeniably extremely rich in a wide variety of food items for birds. The ooze teems with minute animal and plant life, as well as with worms, crustaceans and shellfish. Its surface carries plentiful seaweeds, and these harbour still more animals–especially snails. On the waters that ebb and flow above, fishes flourish in wide variety.

Such a richness in food is of great value to birds like gulls which are to be found all year round as well as to the few species of ducks and waders that breed on estuaries. Outside the breeding season, many other ducks and waders benefit from this food source. Many of these breed in the far north on the Arctic tundra, but move south to overwinter in unfrozen habitats. In consequence, they often have extensive migratory journeys to undertake, and so the estuaries of western Europe are vital 'staging posts'. Here the migrants may pause to rest, recuperate, perhaps moult, and 'refuel' by building up fat reserves, either to keep out the winter cold or to provide the energy necessary for those species migrating even further south into Africa.

Sadly, this estuarine habitat is under threat. Little known, poorly understood and often considered unsightly, it is a prime target for reclamation and subsequent industrial development with ready access by sea. From a conservation viewpoint, it is important that the vital role which this habitat plays in our ecosystem is more widely understood.

In the north and west, much of the European coast becomes spectacularly rocky, with towering cliffs, and here in the summer months huge seabird colonies develop. The safety of cliffs and offshore islands encourages the development of colonies of seabirds often tens or hundreds of thousands strong. The various species, though densely packed, each choose a slightly different nest site, and thus make full use of the terrain.

Just as important, although the seas nearby must be rich in fish, how do the various seabirds share out this resource? As in the case of the structural adaptations of duck or wader beaks, comparing cliff-nesting seabird foods and feeding techniques makes fascinating reading, and includes the spectacular dive and plunge of the gannet, emerging triumphantly with its wriggling prey, to the seemingly impossible food gathering feat of the puffin, which somehow manages to carry as many as sixty sandeels, held cross-wise in its beak, at one time.

Opposite: Herring gulls on a quay awaiting the arrival of the fishermen and the inevitable free meal.

Fulmar, Leach's and storm petrels

Petrels are ocean-going birds that include the
gull-like fulmar and its smaller, sooty relatives, the
storm petrel and the Leach's petrel. They spend
their lives gliding over the waves in search of food,
only visiting land to breed.

Gliders and flutterers

The fulmar, together with the storm petrel and the Leach's petrel, are all related to that giant among oceanic birds, the albatross, as well as to the shearwaters, aptly named after their habit of skimming low over the waves.

The fulmar looks completely different compared to the other two petrels. It is about double the size of its relatives, mainly white and much like a gull. It nests on open cliffs and in summer can be seen all day long near the coast. The storm petrel and the Leach's petrel, on the other hand, are quite small for seabirds (lighter in weight than a song thrush) and are sooty black all over save for a white patch on the rump. They come ashore to their nests, in deep burrows or natural crevices in the rocks, only after dark.

Tubular beaks All petrels are distinguished from other seabirds by their complex beak structure. Viewed close up, the beak is made up of a series of plates of horny material, with clearly visible joints or sutures in between. In addition, the ridge of the beak is topped with a horny tube that gives the group another colloquial name – the 'tube-noses'.

The precise function of this narrow tube is not properly understood. One theory is that it serves these seabirds – most of them extremely efficient high-speed gliders – as an air-speed indicator, in much the same way as does a 'Pitot tube' on a modern aircraft. Another theory suggests that it functions as a genuine nostril. The sense of smell is poorly developed in most birds, but many petrels emit a powerful, musty odour, and returning birds may possibly 'scent out' their mates not only after dark but also deep in nesting burrows.

Success story The fulmar is at the centre of one of the most amazing bird success stories of the last 100 years. For over 900 years, the only known British breeding station was on the remote island of St Kilda, 50 miles west of the Outer Hebrides. Then, in the middle of the 19th century, the Icelandic fulmar population began to expand, and in 1878 other colonies began to be reported on Scottish islands, the first on Foula.

Since then, there has been no stopping the birds extraordinary spread. First the northern islands were colonised, followed by the cliffs of both the east and west coasts of Britain and Ireland, until by 1970 fulmars were nesting on all suitable stretches of rocky coast. Even in some apparently quite unsuitable areas they find a way to succeed. In the Hebrides, there are now nests on the ground in remote and undisturbed sand dunes, and on the cliff-less coasts of southern and eastern England. The birds have even commandeered nuclear power station window sills as the nearest alternative to a cliff ledge.

Fulmars have also moved inland. Nesting was first reported on ruined buildings in the Shetlands, but now quarries several miles

Fulmar (*Fulmarus glacialis*), 47cm (18½in) from beak to tail. Long stiff wings, grey upper parts, white underparts.

Storm petrel (*Hydrobates pelagicus*), 15cm (6in) from beak to tail. Pale wing bar, white rump, squarish tail.

Leach's petrel (*Oceanodroma leucorrhoa*), 20cm (8in) from beak to tail. Diagonal paler wing band, white rump with dark stripe, forked tail.

from the sea in northern England have breeding pairs.

There is no certain reason for this success. It may be that there was a sudden genetic change in the birds themselves, or that the North Atlantic warmed slightly and produced more fish. A more likely explanation is related to the fulmars' diet, which consists mainly of offal. The rise in numbers coincided with the time when whaling reached a peak in the Atlantic – with abundant supplies of offal both at sea and near the shore. Although whaling has now been curtailed, modern fishing (with a great deal of the catch gutted at sea) has taken over this food-providing role.

Above: The fulmar slices through the air like a guided missile, while the much smaller storm petrel, resembling a large black moth, flutters feebly on an erratic flight path. The Leach's petrel is more positive in flight, but retains the erratic flight of its smaller cousin.

Opposite: At their nesting site on an open cliff, fulmars will 'spit' a foul smelling fluid (regurgitated from the stomach) to deter any intruders.

Manx shearwater

Manx shearwaters nest in burrows, and the sound of their wailing calls, coming from underground at dead of night, has inspired legends of trolls.

Manx shearwaters are slender-winged sea-birds about the size of a small gull. As their name suggests, shearwaters at sea skim low over the water, occasionally touching and 'shearing' through a wave-top as they bank and turn. The wings are relatively long and narrow, in comparison with those of a gull, and in flight they are usually held at right angles to the body, with the leading edge held very straight. For much of the time the wings are stiff, and the tips are bowed slightly downwards.

The plumages of adults and young are similar; dark, oily black above, and white below. The boundary between dark and light comes roughly at water level when the birds are swimming on the sea; although apparently very conspicuous, this distribution of colour hides the somewhat vulnerable shearwaters well from predators such as gulls that approach from above, or large fishes approaching from below.

In flight, however, their plumage is conspicuous; together with the characteristic flight pattern, it makes them easy to recognise at all but the longest ranges. They fly fast and low, often vanishing from view in the wave troughs, which may cause some difficulty in spotting them; but then they bank and turn, first presenting a white undersurface, then black upperparts, to the birdwatcher.

Long-distance gliders At sea, shearwaters cover prodigious distances, and are masters of the art of energy-conserving flight. Most often, they fly in a long, shallow glide down and along the ocean wind, then suddenly turn into the wind, using it to gain a violent uplift at the expense of flight speed, before heading off downwind again in another long glide. Shearwaters are seen performing this spectacular type of flight as they pass along the coast, either on migration or, in the breeding season, on fishing excursions. They often fly in groups, usually in a straggling line.

They are most frequently seen off our south and west coasts. In summer they can be watched in the vicinity of any shearwater

Above: A Manx shearwater; the name 'Manx' refers to a historic colony on the Calf of Man. After centuries of breeding there, shearwaters were absent for 150 years, returning in the 1960s.

Manx shearwater (*Puffinus puffinus*). Summer visitor. Sexes alike. 36cm (14in).

Manx shearwater distribution

colony. These are located on the Isles of Scilly, Lundy, Skokholm, Skomer, Anglesey, some of the islands off the eastern Irish coasts, and many of the islands off the rocky western Scottish and Irish coasts.

Island colonies Most shearwater breeding areas are on remote islands, often uninhabited or at most with just a few human occupants. Shearwaters are clumsy on land; they have powerful webbed feet, and their legs are situated close to the rear of their bodies–which makes them effective swimmers. However, this makes walking on land rather difficult for them. They can only drag themselves along at a painfully slow rate. As a result, they easily fall victim to marauding gulls.

Greater black-backed gulls, in particular, specialise in catching shearwaters. It takes these large gulls only a couple of powerful bites to open the carcase and snip the wings off the shoulders. Then, with a few flicks of the gull's strong neck muscles, the shearwater is skinned and ready for eating. Around the nests of these predatory gulls, the discarded shearwater skins accumulate in a gruesome midden. Despite this vulnerability, shearwaters seem to be maintaining steady populations in most of the areas they inhabit.

As dusk falls, shearwaters gather offshore, floating on the sea in huge 'rafts'. They remain there for some hours, deriving a measure of safety in numbers, and venture ashore only when it is completely dark. Most colonies are on the cliff top, or close to the shore of low-lying islands. One striking exception to this norm is more than a mile from the sea and about 600m (2000ft) up on the rocky screes in the heart of the island of Rhum in the Inner Hebrides.

By day, anyone walking along the cliff top could be excused for not suspecting that there was a shearwater colony nearby. There is little outward sign of their presence in daylight except for the occasional carcase of a shearwater that fell victim to a gull the previous night.

At night, especially on a dark and stormy night, the scene changes dramatically. Home-coming birds fly past overhead with a rush of air, and call to their partners in the nesting burrows with extraordinary cackling, cooing and caterwauling calls. Those in the burrows make similar calls, and the sound of these, coming from the ground and after dark, has inspired legends. The troll legends of Norway, in particular, are said to have originated from these weird sounds.

Shearwater numbers Shearwaters are always colonial, but while some new colonies may only hold a few dozen pairs, others are huge. The one on Rhum was estimated to contain over 100,000 pairs in 1976, while the one on Skomer was estimated at 95,000 pairs in 1973. Counting birds such as shearwaters–which have black upperparts, come ashore only after dark, and nest in numbers as

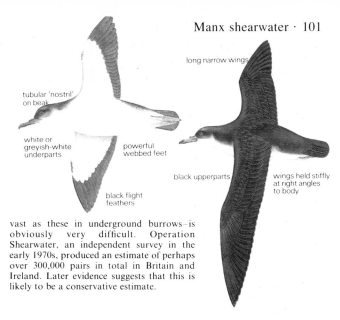

tubular 'nostril' on beak

white or greyish-white underparts

black flight feathers

powerful webbed feet

long narrow wings

black upperparts

wings held stiffly at right angles to body

vast as these in underground burrows–is obviously very difficult. Operation Shearwater, an independent survey in the early 1970s, produced an estimate of perhaps over 300,000 pairs in total in Britain and Ireland. Later evidence suggests that this is likely to be a conservative estimate.

The shearwater's underground nest

Often nests are made in rabbit burrows. The shearwaters evict the hapless rabbits, using their sharp claws and hooked beaks to secure vacant possession of a suitable-sized burrow.

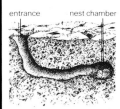

entrance   nest chamber

Above: Shearwater pairs that do not take over rabbit burrows dig new ones for themselves in the soft, peaty soil of the cliff top. A typical burrow consists of an entrance tunnel and a slightly larger nest chamber, which is lined with fronds of bracken and pieces of grass.

Right: A shearwater nesting site, as it appears after many years of burrowing.

Goosander and red-breasted merganser

The goosander and the red-breasted merganser–two quite similar fish-eating ducks–are often called sawbills. They get this name from the tooth-like serrations along the sides of their long, narrow bills. These savage-looking features enable them to take a firm grip on their fishy prey.

Below: The male goosander has a greenish-black head and back, with white underparts.

Bottom left: A female goosander, followed by ten young: she is probably fostering several broods.

Bottom right: Both the goosander and the red-breasted merganser breed in northern Britain, but only the latter breeds in Ireland.

The goosander is a large bird, about 65cm (26in) long, with a wingspan of up to 95cm (38in). The male has a black head, neck and back, with a glossy green sheen. His head bears a distinctive crest of feathers, and his long bill and his legs are reddish orange. His underparts are pure white, contrasting strongly with the head and back. The rump, belly and tail are grey. In flight, even more white shows, as virtually the whole of the inner half of the wing is white, with just a few black streaks; the outer half is black. The female is grey above and white below, with a chestnut head and neck, and a slight shaggy crest. In flight the rear half of her inner wing is white, and the forewing grey.

Arrival of a species Goosanders breed in northern latitudes throughout the Northern

Goosander distribution

Red-breasted merganser distribution

Hemisphere. Rather confusingly, they are known in North America as common mergansers. It has been estimated that there are about 75,000 goosanders in north-west Europe, with between 900 and 1250 pairs breeding in the British Isles, mainly in Scotland. Yet the first definite breeding record of a goosander in Britain was as recent as 1871, when single pairs bred in Perthshire and in Argyll.

There had been rumours of breeding attempts earlier than that, in 1858 and again in 1862, but certainly the goosander was a rare winter visitor to Scotland before the 1870s. However, from about that time it became increasingly common, with winter influxes presumably leading to birds staying for the summer and breeding. By the turn of the century it had spread to most western Scottish counties, from Sutherland to Argyll, and was moving eastwards across the country.

During the first part of this century, breeding spread to the east coast counties of Aberdeen and Angus, and southwards to Renfrew, Selkirk and Dumfries. In 1975 it was estimated that there were up to 950 pairs in Scotland.

The red-breasted merganser This duck is between 50 and 58cm (20-23in) in length, with a wingspan of up to 85cm (34in). The male has a black head, shot with green, ending in a ragged crest. His neck is white, contrasting with a broad chestnut breast-band. His upperparts are mainly black (with a green gloss) and grey, with grey flanks, though a broad white band shows on the closed wings. The underparts are white. The bill and legs are red. The inner half of the wing is white, but crossed by two black bars, and with a dark leading edge. The outer wing is dark.

The female is very similar to the female goosander, but has a larger shaggy crest and a duller chestnut head, and no sharp dividing line between the colour of her neck and breast. In flight, her wing pattern is more obviously barred black and white.

Two fish-eating ducks

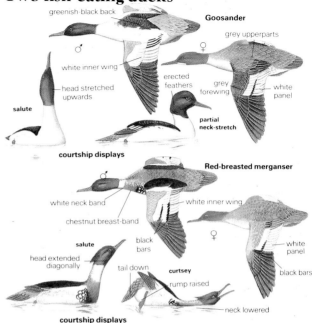

courtship displays

courtship displays

Goosander (*Mergus merganser*). Resident duck, nesting beside upland rivers and lakes. 65cm (26in).

Red-breasted merganser (*Mergus serrator*). Resident duck, mainly coastal. Up to 58cm (23in).

Below left: The red breast of the merganser is really bright chestnut, while the female goosander (below) has a chestnut head.

Both goosanders and red-breasted mergansers have serrated bills, with which they grip their catch. They feed on many fish species, mainly those between 10 and 20cm (4-8in) long.

sharp teeth

Eider, common and velvet scoters

Eiders and scoters are seafaring ducks that dive in shallow coastal waters to wrench mussels and other shellfishes from the rocks of the sea-bed. They have in common a broad, strong bill to crunch the shells of their victims, and in almost all species a proportion of the male's plumage is black.

Seen at a distance, the male eider is a handsome black and white bird, with black sides and tail and a black cap on its head, set off by a white chest, neck, face and back. Closer to, one can see more subtle colouring: pastel green on the back of the head, and soft pink on the breast. The bill is dull green and has a lobe on either side running back towards the eye. In complete contrast, the female is brown all over, much mottled and barred in shades of brown to produce perfect camouflage. This is vitally important when she is sitting on the nest, for she must conceal herself from predators.

The male eider also appears in other plumages, for example during the annual moult in late summer: at this time, he loses the majority of his white plumage and for a

time looks much more like a dark female. Then, during the time when the males are developing their full plumage, there is a period when the black and white patterning is rather variable between individual males.

Another variation is seen in the immature males. Male eiders do not attain their full adult plumage until they are in their second year, and in their first year they have a distinctive immature plumage; this consists of a white breast, with light and dark brown on all other parts of the bird.

Life on our northern coasts The eider breeds commonly all round the coasts of Scotland, except in the extreme south-west; it penetrates into northern England in Northumberland and, on the west coast, at a few locations in Cumbria. It has been estimated that there

Above: When the young eiders have hatched, they are soon able to walk. The parents immediately lead them to the sea, where they learn to swim. Here, three adult females lead seven chicks—doubtless a 'crèche' in which three broods are combined—to the water. Once on the sea, the chicks have survived their time of greatest danger, for they are out of range of foxes and other predators. These chicks may be all that remain of an original total of about 16.

Distribution

◻ eider
◼ common scoter

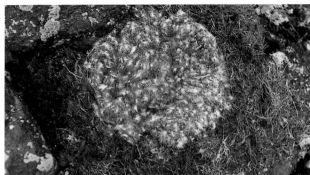

Above: Down falls out of the female eider's plumage, particularly from her breast, and she uses this to good purpose. If she has to leave the nest, she covers the eggs with down (as shown) to conceal them from predators. To keep the eggs warm, she also lines the nest with down. In Iceland and Norway, eiders are 'farmed' or encouraged to breed in special reserves; when they have completed breeding, the down is collected for sale. The down from over 100 nests is needed to fill one sleeping bag.

Above left: A female eider incubates her eggs. Clutches usually contain 4-6 eggs.

Eider (*Somateria mollissima*). Diving duck, resident. 58cm (23in).

Common scoter (*Melanitta nigra*). Diving duck; small breeding population; large wintering population. Length 48cm (19in).

Velvet scoter (*Melanitta fusca*). Mainly a winter coastal visitor. 55cm (22in).

are about 20,000 to 25,000 pairs of eider breeding in Britain, making it our second commonest breeding duck after the mallard.

In most of the breeding locations, the pairs nest several metres apart; each nest is placed in a slight hollow, or in the shelter of a boulder or tuft of vegetation. In certain locations, however, especially where there is a degree of protection, for example on a small islet, or where man actively discourages predators such as foxes, large colonies form, hundreds or even thousands strong.

Eiders are not long-distance migrants: after the breeding season, the parents take the young ducks down to the sea and the families leave the breeding grounds. They gather together in flocks in sheltered estuaries and bays. In some locations on the sea, for example the Moray Firth and the mouth of the Firth of Tay, several thousand eiders congregate.

A crusty meal Eiders eat various kinds of shellfish, including mussels, as well as crabs. They crush these in their powerful beaks,

discard the hard shells and eat the soft meat inside. Because they live most of their lives in tidal waters, eiders have adapted to feeding in a variety of water depths. Thus they can dive as deep as 15m (45ft) in order to reach mussels growing on the sea-bed. They wrench them off the rocks on which they are attached, and bring them to the surface to eat them.

In shallower water, eiders merely upend to reach their food, while in shallower water still they need only dip their heads under the surface to reach the bottom. Another feeding technique is adopted to catch crabs in soft mud. When the mud is covered with a few centimetres of water, the eiders sit over a likely patch and then paddle vigorously with their feet, stirring up the mud and forming a shallow crater. They then probe into the crater with their bills, hoping to feel and then grasp an unwary crab.

Vagrant species Three other species of eider occur in Britain, all as vagrants. All three breed in the Arctic (the king eider most widely) with some colonies in Iceland and many more in Greenland and Spitsbergen. The spectacled eider breeds in north-east Siberia, and Alaska, while the small Steller's eider also breeds in Siberia, with just a handful of pairs in Norway. One or two king eiders and Steller's eiders are seen in most years in the waters around the Hebrides, Orkneys and Shetlands, and some individuals stay there for months or even years.

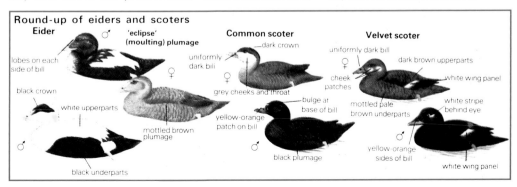

Round-up of eiders and scoters

Eider

'eclipse' (moulting) plumage

Common scoter

Velvet scoter

lobes on each side of bill

black crown

white upperparts

black underparts

uniformly dark bill

mottled brown plumage

dark crown

grey cheeks and throat

yellow-orange patch on bill

bulge at base of bill

black plumage

uniformly dark bill

cheek patches

mottled pale brown underparts

yellow-orange sides of bill

dark brown upperparts

white wing panel

white stripe behind eye

white wing panel

Gannet

Above: Gannets greet each other with raised bills.

A gannetry in spring or summer is a breathtaking spectacle: the cliffs and rocks are white with many thousands of these large seabirds. The air, too, is filled with gannets in soaring flight, each ready to plunge into the sea for fish, perhaps from a height of 30m (100ft) or more.

Gannetry sites

1 Herma Ness; 2 Noss; 3 Foula; 4 Fair Isle; 5 Sula Sgeir 6 Sule Stack; 7 Flannans; 8 St Kilda; 9 Bass Rock; 10 Ailsa Craig; 11 Scar Rocks; 12 Bempton; 13 Gt Saltee; 14 Little Skellig; 15 Bull Rock; 16 Grassholm; 17, 18 Alderney.

The gannet is our biggest and most spectacular seabird, with a body length of about 1m (3ft) and a wingspan approaching 2m (over 6ft). It is essentially a maritime bird, breeding in cliff colonies called gannetries, although very occasionally storm-driven gannets are seen on lakes and reservoirs inland.

Goose-like bird The adult gannet is a large, almost goose-like white bird with a yellow ochre tinge to the head and nape and conspicuous black wingtips. The yellow colour is mostly lost in winter. In flight, its appearance is less goose-like, mainly because the stout neck and beak in front are counterbalanced by a long, pointed white tail, whereas geese have very short tails and a characteristically unbalanced appearance in flight. The wings, long and noticeably slender, are white for much of their length but with mostly black primaries, or flight feathers. Gannets are often seen flying along the shore, maintaining a height of about 10m (30ft) above the water. The steady flight pattern consists of a series of slow wingbeats, followed by a glide. In small flocks, often all or most birds will pause to glide with precisely timed synchrony.

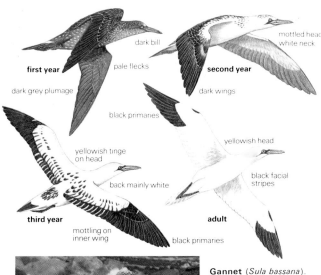

first year
dark bill
pale flecks
dark grey plumage

second year
mottled head
white neck
dark wings
black primaries

yellowish tinge
on head
black primaries
back mainly white

yellowish head
black facial
stripes

third year
mottling on
inner wing
black primaries

adult

In close-up view when perched, the gannet's webbed feet can be seen to be lead grey, with a neat blue-grey line running along each toe and down the front of the 'shin' or tarsus. The beak, stout and dagger-like, is almost 15cm (6in) long, and is silver coloured, with black lines. On the face a patch of grey or bluish naked skin surrounds a glaring eye with a strikingly pale iris.

Remote gannetries Gannets are colonial breeders, and their expansion in numbers over the last hundred years is one of the more striking bird success stories. There are now 18 gannetries off our coasts, no less than 11 of them founded this century.

The current increase in gannet numbers may partly be a restoration to an earlier situation following an intervening decline. Certainly during the 18th and 19th centuries gannets were persecuted by man, the fat and nutritious nestlings being slaughtered for food in tens of thousands by the inhabitants of some of our remote islands. This pressure has ended with the modernisation of our food industry, and with bird protection laws.

At the same time, it seems most unlikely that the current rate of increase, some 3% per annum, can be solely due to the relaxation of hunting pressure. Probably a major additional factor is climatic change, influencing the numbers and location of such surface-shoaling fish as mackerel, on which the gannets feed. Certainly the rate of increase is high for such a large bird which lays only one egg per season.

During the present century, the world population of the gannet has trebled, and with some 140,000 breeding pairs, Britain and Ireland hold 70% of the world total.

Gannet (*Sula bassana*). Resident seabird; 70% of world population found in British Isles. Sexes are alike. Length 90cm (36in), wingspan 1.8m (6ft).

Left: A juvenile gannet. In its first autumn and winter it is dark chocolate brown, flecked with pale grey or white. The plumage develops to the adult stage over four or five years.

Below: Herma Ness gannetry, at the extreme northern tip of Shetland.

Diving for a fish

sighting
the fish

dive may
be over
30m (100ft)

wings are
swept back
on entering
water

Cormorant and shag

Cormorants and shags (below), two of our largest
sea birds, are common around our coasts at all times
of the year, often bobbing about in the water in
their continual search for fish, or standing motionless
with their wings spread out wide to dry.

Groups of large, black, long-necked birds apparently just standing idly around, are a familiar sight on British coasts. They are cormorants and shags. Although totally dependent on diving in water to catch food, these birds have wing feathers that are less water repellent than those of most other water birds. After each feeding session they have to seek an open, breezy place and hang their saturated wings out to dry. At favourite loafing spots, such as low rocky ledges, islets, piers, breakwaters, moored boats and buoys, you can often see several birds standing in a row. Sandbanks exposed at low tide in estuaries are also often used.

Ancient birds The cormorant and shag family has one of the longest fossil records of all birds. Remains of one cormorant-like bird found in Hungary are thought to be 100 million years old. Today there are 31 species of cormorants and shags in the world, including a flightless species found only in the Galapagos Islands.

In the British Isles we have only two species, and shags outnumber cormorants by about four to one. Our species of cormorant has an extensive world distribution and lives in every continent except South America. In contrast, our shag is restricted to Europe and North Africa.

Near-black look-alikes Even experienced ornithologists sometimes have difficulty distinguishing between shags and cormorants.

Of the two species, the shag is smaller and slighter, with a narrower beak. Neither species is really black; shags are glossy green-black with a brownish tinge to their wings and back. Cormorants have white cheeks and chins.

In summer, identification of adults is easier, since both species develop temporary breeding plumage. Shags grow a characteristic recurved crest about 5cm (2in) long. Cormorants grow whitish wispy feathers on their heads, and a white patch on each thigh which is often conspicuous in flight.

Immature shags and cormorants have brown upperparts. Young shags may only be a little paler beneath, whereas young cormorants can be almost white. The plumage of both species becomes darker with each successive moult until they reach full adult plumage in the second or third year.

In common with their close relatives, the pelicans, gannets and frigate birds, shags and cormorants have patches of bare skin around the beak and eyes. These are analogous to the pelican's enormous fish-carrying pouch. *Phalacrocorax*, the Latin name for shags and cormorants, refers to these patches, and means 'bald raven'. The name cormorant is apparently an English corruption of the Latin *Corvus marinus*, or sea crow.

Cormorant
adult

Shag
adult

white cheeks

adult in breeding plumage
drying wings

Cormorant

white thigh patch

Shag
(Phalacrocorax aristotelis); 76cm (30in) from beak to tail. Found all round the coast of the British Isles and occasionally inland. Population currently on the increase. Resident.

Cormorant
(Phalacrocorax carbo); 90cm (36in) from beak to tail. Less common than the shag, but more widespread, being found inland as well as around our coast. Resident.

Oystercatcher

With its pied plumage, pink legs and red bill the oystercatcher is one of our most distinctive shore birds. It has several strange patterns of behaviour, including an unusual 'piping display' performed in the breeding season to defend its territory.

Oystercatcher *(Hematopus ostralegus).* Resident wader, found on rocky shores (exposed headlands as well as sheltered bays), mud flats and sometimes inland, particularly in Scotland. Length about 40cm (17in).

Most of our coastal waders are dull brown and difficult to distinguish from each other, but the oystercatcher is an exception. Its orange-red bill, red eyes and pink legs stand out strongly from its stark black and white plumage. Yet if you come across an oyster-catcher while it is quietly feeding it can seem an inconspicuous bird, particularly if its back is turned towards you. Only when it is disturbed and looks up does it reveal its remarkable colouring.

Sexes alike Male and female oystercatchers are similar in appearance. The upperparts are predominantly black, with white wing-bars, rump and base of the tail. During the breeding season in spring and summer the black part of their plumage becomes glossy. In winter it is duller and the birds develop a white collar round the front of their necks. Young oyster-catchers retain the white collar and duller plumage all the year round.

The adult bill is orange-red, tending to become yellower towards the tip. In younger birds the tip is duller yellow-brown. The bill is about 7cm (3in) long, the female's being slightly longer than the male's. The legs of the adult are pink but in young birds are greyish. The colour of the eyes also develops as the birds mature. In their first year, oyster-catchers have brown eyes. As they grow older, these become yellow, then orange and finally red by the time the birds reach adulthood. The red of the eye is accentuated, again primarily in the adult, by a ring of red feathers surrounding it.

Coastal and inland habitats Oystercatchers occur in a variety of habitats, primarily coastal. On rocky shores they feed on both exposed headlands and sheltered bays, though the number of oystercatchers found there is never·great. Larger numbers are found on mud flats, where the birds can probe for worms and shells. On extensive mud flats, such as those of the Wash, Morcambe Bay, Solway Firth and the Burry Inlet, huge winter flocks numbering 10,000 or more can be seen. As high tide approaches the birds fly off noisily in flocks to roost together in dense packs above the high-water mark.

During the last hundred years oystercatchers have been moving away from the coast to take advantage of inland feeding sites—after all, probing for worms in soil is much the same as probing for worms in mud. In northern Britain and particularly in Scotland they are now common farmland birds often seen feeding in association with lapwings, rooks, starlings and those other inland invaders of recent years: gulls. The reason for this movement is not known, but increasing human disturbance of the coast, and even a genetic change in the birds themselves, have been suggested.

Oyster catchers no more The name 'oystercatcher' is a misnomer, for the bird rarely eats oysters these days. Inland feeders live off earthworms and other soil invertebrates; coastal dwellers eat mostly crabs and shellfish such as limpets, cockles and mussels, though worms are commonly eaten.

adult

broad white wing-bars and white rump

pink legs

white underside

chick

short black bill

legs dark at birth

Above: A pair of oystercatchers during the breeding season. In winter their coats are much less glossy and the birds develop an irregular white collar round the front of their necks.
Oystercatchers usually mate for life and, during the breeding season, are strongly territorial.

Right: In winter oystercatchers form themselves into large flocks.
To identify an oystercatcher in flight, look for the white underparts with black head and wing tips. Of the more colourful parts of an oystercatcher, only its pink legs are distinct in flight.

Turnstone and purple sandpiper

Our wintering waders are generally seen on mudflats and estuaries, except for two: the turnstone, which visits rocky shores as well as beaches and nearby fields; and the purple sandpiper, which is a true specialist of the rocky shore. The two species can be seen together in mixed flocks.

Above: A mixed flock flies along the strandline between feeding grounds. About a third of them are purple sandpipers and two thirds are turnstones. The purple sandpipers are slightly smaller, dark birds with long, down-curved bills. The turnstones can be identified by a white stripe along the back and an extra wing stripe, which shows as a clear white area, often L-shaped, almost on the shoulder.

Those of us who brave winter weather to walk around muddy shores are probably familiar with the most noticeable features of a typical wader – a long bill for probing into the mud for hidden food, and long legs to permit the bird to walk in the shallow water among breaking waves without getting its belly feathers too wet. It is somewhat surprising, therefore, to discover that these features are little used for these purposes on the breeding grounds, for most waders breed during the short summer of the high Arctic, where their staple diet consists of the myriads of midges and their larvae abounding on the tundra.

Two of the waders that visit our coasts in winter have tended to forsake the mud and manage, instead, to eke out a living from our rocky shores. These are the purple sandpiper and the turnstone. Like other waders, they breed in the Arctic, except that in some recent years perhaps one single pair of purple sandpipers has bred in an unpublicised locality in Scotland. For all practical purposes, therefore, the two species are migrants visiting Britain and Ireland for the winter months only.

The purple sandpiper This species is almost entirely restricted to rocky shores during its stay in Britain and Ireland. It is a stocky bird, about 20cm (8in) long, and is usually found feeding in small flocks. The head and breast are sooty brown, while the back is a little

Purple sandpiper (*Calidris maritima*). Winter visitor to rocky shores all round Britain and Ireland. Though classed as a wader it is very much a rocky shore specialist. Sexes are alike. Length 20cm (8in).

Turnstone (*Arenaria interpres*). Winter visitor to rocky, sandy and muddy shores round Britain and Ireland. Frequently lifts stones to find prey. Sexes are alike. Length 23cm (9in).

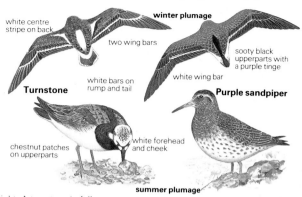

white centre stripe on back

two wing bars

winter plumage

sooty black upperparts with a purple tinge

white wing bar

white bars on rump and tail

Turnstone

Purple sandpiper

chestnut patches on upperparts

white forehead and cheek

summer plumage

darker, at close range showing a purplish tinge. The eye is surrounded by a fine white ring. The throat, belly and under-tail are white, and in flight the upper wing shows a white wing bar.

In addition to being stocky, the purple sandpiper also appears somewhat squat, for its legs are a little shorter than many of its mud-dwelling relatives. A useful identification feature is that the legs are yellow, as is the base of the slightly down-curved bill.

As the birds develop their breeding plumage, brownish feather edgings on the back give them a more mottled appearance. Some-

Right: A turnstone in full summer plumage. You can see varying degrees of summer plumage on turnstones in Britain and Ireland, for in spring some of them begin their seasonal moult before departing for the breeding grounds; and in autumn some arrive with their breeding plumage still showing. However, such birds are in the minority and it is commoner for turnstones in Britain and Ireland to be seen in complete winter plumage. Purple sandpipers, too, are sometimes seen in summer plumage, but this is normally only in spring, for in autumn they almost all arrive in winter plumage.

Below: A purple sandpiper resting on a shingle beach. This bird is clearly in winter plumage, looking dark with a slight purple tinge. The shingle is a good place for roosting after tirelessly hunting for food amid the harassment of the waves.

times this occurs before they migrate northwards in spring, so that you can see purple sandpipers that look lighter than usual while they are still on our shores.

The turnstone Squatness and stockiness are features the purple sandpiper shares with the turnstone, but the latter is a little larger, being around 23cm (9in) long, and with much more boldly marked plumage. In winter the back and breast are dark grey-brown, and while the head is the same general colour it has suggestions of white markings behind the eye and on the cheeks. The throat and belly are white, the latter being separated from the dark breast by a clearly defined line. The contrast between the dark breast and the white throat and belly gives the appearance of a distinct, dark breast band.

In flight, even a winter plumage turnstone is readily distinguished from the purple sandpiper, for it is much more strongly patterned, with a double white wing bar and broad black and white bars on the rump and tail. The turnstone's legs are generally orange and its pointed bill is black.

In summer, the turnstone takes on a completely new appearance, to become one of our most striking shorebirds. The head and breast become strongly patterned in black and white, and the back develops rich chestnut patches, giving a 'tortoiseshell' look.

Dunlin and sanderling

In spring, large numbers of these dainty waders gather on our shores before setting off for their summer grounds far to the north. Just a small population of breeding dunlins is left behind.

Above: A sanderling in its summer breeding plumage. Although the sanderling does not breed in this country it can be seen here in full breeding plumage in the spring when it migrates north along our coasts.

The dunlin and the sanderling are both small gregarious waders often seen on our larger expanses of mudflats and long sandy beaches, especially in the winter and during the spring and autumn migrations. Indeed, the dunlin is our most common wading bird in mid-winter; some 700,000 individuals are found around the coasts of Britain and Ireland at that time of year – more than twice as many as any other wader. Dunlins also breed here, though in far smaller numbers, but the sanderling is a winter visitor or a migrant; it never breeds in the British Isles.

Delicate dunlins At about 18cm (7in) long, the dunlin is one of our smallest waders. Throughout the year, it can be seen at almost any estuary, muddy beach or harbour. Inland, it is surprisingly common; sewage farms, flooded fields and the shores of reservoirs are good places to see dunlin in winter, and in summer it can be found in the moorland areas where it breeds.

The dunlin is easy to recognise in the summer because it has a characteristic black patch on its belly. The upperparts are a rich rufous brown streaked and spotted with black. The breast is heavily streaked with brown. In the autumn, the dunlin moults to its winter plumage, losing both its body and wing feathers (in spring, when it regains its breeding plumage, only the body feathers are moulted and replaced). The dunlin's winter plumage is quite drab and inconspicuous, the upperparts being grey-brown and the underparts a dull white.

Dark-shouldered sanderlings The sanderling is slightly larger than the dunlin and usually inhabits sandy estuaries and long sandy beaches. In Britain, it is most often seen in its winter plumage, which is much more striking than that of the dunlin. Its underparts and much of its head are pure white and its back and wings are pale grey. Often, there is a dark patch on the 'shoulder' of the wing (technically called the wrist).

Like the dunlin, the sanderling moults its body and wing feathers in the autumn and just its body feathers in the spring. Its summer plumage resembles that of the dunlin, except that it has a white belly. The best chance of

Dunlin (*Calidris alpina*). Resident wader; numbers augmented in winter by migrants from the Continent and Greenland, when it becomes our commonest coastal wader. It is also found inland, and breeds in moorland areas. Length 18cm (7in).

Sanderling (*Calidris alba*). Winter-visiting wader, confined mostly to sandy beaches and estuaries. Length 20cm (8in).

seeing a sanderling in full breeding plumage is in spring, when many birds migrate north along our coasts, having just grown a new set of body feathers.

Beak differences A good way to tell the difference between the dunlin and the sanderling is to look at the beak. British dunlins have downward-curving beaks about 3cm (1½in) long, whereas the sanderling has a shorter (2.5cm/1in), straight beak. There is considerable variation in beak lengths among dunlins, the British birds in general having shorter beaks than those breeding further north. For example, Canadian dunlins have beaks averaging about 4.5cm (1¾in).

The beaks of these two species are different because they have different methods of feeding. The dunlin, when feeding, walks with a purposeful air, head held low, constantly pecking at the surface of the mud and probing for tiny molluscs. The tip of its beak is particularly sensitive and allows the bird to detect, by touch, food lying below the surface of the mud.

The sanderling, on the other hand, feeds at the water's edge, hurrying back and forth like a clockwork toy following each wave as it breaks and recedes. It can be seen skilfully snatching small creatures such as sandhoppers from the edge of the surf.

Both dunlins and sanderlings feed until high tide and then fly off to special roosting

The dunlin and sanderling, in summer and winter plumages. In flight, both show a white wing-bar throughout the year, though on the sanderling it is much more prominent. In winter, flocks of dunlin can be seen flying along the coast and flashing grey or white as the birds manoeuvre in unison.

Below: Outside the breeding season the best places to see dunlin are estuaries, beaches and harbours, where food is always plentiful.

sites on shingle banks and marshes or, sometimes, on grassy fields. There the birds gather in their thousands for two or three hours until the tide has retreated and they can return to feed. Both on the ground and in flight the two species form their own groups. In the winter, a large flock of dunlins flying to or from the feeding and roosting areas can be a marvellous spectacle. Each bird in the flock flies in precise formation only a few inches from its neighbour, and with each change of direction the colour of the flock changes. First, you see the birds' dark upperparts then, as they swerve to one side, the dark changes to the white of their underparts.

Migration routes Most dunlins seen in Britain, and all sanderlings, are winter visitors or passing migrants. Migrating sanderlings arrive in the British Isles each July and August from their breeding grounds in Greenland and Siberia. Some spend the winter here and the remainder fly on south to France, the Iberian Peninsula and Africa. In May, our wintering sanderlings return to their summer grounds, joined by migrants passing through Britain from further south.

Britain is one of the few countries in the world with both breeding and wintering dunlins, so their passage through Britain is not as distinct as sanderling migrations.

Curlew and whimbrel

The curlew (above) is a common British wading bird, while its relative the whimbrel is scarce, being chiefly a bird of the Arctic. But you may see whimbrels flying past on their migratory flights to Africa in autumn, and on the way back in spring.

Curlew (*Numenius arquata*).
Largest European wader. Resident, breeding in moorland, grassland, marshes and dunes. Winters on estuaries and coasts. About 50,000 breeding pairs. Length 53-58cm (21-23in).

Whimbrel (*Numenius phaeopus*).
Summer visitor, smaller than curlew. Breeds in dry moorland and grassland in north Scotland and Shetlands. Under 200 breeding pairs. 41cm (16in).

The curlew is a truly unmistakable bird: a large, robust wader, common on estuaries in autumn and winter, and familiar in the west and north as a breeding bird of inland pastures and hayfields in spring and summer. Its silhouette, with long legs, slightly hunched attitude and long, curved bill is unlike that of any other bird except for the whimbrel which, although it looks similar to the curlew, is rarely seen in Britain. Look closely at the curlew and you will see that its strong legs are a delicate pale grey, while the plumage is a warm ashy brown, paler below, and streaked with darker brown on the neck and upperparts. Like other large waders it has a long neck, but the most remarkable feature is the surprisingly long, downward curving bill.

On the wing, curlews are bulky birds with strong, steady flight, less rapid than most other waders and looking a little like gulls at a distance – even in their habit of dropping down to their feeding grounds on estuaries in a long, planing glide. They are shy and wary birds, whose measured, dignified movements set them apart from the scuttling activity of the mass of other waders on the shore.

Introducing the whimbrel The much scarcer, but less timid, whimbrel is superficially similar to the curlew, but the main differences are a shorter and less curved bill, shorter legs and a distinctive pattern of two dark bands of feathers on the crown. In general, it is a slightly darker and smaller bird than the curlew, although if it were not for the simple and distinctive call of the whimbrel it is probably fair to say that a great number of individuals passing through on migration would go undetected.

Whimbrels are essentially birds of passage in Britain, and so if you hear the sound of a whimbrel at all, it is likely to be flying overhead, giving its presence away by a call of about seven rapid, whinnying notes. Whimbrels stay to breed only in small numbers, chiefly in the north of Scotland and the Shetland Islands. In their northerly habitat they replace the curlew, which is a bird of the temperate zone. They breed chiefly in the Arctic zone all round the northern hemi-

How shore birds share their prey

The many birds that feed on estuaries and mudflats do not all compete for the same food. The curlew and the whimbrel can locate deep-burrowing creatures with their long, sensitive bills. For shorter-billed species of birds, such as shelduck and oystercatcher, there are shallow-burrowing shellfish, while turnstones and gulls feed on surface-dwelling crabs and mussels.

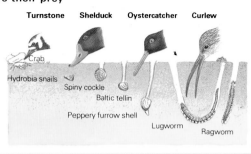

Turnstone Shelduck Oystercatcher Curlew

Crab

Hydrobia snails

Spiny cockle

Baltic tellin

Peppery furrow shell

Lugworm

Ragworm

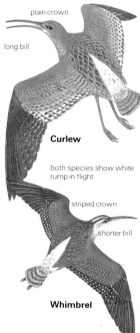

plain crown

long bill

Curlew

both species show white rump in flight

striped crown

shorter bill

Whimbrel

Far right: Adult curlews incubate their eggs for just over four weeks and the young hatch at about the end of May. The curlew and whimbrel, in common with other large birds, have only one brood per year, but lay a replacement clutch if the first one is lost.

Below right: Curlews lay four green-brown eggs, which are large and strongly pointed. The chicks have short beaks, which grow rapidly during fledging.

sphere. They nest on dry moors and old peat hags (mounds), and although much of this habitat exists in northern Scotland, the whimbrel remains a very scarce breeding bird in Britain, which lies at the southern limit of its breeding range. Fewer than 200 pairs of whimbrels breed in Britain each year.

The curlew in spring The return of the curlew to its nesting fields is one of the unfailing signs of spring. There are few sounds that are more welcome at the end of a long winter than the strident, bubbling song of the curlew. The song begins with a series of slow, graceful notes and then gains momentum, strengthening and rising in pitch to a rapid trill before descending again.

Common, wood and green sandpipers

Sandpipers are among the most dainty of our wading birds. Three species are found in Britain, of which only one is common here. The other two are migrants on their way to or from their breeding grounds.

Several species of small and medium-sized waders are known as sandpipers. They all have pointed beaks with which they probe mud for food, in typical wader fashion. But, because their beaks are not as long as those of many waders, they can also feed by pecking at morsels on the ground.

Of the three species of sandpiper found in the British Isles one, the common sandpiper, is a summer visitor and breeds here in large numbers. The other two species, the green sandpiper and the wood sandpiper, are sometimes seen in the spring and autumn on their way to or from their breeding grounds in north-east Europe. They are known as passing migrants. Both, however, occasion-

ally breed in this country in very small numbers.

Which is which? The common sandpiper is the smallest of the three species and it has the shortest legs and neck. It has dark olive-brown upperparts, with a dark rump and tail. The underparts are white except for some brown streaks on the neck and breast.

On the ground, the most distinctive feature of this species is the way it constantly bobs its head and tail up and down. In flight, it can be distinguished from other sandpipers by a conspicuous white wing bar.

The other two sandpipers are similar to each other, especially when seen on the ground. Both have dark upperparts speckled

Above: The common sandpiper, seen here at the edge of a loch in Scotland, is the only sandpiper to breed in large numbers in the British Isles.

Common sandpiper (*Actitis hypoleucos*). At 19cm (7½in) long, the smallest of the three species. It is a summer visitor, arriving in April.

Green sandpiper (*Tringa ochropus*). Length 23cm (9in); the largest of the sandpipers. Passing migrant sometimes seen in spring or autumn. A few pairs have bred in Britain.

Wood sandpiper (*Tringa glareola*). Length 21cm (8in). Like the green sandpiper, usually seen as a passing migrant, though a few pairs now breed here.

Above: The common sandpiper is widespread in upland Britain and Ireland, whereas the wood sandpiper is confined to a few sites in the Scottish highlands.

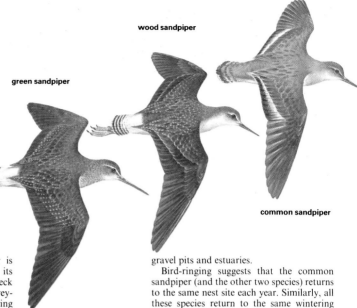

green sandpiper

wood sandpiper

common sandpiper

with buff, though the green sandpiper is darker (almost black) and in winter its speckling is reduced to a few flecks. The neck and breast in both species are pale grey-brown; in the green sandpiper this colouring is sharply demarcated from the white belly, whereas on the wood sandpiper the two areas merge. Both species have a white rump, and a paler face than that of the common sandpiper.

The best way to tell the wood and the green sandpipers apart when they are flying is to look at their legs. On the green sandpiper they are greenish and reach only as far as the tip of the tail, or a little further. On the wood sandpiper they are yellowish and reach well beyond the tail. Another difference is in the undersides of their wings. These are dark on the green sandpiper, contrasting with its white belly, but on the wood sandpiper the undersides are buff-white. Neither species has the white wing-bar of the common sandpiper.

One final way to distinguish between the three species is by their calls. The green sandpiper gives a ringing three-note call: 'tluit-weet-weet'; the common sandpiper utters a shrill piping 'pee-wee-wee', while the wood sandpiper has a shrill repeated 'chiff-iff-iff'.

The common sandpiper In April, after wintering in Africa, the common sandpiper migrates to Europe for the breeding season. During migration it can be seen in many parts of Britain on its way to its breeding grounds, and it becomes widespread again in the autumn as it heads back to Africa for the winter. But during the breeding season it is confined to upland areas of Wales, Scotland and the north of England. It is also common in the west of Ireland.

Common sandpipers breed beside clear streams, rivers and lakes. In the spring and autumn, during migration, good lowland sites to see them include reservoirs, flooded

Below: The nest of a common sandpiper is a simple hollow scraped out of the ground, sometimes lined with vegetation and usually sited beneath overhanging plants at the side of a stream or lake. The eggs (usually four) are laid in May or June. They are pale cream, speckled with reddish- or blackish-brown. Both parents help to incubate the eggs.

gravel pits and estuaries.

Bird-ringing suggests that the common sandpiper (and the other two species) returns to the same nest site each year. Similarly, all these species return to the same wintering area.

Exhilarating display flight Once the common sandpiper has reached its breeding ground, the male stakes a claim to an area that will be his breeding territory and defends it against rival males.

He also needs to attract a mate. To do this he performs a display flight, flying round and round, often soaring high into the air then descending steeply with stiff or quivering wings. Sometimes a female joins him and the pair fly round and round in fast pursuit flights. During these displays the birds sing a series of rapid trills and liquid notes.

Ringed plover

The ringed plover's plumage pattern serves two contrasting purposes: during nesting it is camouflage, and yet in display it is vivid and eye-catching.

Above: A ringed plover at rest on turf. There are two ways you can tell it is not a little ringed plover, even without seeing both birds together: this bird lacks a yellow eye ring, and there is no white border at the back of the black band on the forehead. The ringed plumage is good camouflage, but also has a vivid visual effect when the bird adopts a demonstrative posture: thus it plays a part in the highly developed display behaviour of the species.

Leap-frog migration

From extensive northern breeding areas, most of the world's ringed plovers migrate long-distance to Africa. In doing so, they 'leap-frog' the ringed plovers of Britain and Ireland, some of which migrate 'short-haul' to the Spanish and French coasts, while others winter on the south coast of England, or even nearer their breeding sites.

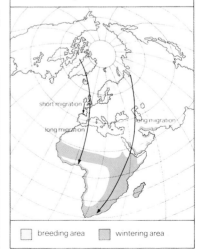

short migration

long migration

long migration

☐ breeding area ☐ wintering area

Ringed plovers can be found on virtually every beach in Britain, at least for part of the year. They are selective in summer, choosing shingle, shell and sandy beaches, but some disperse in autumn to join flocks of other waders on mudflats and estuaries.

Confusion of identity In Britain, the only bird likely to be confused with the ringed plover is the little ringed plover. Both are aptly named since, especially in summer plumage, they have conspicuous black and white rings or collars on the head and neck. The difference in their size is only slight, so plumage features provide a much better way of distinguishing them.

The head pattern of both species is com-

Ringed plover distribution

Identification features

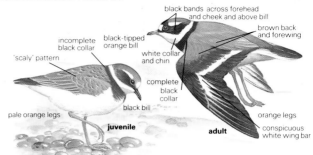

black bands across forehead
and cheek and above bill

brown back
and forewing

incomplete
black collar

black-tipped
orange bill

white collar
and chin

'scaly' pattern

complete
black
collar

pale orange legs

black bill

juvenile

orange legs

adult

conspicuous
white wing bar

plicated. Each has a pale brown and black cap and a white forehead. Each is also black in front, behind and around the eye, and there is a white collar and chin, and a second black collar below this. However, of the two species, the ringed plover has more black on the crown, and it also lacks the yellow eye ring and a white border at the back of the black forehead band, which are characteristic features of the little ringed plover. The ringed plover's best distinguishing feature is a bold white wing bar, totally absent from its relative.

Such striking patterns prompt one to ask what purpose they serve. Recognition of other individuals of the same species is one obvious answer, but a study of the behaviour of these birds shows that two other factors are important: camouflage and display. It might seem surprising that the same plumage should suffice to enable a bird to be either inconspicuous or conspicuous, but this is certainly true of the ringed plover.

Camouflage for nesting Effective camouflage is essential during the breeding season because ringed plovers nest on the ground on wide, open beaches. Shells and pebbles typically give a very varied pattern of stripes and curves in a wide range of colours and shades, and the ringed plover's plumage blends perfectly into such a background. Even sandy beaches usually have a scattering of seaweed and stones which the plover can mimic.

The nest is a shallow depression, lined with small stones and odd bits of vegetation collected nearby. Predictably, the eggs are stone-coloured, being grey to buffish in ground colour, spotted and blotched with black and grey. They are laid one every day or two, four eggs being the usual clutch. The chosen site always has a good all-round view – rocks and other obstacles are avoided – so the incubating bird is able to watch for danger.

On the approach of a predator, or perhaps someone walking along the beach, two alternative strategies are usually possible. If the intruder is unlikely to approach closely, the incubating bird bird may sit tight and rely on its own camouflage for protection. How-

Above left: The ringed plover is a sand and shingle nester, and the form of its nest is typical of all the wading birds: a simple scrape in the ground. The pointed eggs are laid in May, June and July.

Ringed plover
(*Charadrius hiaticula*).
Wader breeding on beaches.
Partial migrant, some birds
wintering on mudflats and
estuaries in the British Isles.
Sexes alike. Length 15cm
(6in).

Below: The distraction display is performed in order to lead an intruder from the nest. The bird feigns injury and runs or shuffles along with one wing raised and the other dragging over the ground or (as here) folded.

ever, if the intruder is likely to come within a few yards of the nest, the better alternative is to leave the nest quietly, run some distance and then fly to safety. The logic behind this course of action is that the nest and eggs are even more difficult to see than the incubating bird, and unless the intruder knows exactly where to look they are almost impossible to find. When the danger is past, incubation can be resumed. Like other waders, ringed plovers have very rapid flight, so it would be possible for them simply to wait and then fly to safety at the very last moment, but this sudden movement would almost certainly reveal the nest site and so jeopardise the eggs.

High failure rate Incubation is shared more or less equally between the two sexes, changeovers occurring at least once each hour throughout the day and night. Off-duty birds usually fly off to feed or stand sentinel on a raised piece of ground nearby, ready to sound the alarm when necessary. Incubation lasts 23-25 days, typical for waders but about twice as long as the average garden bird.

Redshank and spotted redshank

The redshank, famous for its bright red legs, is called the 'sentinel of the marshes' for its habit of calling loudly to warn of approaching intruders.

Above: On mud or a grassy nesting meadow, the redshank is a shy and restless bird. When it is suspicious, it bobs both its head and its tail as it walks along – just like the various sandpipers, which belong to the same genus.

The redshank is a slender, medium-sized, grey-brown wader with striking bright red legs. (In young birds, however, the legs are a dirty yellow.) The beak is long and thin, dark brown at the tip but deep red near the face. In summer, the redshank's back is a warm golden brown, with black patches, and the head and neck have well-defined black streaks. In winter the back is grey-brown with darker flecks, while the head and neck are greyish with sooty streaks. The flanks are speckled and streaked grey-brown, shading to a pure white belly.

Recognising redshanks By far the most conspicuous plumage feature of the redshank – in summer or in winter – is its pattern in flight. The rump is white and a broad white streak extends up the back between the wings. The tail is white, with narrow brown bars, and the wings are brown, but with a very broad white bar along their trailing edges. This striking pattern, coupled with the continuous noisy calls the bird utters, makes the redshank one of the easiest waders to identify.

In flight the redshank is vigorous, fast and rather erratic, somewhat reminiscent of a snipe in its sudden changes of direction. Often, immediately after landing, the redshank lifts both wings vertically over its back, as if stretching to relieve tired muscles after a long flight.

When walking it is normally a slow and graceful bird, something that is particularly apparent as it moves among other waders on the mud. Except at high tide, when all species are forced to pack together on the few remaining spots of dry land, redshanks rarely form large flocks.

Musical calls All of the redshank's many calls have a special musical quality, even the noisiest and most frantic of its alarm notes. The commonest notes, uttered by undisturbed birds, are a single beautiful but slightly mournful 'tuuu', and a trisyllabic 'tu-hu-hu'. The song, a series of yodelling variations on the calls, includes a 'tu-oodle' sound. It may be produced by a male standing on a prominent song perch – an old fence post, for instance – or in a yo-yoing hovering display flight.

Redshank (*Tringa totanus*). Resident wader, found inland in the north, and on eastern and southern coasts, on damp marshland, flooded fields, estuarine marshes and saltings; joined by migrants in winter. Length 28cm (11in).
Spotted or **dusky redshank** (*Tringa erythropus*). Passage migrant, appearing in Britain in April and May, sometimes overwintering on estuaries in south and south-east England and western Ireland. Length 30cm (12in).

Redshank
golden brown back
white rump

summer

white wing bars

white back and rump

Spotted redshank
sooty black plumage

Redshank chick

grey and white plumage

grey-brown back

Spotted redshank

drab yellow legs

Redshank   **winter**

Above: Redshank in roosting posture. Redshanks are resident here, but harsh winters can take a severe toll. The winter of 1962-3 eliminated the breeding population of redshanks in Devon and it took a decade before they reappeared there.

Below: Spotted redshank in autumn plumage. At this time of year, it can be told from its relative, the redshank, by its larger size and paler colouring. Also, its legs and beak are noticeably longer.

The spotted redshank A relative of the redshank, the spotted redshank is a slightly larger bird with longer legs and beak. In flight its white back, visible between the wings, is conspicuous, but the white trailing edge to the wing, so obvious in the redshank, is lacking. The wing feathers are delicately barred and spotted with white instead of being uniformly brownish grey.

Towards the end of the spring passage in May, some migrant spotted redshanks start to acquire their spendid full breeding plumage. They become sooty black all over, with a few grey crescent-shaped bars on the breast and belly, and upperparts flecked with white spots, against which the reddish beak and long dark red legs are well set off. This beautiful plumage gives rise to the most commonly used colloquial name: dusky redshank.

This bird's delicate, rapid pecking technique of feeding is much the same as that of the redshank, but the spotted redshank takes advantage of its longer legs and can be seen wading out from the margins of marshland dykes or lagoons and feeding on small surface animals even when the water comes halfway up its flanks. At all times, though, the flight call is characteristic and unmistakable: an emphatic, two syllable 'chewitt', carrying well over the mudflats.

Avocet

The avocet is a beautiful bird with long grey-blue legs, startling black and white plumage and a gracefully up-curving bill. It is very rare—your best chance to see this wader is through the viewing slots of a hide on one of two RSPB reserves.

Above: The avocet is an elegant, graceful bird with a strongly up-curving black bill about 9cm (3½in) long. It feeds on small invertebrates on the shoreline.

Although the avocet is still a rare British bird, there is certainly never any problem of identification or recognition. The snow-white plumage is strikingly marked: on the outer third of the wings there are convergent black bands on the back and across the wing coverts, and the nape and top of the head are also black. The most unmistakable recognition feature is the up curved bill. The avocet is a wading bird and frequents seashores where it feeds on invertebrates living in shallow water.

Speedy swimmer Most waders can swim adequately if necessary; but the avocet does so more easily than most because, unlike most waders, its feet are partially webbed. It frequently gets out of its depth when feeding, swimming positively and quickly to the next shallow area, and occasionally upending for food items while swimming. A characteristic feature is its walk—it has a brisk and busy gait and holds its body almost horizontal, carrying its neck in a graceful forward curve.

Pairing and nesting In most waders court-

ship display is prominent and often lively, but avocets are remarkable in having virtually no courtship display. Male and female pair in spring and the bond between them appears to be strengthened through mating.

Although courtship is limited, the avocet's mating ceremony is distinctive and attractive. The female adopts an inelegant position of readiness in thigh-deep water. This stimulates the excited male to execute a particular dance in which he runs round the rear of the female several times from one side to another before mounting. After mating he jumps to one side of the female and both run forward together for several yards. Often one of his wings extends over the back of his mate—a touching gesture in human terms. The avocet's call is an unvarying 'kloot' or 'kluit'—the latter being the Dutch word for avocet.

The avocet is a gregarious bird which lives in colonies during the breeding season. This is probably a result of specialised breeding and feeding requirements, and a consequently limited choice of sites.

The parents scrape out a nest hollow on

Opposite: The shallow brackish water pools which form on saltmarshes are favourite feeding areas for the avocet.

Above: Apart from its more obvious attributes, the avocet is distinguished from other waders by its partially webbed feet.

adult using
sweeping motion
of bill to feed

up-curving bill

adult in defence
posture protecting
chick

chick with
camouflage
coloration

drooping wings

Left: In cloudy water, where the avocet cannot see prey clearly, it traps its food by feel. The bird holds its bill slightly open under water, sweeping from side to side to catch small invertebrates. In clear water or from the surface, it pecks at its prey.

Below: Both parents incubate the eggs using their brood patches—feather-free areas that give direct contact from the adult's skin to the eggs and so transfer heat. The chicks are a sandy, brownish colour on top, which provides some camouflage.

sandy ground close to the water. They sometimes collect and arrange dead grass or other vegetation around the nest scrape, but they do not build a nest as such. Both parents share in the incubation, which begins once the final egg is laid and lasts for 22-24 days. The chicks start to feed themselves almost immediately after they hatch, pecking for insects and shrimps on the surface of the mud.

Feeding habits The avocet's feeding technique is unique among waders. It frequents saline and brackish pools and its food comprises the narrow range of creatures which can tolerate varying levels of salinity and desiccation – these include several species of shrimp, water beetles, midge larvae, aquatic flies and ragworms. The bird feeds by sweeping the upturned bill from side to side as it moves through the water.

The availability of food differs as lagoon water evaporates in summer and salinity increases. This is a critical factor in the survival of avocet young. The size of a family feeding territory is determined by the abundance or scarcity of food. The adults take their brood to areas rich in food and defend

them aggressively from neighbouring families in a manner which contrasts with their mutual tolerance in nests positioned close together before the eggs hatch.

Numbers and distribution The avocet's numbers in the British Isles are on the increase today – an astounding fact considering that before World War II they had not bred in Britain for over 50 years. Although the full extent of the avocet's former breeding distribution and numbers in Britain is not known, it was probably never great, and almost certainly restricted to coastal areas in the south eastern part of Britain between the Humber estuary and the Sussex coast. What is known for certain is that the avocet's decline occurred well before the end of the nineteenth century. The drainage of fens and coastal marshes was a root cause of the decline; later, egg collecting and shooting for mounted specimens completed it.

In 1947, when access was again permitted to many of the east coast areas which had been fenced off during the war, it was discovered that avocets were breeding in two sites in Suffolk: Minsmere Marshes and Havergate Island, near Orfordness.

Gulls are generally but not exclusively coastal birds; and at least six species are common around the British Isles. Here we look at four of our larger, familiar gulls: the herring, the lesser black-backed, the great black-backed and the common – which is not quite so commonly seen as its name suggests, except in Scotland and Northern Ireland. These four gulls are difficult to tell apart, especially the immature birds.

Herring gulls are the most numerous of our gulls. They breed all round the coasts of Britain and Ireland, except the stretch from Flamborough south to the Thames. In this area only a few isolated pairs have been recorded – in north Norfolk and Orfordness. The further north and west you go, the more abundant herring gulls are. In 1969-70 there were more than 333,000 pairs – 157,000 in Scotland, 52,000 in Ireland, 70,000 in England and 54,000 in Wales and the Channel Islands. These numbers are increased in winter by visitors from north-west Europe.

Herring gulls nest along the steep cliff edges, among rocks, on ledges and stacks and sometimes on shingle banks or in sand dunes. Many nests are isolated, but where there are plenty of suitable sites then something like a colony develops – though this is more because of opportunity than design.

Herring, common and black-blacked gulls

Identifying gulls by sight is not easy, nor can you rely on habitat as a guide. Although we associate these birds with our cliffs and shore-line, not all are coastal.

Above left: The herring gull, an opportunist feeder, is a persistent scavenger behind trawlers and also finds food on ploughed fields and refuse tips.

Below: The herring gull frequents rocky coasts and cliffs while the lesser black-backed gull prefers flatter sand dune areas or grassy cliffs. The great black-backed gull nests on rocky coasts, as does the common gull which also nests inland in northern Scotland.

Herring gull

Lesser black-backed gull

Great black-backed gull

Common gull

Lesser black-backed gulls often breed close to or in mixed colonies with their close relatives the herring gulls. Their distribution is similar but their numbers are smaller – under 50,000 pairs.

Lesser black-backed gulls always nest in dense colonies well back from the edge of the cliff. They may even take to islands in lakes. Unlike herring gulls, newly hatched lesser black-backed gull chicks leave the bowl of the nest as soon as they have dried out, to find shelter from predators. They hide in vegetation such as bluebells and bracken. Another difference is the lesser black-backed gulls' defensive behaviour: they attack any intruders into a colony with threatening dive-bombing displays that avoid actual physical contact.

Great black-backed gulls, as big as geese, are the largest of our four gulls. Juveniles in their first year are darkly mottled; their plumage patterns in subsequent years are similar to those of the lesser black-backed and herring gulls.

They are birds of the north Atlantic, with a steadily increasing range and population. They have colonized the east coast of Scotland since 1960 and are found all around Ireland. Elsewhere in the British Isles, nesting is confined to western and northern coasts and there are few nests from the Forth to the Isle of Wight.

Great black-backed gulls tend to nest singly, on the top of outcrops, stacks and on small offshore islands as well as in lakes. The same pair may occupy a site for years. There is a colony of 1800 pairs on North Rona, but this is exceptional.

Common gulls breed all round the northern hemisphere, but their name is ill-chosen in England and Ireland. The greatest numbers are in the Scottish Highlands and northwest Ireland. They are as much birds of inland waters as coastal species. No census of these birds exists in Britain because so much of the terrain is hard to cover. However, isolated pairs have nested at Dungeness, Anglesey and in the Pennines.

Common gulls are the smallest of this group of gulls – markedly smaller than herring gulls. They are best distinguished by the lack of a red blob on the tip of the lower beak, which also makes their head look rather pointed. During the breeding season common gulls are so rowdy that the noise can be unbearable. Both sexes take up a non-stop, shrill, rapid chorus of 'keeya-keeya-keeya', passing it on from group to group. As with other gulls, their vocabulary is extensive, but they hardly call at all in winter.

Great black-backed gull *(Larus marinus)*, 70-75cm (27-30in) long, wingspan 165cm (65in). White except for black mantle and wings. Legs are pale flesh pink.

Lesser black-backed gull *(Larus fuscus)* (left), marginally smaller than herring gull. Dark slate-grey back, yellow legs.

Herring gull *(Larus argentatus)* (right) 55-60cm (22-24in) long. Wingspan 130cm (52in). Pale silvery back, flesh-pink legs.

Common gull *(Larus canus)*, 45cm (18in) long, wingspan 120cm (48in). Back is mid grey, legs greenish-yellow. Unlike others, no red spot on beak. Smallest of this group.

Common and Arctic terns

The Arctic tern is one of the world's greatest travellers, and the common tern is not far behind it; these two maritime birds, both notable for their graceful flight and endurance, well deserve their popular name of 'sea swallows'.

Below: Common terns calling. Despite their propensity for long-distance travel, common terns can be seen from spring until mid-autumn, feeding close inshore near many coastal resorts.

Terns have aptly been given the popular name 'sea-swallows', for they are perhaps the most graceful and elegant of our seabirds. Silver-grey and white, with darker wing-tips and black cap, and long tail streamers, they are smaller and much slimmer than any of the gulls. All are migrants, travelling to fish in the oceans of the southern hemisphere during our winter, and returning to our coasts to breed in the summer.

The two species most often seen off British coasts during the summer months are the common tern and the Arctic tern. Both fit the general description above, and are so similar in size, shape and plumage that they may often be very difficult to identify with certainty. Because of this, birdwatchers have coined the jargon term 'comic terns' for those whose identity has not positively been confirmed.

Telling them apart If a really close view can be obtained in good light, then you can see some plumage differences which distinguish the two. In a mixed group (and on passage mixtures of the two are often seen) standing on a beach, Arctic terns are noticeably shorter in the leg than common terns: they are so short-legged in fact, as to seem to be sitting rather than standing. Especially during the height of the breeding season, Arctic terns have a totally blood-red beak, while common terns have black tips to their orange-red beaks, often extending to half the beak's length.

long tail
streamers

pure red
beak

Arctic tern

black-tipped
beak

summer plumage

Common tern

darker plumage
than adult

white
forehead

blackish beak
with red base

**Juvenile
common tern**

Terns in spring During the breeding season, terns fish close inshore, 'flickering' along lazily in the air a few feet above the waves before suddenly turning and plunging head-long into the sea. Often these dives result in an audible 'plop' and a considerable splash, but the bird penetrates only a few inches rather than submerges deeply.

Arctic terns are colonial breeders, and the colonies may be thousands strong. They are birds of the Arctic, as their name suggests, nesting on barren beaches and tundra. The nest is a shallow scrape, lined with fragments of shell and sometimes vegetation, and con-taining one, two or three eggs which are incubated for about a month. The young wander about soon after hatching, and fly four or five weeks later. In Britain and Ireland, not surprisingly, they are birds of remote islands and beaches in the north and west.

Generally, Arctic terns shun areas dis-turbed by man, but at one of their more southerly breeding colonies, on the Farne Islands, they have become accustomed to the regular but well-managed parties of visitors that are allowed to pay brief visits.

Above: An Arctic tern brings food to the nest after a fishing flight close inshore. The prey is usually small fish or shrimps, and the fish are caught one at a time, not in a beakful as with puffins. Early in the season the male feeds his mate, an activity known as courtship feeding.

Arctic tern (*Sterna paradisea*); summer visiting seabird, almost entirely coastal. Breeding range more northerly than that of common tern, wintering grounds more southerly. Length 36cm (14in).

Common tern (*Sterna hirundo*); summer visiting seabird, mainly coastal but sometimes nesting inland; length 36cm (14in).

Below: A common tern alights at its simple nest.

Towards the end of the summer, as the adults moult into winter plumage, beak colours become drabber and this feature is less reliable. Both species acquire white foreheads in the autumn. Young birds have blackish beaks and so cannot be separated by this feature. Again, with the birds seen at rest, the tail streamers of the Arctic tern (part of the origin of the term 'sea swallow') extend for a couple of inches or more beyond the folded wing tips, while the common tern's streamers and wings are about the same length.

Perhaps the best separation feature of all is the wing pattern, seen when the birds are in flight. The primaries, or flight feathers, of the Arctic tern appear slightly translucent in the light, giving the impression of an almost luminous white patch in the outer section of the wing. This noticeably bright area has only a very narrow grey-black border along the leading edge of the outermost feather and along the trailing edge of the outer part of the wing. In contrast, the common tern has a pale smoky-grey outer half to its wing, above and below, and its grey-black feather margins are more extensive, especially on the upper wing surface.

Listen to the call There are also slight differences in the calls of the two species, but these require a great deal of experience before they can be successfully used as an identification feature. Both have a long-drawn-out 'keeee-yaaaah' call. In the com-mon tern, the emphasis is strongly placed on the first syllable, which forms the longer part of the call, while in the Arctic tern the two syllables have roughly the same length and emphasis. On migration, the common tern uses a 'kik-kik-kik' call which can sometimes be distinguished from the higher pitched, whistling 'kee, kee' of the Arctic tern.

Puffin

The puffin, with its clown-like face, multi-coloured
beak and quizzical expression, seems designed to
attract our sympathy–and well it might. With the
sharp decline in distribution and numbers, as well as
the ability of some bird predators to kill them in
mid-air, puffins need protection.

The puffin, in its 'dinner-jacket' of black and white feathers and colourful banded beak, is one of our most charming birds. It belongs to a family of seabirds–auks–which includes guillemots and razorbills. All auks characteristically hunt fish beneath the sea surface, and remain at sea outside the breeding season.

The puffin is a difficult bird to study in detail: comings and goings about the puffinry (as a colony of puffins is called) are notoriously erratic, and it nests in a burrow too deep and dark to permit eggs or young to be seen.

Distribution and dispersal For most of the year puffins live on our remote, almost inaccessible, northern coasts–particularly around uninhabited islands in the Orkneys and Shetlands. They once flourished along the Channel coast, but have now virtually disappeared from this region. In the east only suitable cliffs from Flamborough Head northwards support colonies. There are more puffinries on the western, generally rocky shoreline of Britain and Ireland. Here, the population increases towards the north.

In winter, puffins disperse widely from their breeding colonies, remaining at sea in ones or twos, not in the large groups (rafts) favoured by other auks. Some puffins stay in the North Sea or in the Bay of Biscay, while a few move south into the Mediterranean .

Puffins remain further out to sea than guillemots or razorbills, and most spend the winter scattered over the north Atlantic, feeding mainly on plankton. Even juvenile birds range far and wide: two nestlings ringed one year on St Kilda, off the Outer Hebrides, were recovered the following winter over the Newfoundland Banks.

Once a puffin moves away from its breeding site in winter, its brightly coloured beak turns a dull grey. The crisp margins of the black plumage also become blurred and the white areas of the face, breast and belly turn greyish. The puffin sheds the odd patch of wrinkled yellow skin at the corners of the mouth, as well as the horny red and grey triangles round the eyes.

Breeding sites The puffins return to their puffinries at varying times in spring. Many of

these sites are large, and some, with tens or even hundreds of thousands of pairs, are enormous. The Farne Islands are a good place to see puffins, on the National Trust reserve, but there are also large colonies on the Scilly Isles, Bempton Cliffs in Yorkshire and Skomer off the Pembrokeshire coast. Puffins are sensitive to the presence of humans, so all the best places to see them are inaccessible.

Some puffins live in holes in sea cliffs, while others choose the extensive screes and tumbled boulders at the head and foot of the cliffs. Most puffins, however, nest in grassland burrows, usually close to the cliff top. Here they either dig burrows themselves, making use of the long sharp claws on their strong feet, or they take over a disused rabbit hole or Manx shearwater burrow.

The grassy slopes favoured by puffins are usually covered in pink thrift, white sea-campion, and often harebells–all flourishing on the guano deposited by the seabirds. This forms an attractive back-drop to the puffins' social gatherings at burrow entrances,

Above: Although puffins do not have an elaborate courtship display, the male and female bow to each other in a 'courtly' manner, and nibble one another round the back of the neck.

Opposite: As their young grows, the adults visit the burrow regularly with sand eels or similar fish held cross-wise in the beak.

Puffin (Fratercula arctica); about 25cm (10in) high. Distribution on coastal, rocky shores, particularly western Britain, Ireland and northern offshore islands.

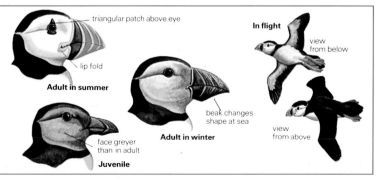

Beak-full of colour
The huge, comical-looking, parrot-like beak of the puffin, is only coloured with red, blue and yellow bands for display in the summer breeding season. The adult sheds the horny outer sheath at the end of summer. It then grows a much smaller, slimmer and strictly functional grey winter beak—much the same size as that of the youngsters. This beak change is accompanied by plumage colour changes.

triangular patch above eye

In flight

view from below

lip fold

Adult in summer

beak changes shape at sea

view from above

face greyer than in adult

Adult in winter

Juvenile

Songbirds and garden birds

Many of our most familiar, everyday birds are included in this chapter, as are many of the most popular: their popularity largely due to the richness and variety of their song.

It is well worth considering the origins of this group of birds. Some 2000 years ago, much of Europe was covered in forest. Oak, ash and lime grew in the lowlands, beech grew on the chalky soils, conifers grew on the sands and in the uplands, and water-loving species like alder and willow grew in the substantial wetland areas which existed in river valleys in the days before land drainage. Man was of course present then, but in very small numbers. As the human population grew, so did the need for a more sophisticated farming system to produce food. To raise crops and stock, it was necessary to make clearings in the woodland cover.

Most of these clearings would naturally be near to centres of population, and these in turn would have been located in the most hospitable areas—mostly in the milder, drier lowlands. Hence most of today's remaining forests are in the remote and wet northern and western uplands. In the last 500 years these clearings for farming have expanded more rapidly, both to feed a fast-growing population, and to provide a surplus for export, for building houses and ships, and for fuel. Now we are left with only a residual pattern of cover which varies from the still predominantly wooded northern areas to the 'prairie farming' expanses of some fertile lowlands—a matrix of fields and woods with an interlinking network of hedges and spinneys.

Overall, this process has probably been extremely beneficial to birds. While it is true that some larger forest-loving birds (like the honey buzzard) will have suffered, continuous, dense mature woodland is a relatively poor habitat for birds, and therefore not particularly rewarding for birdwatchers. Creating farmland has vastly increased the woodland 'edge'—the area most preferred by birds in that it provides shelter, some food and nest sites, but also allows access to other food sources in the fields.

Thus it is this matrix that supports throughout the year large numbers of our wide range of resident seed and fruit-eating birds—each well supplied because of the variety of plants that grow *outside* the mature wood—and which holds many of our summer visitors (such as the warblers), that are primarily insectivorous, because on such a varied habitat a wide variety of insects naturally flourish.

Of these farmland and hedgerow birds, a considerable number have proved adaptable enough to consider our gardens as an extension of their preferred habitat: blackbirds, robins and blue tits are typical examples. Some—the feral pigeon and the house sparrow come to mind—have even adapted well to the apparently stark conditions of the hearts of our cities. Yet others have been encouraged to change their lifestyle. The blackcap is one such bird: a migrant, and largely insectivorous, it is now wintering regularly in northern Europe where its natural food is augmented by garden bird-feeding tables.

Opposite: A great spotted woodpecker swoops from its nest hole in the trunk of an oak.

Woodpigeon, collared and turtle doves

Pigeons and doves vary in size and colour but all have a plump body, small head and slender beak. They have succeeded in adapting to Man's urban sprawl, and have withstood the threat of the shotgun by rapid flight and consistent breeding.

Below: Turtle doves are thinly distributed on farmland south of a line between Durham and Lancashire (they are scarcer in west Wales and Cornwall). Their main food plant, which grows here, is fumitory.

There are about 300 species of pigeons and doves in the world, five of which occur in the British Isles. Whether you call them 'pigeon' or 'dove' is a matter of personal preference – though generally pigeons are large birds with short, square tails, and doves are more slightly built with long, rounded tails.

Cliff cousins Multicoloured town pigeons are a common sight in urban areas on buildings, statues and railway stations as well as in gardens. They are domesticated descendants of the rock doves, which now live only on remote sea cliffs in north and west Scotland and the Atlantic coast of Ireland. These 'true' rock doves also occur around the Mediterranean, on coasts and near inland cliffs. In Britain, however, it is their town cousins that thrive, with buildings for nest sites, ample supplies of bread and other scraps for food, and an extraordinary tolerance of Man's proximity.

In the early days of agriculture, most farms had a dove-coat, containing free-flying, domesticated rock doves, which were bred for their different colours and racing abilities. The domestic birds look quite different from the cliff-dwelling ones, but extensive interbreeding between the two has 'contaminated' all but the most remote rock dove colonies. However, breeding feral populations tend to revert after a few years to the 'blue' colora-

tion found in true rock doves.

Stock doves are easily confused with rock doves. Both have iridescent-green neck patches which they use in courtship display, but stock doves are less gregarious, more inconspicuous birds and lack the bold markings of their relatives. Once found only in south and east England, they have spread throughout Britain with the increase in agriculture.

Woodpigeons have also increased dramatically in number and range, and are even colonising the Outer Hebrides and Shetland Isles. They are unusually tame birds in urban areas where their numbers are increasing. A broad, white crescent bisects each wing. It is concealed when the wings are folded; in flight, however, it is obvious and recognised by other pigeons as a hazard-warning signal. Woodpigeons are larger than other British pigeons and have proportionately longer tails than stock doves. A good way to identify woodpigeons is by their bold white neck patch or ring–hence their other name 'ring' dove.

Collared doves take their name from the incomplete, white-bordered but otherwise black neck collar. The smallest of our resident species, they spread from the Continent and have colonised most of the British Isles in the last 25 years with a dramatic population explosion. Associating closely with Man and his cereal grain, collared doves are now common birds in villages and suburban areas.

Turtle doves are even smaller than collared doves, with a shorter, more rounded tail. They fly in a dashing manner, with quick flicking wing-beats, and when overhead the white belly appears outlined by darker wings and tail. Turtle doves spend the winter in Africa, and return in late April to May.

Cooing songs Pigeons and doves have a characteristic, monotonous call which they use to establish territories. The establishment of territories helps to separate nests and reduce the dangers from predators. Wood-

1 Rock dove/feral pigeon
(Columba livia)
2 Stock dove
(Columba oenas)
3 Turtle dove
(Streptopelia turtur)
4 Collared dove
(Streptopelia decaocto)
5 Woodpigeon
(Columba palumbus)

Above: Unlike most birds, a woodpigeon does not need to lift its head to allow water to drain down the throat with each gulp.

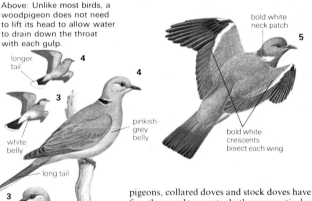

pigeons, collared doves and stock doves have five, three and two-note rhythms respectively; they repeat each phase several times in succession. Male collared doves also have a nasal-sounding song which is often mistaken for the call of the cuckoo. The cooing of domestic and feral pigeons is well-known and seems not to have changed from that of rock doves. The turtle doves' soothing purr, which they sing hidden in deep cover, can easily go undetected.

Display flights Pigeons and doves also advertise their territory by flying in display positions. Rock and stock doves glide with wings held stiffly in a 'V'. Turtle and collared doves fly up and then parachute down with tail fanned and wings held below horizontal level. Woodpigeons have an undulating display-flight; they fly up, stall and 'clap' their wings two or three times, and then glide down before repeating the process. The claps, made on the downstroke of the wing-beat, are similar to the crack of a whip–contact between the wings is not important.

Cuckoo

The cuckoo, whose call is so familiar in early summer, comes here to breed, but it neither builds a nest nor cares for its young–other birds do that for it!

The cuckoo is frequently heard but, being a shy bird, is seldom seen. The one British breeding species is extremely vocal from the moment it arrives here from Africa in mid-April. It sometimes calls on the wing, but usually waits until it alights before uttering the familiar, far-carrying 'cu-coo'. Occasionally the cry is 'cu-cu-coo' which, with other

variants (and contrary to popular belief), can be heard at the start of the season as well as near the end. A much lesser known call is a comparatively subdued liquid bubbling sound. It is likely that most of the 'cu-cooing' comes from the male and most of the bubbling from the female, but both sexes can make these calls. Both also use a deep 'grow-ow-ow' sound. Strangely enough, cuckoos often seem to call with their beaks closed.

The only view you're likely to have of a cuckoo is as it hastens by on a direct, level course, its rapidly beating wings held mainly below the body, or as it glides the last few yards to a perch. It is a long-tailed, hawk-like grey bird with barred underparts and bright yellow eyes, and often perches horizontally with wings drooping. Cuckoos' feet, which have two toes pointing forwards and two pointing backwards, like those of a parrot, are adapted to make perching and scrambling about in branches easy, but it makes the birds clumsy waddlers on the ground.

The cuckoo is insectivorous, feeding on the

Above: A young cuckoo about two weeks old. Juveniles are often reddish in colour and can be further distinguished by a pale patch on the nape. Occasionally, when two cuckoo eggs have been laid in the same nest, the foster parents find they have two chicks to rear because neither has succeeded in evicting the other.

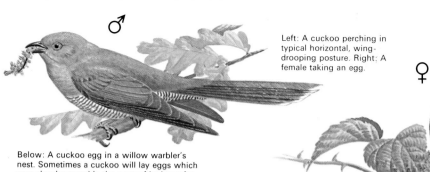

♂

Left: A cuckoo perching in typical horizontal, wing-drooping posture. Right: A female taking an egg.

♀

Below: A cuckoo egg in a willow warbler's nest. Sometimes a cuckoo will lay eggs which very closely resemble the eggs of its host; for example, blue eggs which match those of the dunnock, a frequent host species.

Above: A newly hatched chick ousting the host's egg from a nest. The instinct to do this is very powerful and lasts for about four days.

caterpillars of magpie moths and the larvae of sawflies and other insects; it is also unusual in being an avid devourer of hairy caterpillars and brightly coloured ones which warn of an unpalatable taste – insects normally avoided by birds.

Take-over bid The breeding season begins as soon as the cuckoos arrive in Britain. The males display excitedly, sometimes several of them together: calling loudly, they sway from side to side, bobbing up and down and even spinning round, their large, decorative tails raised and fanned out.

While the males display, the female cuckoo keenly defends her own territory, at the same time observing possible host species – birds smaller than herself such as willow warblers, meadow pipits, dunnocks or even robins. Her aim is to find out where they are building and when they start laying their first eggs. After days of careful watching, the female chooses a nest with an incomplete clutch of eggs – usually with just one egg – where incubation has not yet started. Between mid-afternoon and eight in the evening – a time when her victims are likely to be away feeding (because their eggs were laid in the morning) – the female cuckoo flies straight to the nest, ignoring any small birds which mob her in mistake for a hawk. She takes an egg out of the nest and holds it in her beak while she quickly lays one of her own in its place. Finally, she eats or discards the egg.

Cuckoos' eggs have been found in the nests of over 50 different British birds. Some of these nests – such as the hole type – seem rather unsuitable. Where the nest is in a hole too small for the cuckoo to enter, she clings with outspread wings and tail against the opening and ejects her egg into the nest. If this fails and her egg rolls aside she abandons it, making no attempt to pick it up.

Most small birds lay an egg a day, but the cuckoo lays every second day, presumably to give herself time to find all the nests she needs, for she may lay a dozen or more eggs. When her final egg is laid the female cuckoo's task is over, and she takes no further part or interest in her progeny's future. Nor does the male. He stops singing by the end of June and then he, and all other adult cuckoos, are free to fly back to Africa. They leave in July, the earliest of our summer birds to go.

Fooling foster parents An intriguing feature of the story is the foster parents' generally willing acceptance of the cuckoo's egg. Occasionally the put-upon fosterers react by burying the alien egg under a fresh layer of nesting material; a very few species, such as the blackcap and the spotted flycatcher, seem to become cuckoo-resistant, readily deserting the nest if a cuckoo lays her egg in it. Most cuckoos avoid the nests of these species. The female cuckoo's biggest risk is that her egg may be rejected. Perhaps her main reason for removing an egg before depositing her own is to minimize suspicion in the fosterer's mind. Sometimes two or even three cuckoo eggs are found in one nest, but they are almost invariably laid by different birds – something which is easy to check since the eggs of each cuckoo are individually marked and can be recognised from year to year.

Whenever possible a female cuckoo, all her life, lays in the nest of only one kind of host species. The females are grouped into various clans – such as the meadow pipit cuckoos (probably the commonest clan in Britain), hedge sparrow cuckoos (mainly in woodlands and hedgerows) and reed warbler cuckoos (in aquatic habitats).

Migration route
Adult cuckoos leave in late July, flying through Italy and across to Africa. The young follow in late August, finding their solitary way by instinct only.

breeding area
wintering area
→ route

Swallow

Every spring, swallows make an astounding journey from their winter quarters in South Africa. They travel nearly 5000 miles in one month, arriving here in early April to nest and breed and take advantage of our plentiful supply of insects.

Above: Young swallows about to receive a few welcome morsels of food from an assiduous parent. In their nest high up in the corner of an outbuilding, the young are generally fairly safe from predators; the adults warn of the presence of an inquisitive cat (or human) with a series of loud, sharp alarm calls, but use a longer, shriller and more penetrating cry if a bird predator—such as a hobby—appears.

According to the proverb, one swallow doesn't make a summer, but to many people the return of this bird each year is a sure sign that winter is at an end and summer just round the corner. As the weather gradually warms up in spring the flight paths swallows take on their migration journey north from South Africa can be mapped right across Europe. The first swallows appear in southern Britain on or around April 10, but the north of Scotland may have to wait until early May before the breeding birds arrive.

Food supply is the vital factor controlling both arrivals and departures. Swallows feed by catching insects on the wing, and in good weather you can often see them flying low over water meadows or skimming along a river, above a hayfield or even the local cricket pitch. In cold, wet or windy weather they gather in large flocks to concentrate on places where insect food remains available, often down-wind of large bodies of water where insects may be hatching, or in the lee of a wood or hedge where there is shelter. In temperate northern areas such as Britain where the birds breed, the summer supply of food is very good and is fully exploited by the migrants arriving from the south. In winter however there are few if any flying insects and any swallows rash enough to remain would soon starve to death.

A question of identity There are four species of fork-tailed, aerial-feeding birds which come to Britain for the summer months and which, at first glance, may be confused with each other. One, the sooty-black swift with its sickle-shaped wings, is not closely related to the swallow. The other two, the house martin and the sand martin, are members of the same family group as the swallow—the hirundines. The house martin has a patch of white on the back at the base of the tail while the sand martin can be distinguished by its dark brown upper parts and small size. The swallow has a longer and much more deeply forked tail than the other species, and the sleek, burnished blue of its head, collar and back, rusty red chin and pale pinky-brown undersides make it unmistakable.

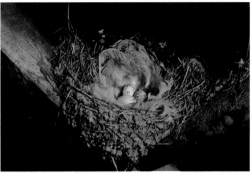

Left: The angle between rafters in a barn or shed is a favourite nesting place for the swallow, providing a firm base for the cup of mud reinforced with dried grass. A lining of hair and feathers makes a soft bed for eggs.

Swallow (*Hirundo rustica*), also known as the barn swallow; 19cm (7½in) from beak to tip of tail; distribution widespread throughout the British Isles from spring to autumn.

Raising a family The first swallows to arrive—the males—are quick to establish their nesting sites; females arrive soon after. Pairs are formed with aerial display flights, mutual preening and exploration of the chosen site. Swallows show a very positive preference for buildings as breeding places, choosing a variety of barns, sheds, garages and porches. The main body of the nest is made with pellets of wet mud cemented together and is lined with hair and feathers and sometimes dried grasses.

The first clutch of four or five white eggs with reddish markings, laid fairly quickly, is incubated by the female and hatches after 14 or 15 days. The youngsters are fed by both parents for about three weeks, until they fledge, and then for a few days more while they fly around the nest site. After that, the young birds disperse and the adults set about raising a second brood. Some assiduous pairs manage to rear three broods successfully.

The birds you see gathering in flocks on the telephone wires for the autumn migration are generally young individuals. These birds do not have the pressing family responsibilities of the adults and spend their time gener-ally making themselves familiar with the area to which, if they survive, they will return the following year to breed. Young birds are also the main occupants of the massive autumn roosts that form in reed beds throughout the country.

Migrating millions For centuries it was believed that swallows hid themselves in mud at the bottom of ponds throughout winter. People found it difficult to account for the sudden disappearance of the species every year in any other way. Even Gilbert White, the 18th century Hampshire naturalist famous for the accuracy of his observations, did not dismiss this idea completely. By the end of the 19th century, however, the migration of birds was established as fact, proved conclusively by the tracing of ringed birds. The 10,000 miles that swallows fly on migration to South Africa and back each year is a fact every bit as astonishing and marvellous as the supposed six month hibernation period under water.

Migration starts as early as the end of July in some years, and is in full swing from mid-August to the end of September.

How to tell adults from young

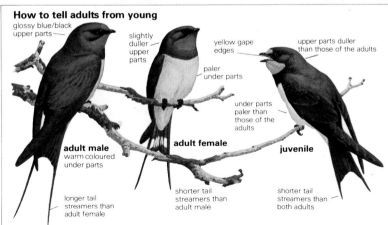

glossy blue/black upper parts
slightly duller upper parts
yellow gape edges
paler under parts
upper parts duller than those of the adults
under parts paler than those of the adults
adult male warm coloured under parts
adult female
juvenile
longer tail streamers than adult female
shorter tail streamers than adult male
shorter tail streamers than both adults

At first glance, male and female swallows look very similar. But the male has much longer, thinner-tipped outer tail feathers than the female; also the male's chestnut or rust-red forehead and chin is often richer and darker than the female's. Both sexes share the glossy, deep blue upper parts, pinky-brown underside and white spots on the inner tail feathers. You can distinguish the juvenile in autumn by the short, blunt outer tail feathers and very pale forehead and chin.

Swift

Swifts spend their lives in the air–feeding, sleeping and even mating on the wing. Once fledged, they do not set foot on the ground–not even on a perch–for two years or even more.

The swift is the most aerial of our birds. Every aspect of its anatomy and biology underlines its commitment to this mode of life. The swift rarely breeds until it is at least two years old, and entering its nest hole is its first contact with anything solid since it fledged. If a swift is accidentally grounded, its legs are so short and its wings so long, that the bird has little chance of getting airborne again.

Wing design The most obvious outward indication of specialisation is the wings–slender, sickle-shaped and extremely long. Much of this length comes from the unusually long primary feathers–the outer section of the wing.

The primary feathers provide the forward power for flight and–in most birds–are roughly equal in length to the secondary feathers which produce aerodynamic lift. But the swift's extra long primaries give greater power and make it one of the fastest birds, capable of speeds of over 60mph and perhaps even twice this in dives or if pursued by a falcon such as hobby.

Aerodynamics The streamlined body is shaped like a torpedo, with a blunt, rounded head and a body gradually tapering to a short, forked, tail. You might expect the bird to have a slender pointed head which would penetrate the air better, instead of the blunt front that appears to act as a buffer against the wind current. But the swift's shape is actually in perfect agreement with the engineering principles involved. The tapered rear end reduces the turbulent eddies of air *behind* the bird which would otherwise create a partial vacuum, or 'drag', and so slow the swift down.

The swift has few body projections interfering with airflow: the feet are tiny, and tucked into the feathers; the visible part of the beak is pointed, and extremely small; and the eyes, though large, are deep-set in slots–similar to the headlights of a sports car which are recessed in the smooth fibreglass body shell. The swift's body feathers serve a similar function in producing an unimpeded airflow over the body.

High-flyers In flight, swifts are capable of climbing up to 3000m (10,000ft). At these great heights they seem to spiral on set wing positions, certainly for long enough to obtain the necessary 'catnaps' of sleep. Sometimes swifts ascend to such altitudes in pursuit of their insect prey. They are highly specialised feeders, taking only flying insects and spiders drifting on gossamer-thin threads.

Behind the minute beak lies an enormous gape: the mouth literally opens from ear to ear, and when wide open occupies a large proportion of the front of the bird. The swift is ideally adapted to effective feeding on the wing, sweeping back and forth through the air, with its mouth gaping open, collecting small insects ('aerial plankton'), in much the way a whale scoops plankton from the sea.

Above: The swift grips on to brickwork, aided by four needle-sharp claws (below) which all point forwards. Its legs and feet, though small in proportion to the rest of its body, are very muscular.

Where to watch them One of the best places to watch swifts is over reservoirs in early summer as they feed on insects. Another good viewing site is marshland – here, using high speed passes, the swift catches the myriad midges that dance in smoke-like columns. In summer, insect abundance is controlled by the weather. In long, cool, rainy periods flying insects can become scarce, and in fine spells they may be at a great height, often accumulating at the junction of cold and warm air fronts.

Radar tracking Mobile and speedy, swifts may travel hundreds of kilometres daily in search of food. Striking evidence of this is provided by some remarkable film (taken by Marconi Ltd) of a radar screen in south east England. Many birds, swifts included, are large enough to leave a blip or 'echo' on modern radar; this spectacular film – covering a summer afternoon and the following night – shows the radar screen covered by a mass of blips caused by London swifts rising high into the sky at dusk. The blips show a rapid movement north to the Wash, where the birds congregated. Here they fed on the insects massing at a cold/warm front junction over the North Sea, before returning to their nests in the city.

Acclimatised young Nestling swifts are as well-adapted as their parents to the vagaries of the British summer which affect their food supply. Since their food is so specialised, they are more vulnerable than most young birds to shortages which may last several days. The young swifts have a survival mechanism that allows them to go gradually into a torpor – a sort of short-term hibernation.

Their body temperature falls, pulse and breathing rates are reduced to a minimum and growth ceases. The nestlings survive on a tick-over metabolism (using as energy their stored body fat),

long primary feathers

sickle-shaped wing

short forked tail

Above: With long slender wings and body built to much the same design as high-speed, high altitude reconnaissance aircraft, swifts have difficulty manoeuvring in confined spaces. You can distinguish swifts from martins and swallows which have much lighter bellies when viewed from below.

Right: In common with many other birds that nest in dark cavities, the swift's eggs are white and rather spherical. In a new site the nest may be composed of no more than a few bits of mortar arranged in rough circle.

Below: Occasionally both adults roost in the nest hole, sharing the cramped quarters with the eggs or, more uncomfortably, with well grown young.

House martin

House martins, among the most aerial of all our birds, feed and even roost on the wing, coming down to earth only to collect mud for their nests.

The house martin is a familiar summer visitor to nearly all parts of Britain and Ireland. It is an almost entirely aerial species and is often confused with its close relative, the swallow. However, house martins' tails are more shallowly forked than those of swallows, and house martins also lack the chestnut colour seen on swallows. The crucial field mark of the house martin is the white patch on the rump, which is very prominent when the bird is flying. The sand martin, our third member of the hirundine family, is brown, in contrast to the metallic blue of the house martin. (The swift, though superficially similar to the hirundines, is much larger and lacks the white rump: also, it has an even smoother, narrower 'sickle' shape in flight than any of the hirundines.)

Both the swallow and the house martin build nests of mud, plastered on to the walls of buildings or the ends of rafters. The structure of these two birds' nests is quite different, however. The swallow's nest is a simple cup, generally placed inside a building rather than on the outside. The house martin produces a rather more elaborate structure, generally on the outside of a building: when complete, this forms an almost complete quarter globe with a narrow slit entrance on the outside top edge.

Spring arrival The first sightings of house martins each spring generally occur in early April, but most birds do not arrive until the end of this month, or early May. Stragglers continue to appear until the end of May and even during June. They are therefore later in arriving than both sand martins and swallows, but a little earlier, on average, than swifts. The first migrants search out areas where food is in good supply, and often congregate around the shores of lakes or reservoirs, for there they are able to find newly hatched insects.

The house martin's flight is not as acrobatic as that of the swallow, nor as direct and speedy as that of the swift. House martins are frequently seen hawking very high in the sky, but if the weather is cold they fly very low in the shelter of a hedge or bank. Because of their startling white rumps they are often much more conspicuous under such circumstances than the other hirundines and the swifts, all of which often feed together with them. A wide variety of aerial insects are taken, as are many species of gossamer spiders floating about in the air on threads of silk.

Mud collectors In order to build their nests, house martins must abandon their aerial life temporarily and come down to the ground to collect mud. Here they are not very agile, and walk with a pronounced 'waddle'. The mud may be gathered from the fringes of a pond, a muddy gateway or, most often, from a

Above: House martins start their nests about 7cm (3in) below the eaves and build steadily upwards. A nail in the wall is a useful keying point from which to start.

Opposite page: A multitude of house martins roosting on telephone wires before migration. They are smaller than swallows, with whiter undersides.

House martin distribution

Left: House martins are not timid and often allow a close approach, particularly if you are in a car and they are collecting mud from a roadside puddle. Seeing them at close quarters, you can appreciate the fascinating tiny white feathers that cover their legs. If dry weather removes the supply of mud, some people do the house martins a kindness by leaving out a bowl full of a mixture of earth and water.

roadside puddle. In really dry weather nest building may be held up for weeks through lack of mud, and birds may have to fly long distances to fetch it.

Observations of nest-building house martins have shown that it takes the birds roughly a fortnight to complete a nest. Many blobs of mud tend to be lost at the very start, in the process of keying the nest to the wall. Often the birds use a nail in the wall, a gutter bracket or a window hinge as a support. The complete nest may contain roughly 500cc (30 cu in) of mud, comprising more than 2500 beakfuls. The bare mud is then lined with feathers, grasses and straw. Much of the lining material is caught in the air, but some is picked up off the ground.

The brood in the nest The female lays a clutch of four or five white eggs, which are incubated, with the help of the male, for about two weeks. The young are fed in the nest, by both parents, for 18 or 19 days before they fledge. Most pairs are able to rear two broods, and three broods are not uncommon. The young from the first clutch often help their parents to feed later young, and the whole of this extended family may live crammed into one nest. There have been records of 13 birds living together in this way. Alternatively, a new nest may be constructed as a dormitory for the fledged young.

Man's dependant? In recent years, house martins have been recorded breeding much

nearer the centres of many British cities than before. This is a measure of the success which the various Clean Air Acts have been able to achieve. Earlier this century, so much smoke was emitted that there were few if any of the insects needed by house martins in inner city areas.

Going back further in the history of the species, it is interesting to speculate how many (or how few) pairs of house martins there may have been in Britain and Ireland before man built dwellings on a large scale. There are certainly a handful of natural house martin colonies on coastal cliffs, in quarries and along river banks, but over 99% of all British breeding pairs now nest on buildings.

House martin (*Delichon urbica*). Aerial bird making an elaborate mud nest, usually on walls. Summer visitor. Sexes are alike. Length 12.5cm (5in).

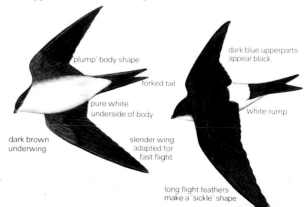

plump' body shape

forked tail

pure white underside of body

dark brown underwing

slender wing adapted for fast flight

dark blue upperparts appear black

white rump

long flight feathers make a 'sickle' shape

Great and lesser spotted woodpeckers

You can tell a spotted woodpecker by its frenzied activity even before you come close enough to recognise its brilliant colouring. Its persistent drumming against wood to attract a mate and proclaim territory is unique among British birds.

A male great spotted woodpecker removing wood excavated from its nest. In northern Britain nests are made in birch or pine, but in the south in hardwoods.

The great spotted woodpecker is both the most numerous and widespread of our woodpeckers, occurring in almost all areas where there are suitable trees. Strangely enough, the great spotted shares with its relatives a complete, unexpected, difficult-to-

explain absence from the whole of Ireland, even though there is abundant suitable woodland. There have been occasional sitings in Ireland, but these seem to be of Continental migrants blown off-course in autumn, and none has stayed to breed. The lesser spotted woodpecker is much less common than the great. It does, however, share many characteristics of the great, and has all the same adaptations, though they are reduced in scale.

Woodland bird The great spotted woodpecker prefers stands of timber where at least some of the trees are mature, usually with a few dead or dying branches. It lives in both deciduous and coniferous woodlands, or a mixture of the two, but is scarcer in closely planted coniferous plantations without old or decaying trees. Where good hedgerows are still common, it penetrates deep into agricultural land, feeding and nesting in the tall trees of the hedge, or in spinneys and copses linked by the hedgerow network. It is unusual to find great spotted woodpeckers in isolated clumps of trees.

The magnificent old trees of parkland offer an ideal habitat, and through parks the great spotted woodpecker sometimes penetrates into urban areas. It is a common species of large old gardens, with big trees, that meet the surrounding countryside.

Striking colouring With its pied plumage and scarlet patches, the great spotted woodpecker is a conspicuous bird. Its normal year-round call, a harsh and far-carrying 'tchack', or its staccato breeding-season drumming, quickly draw attention to its presence. Its deeply undulating method of flight, too, is conspicuous and characteristic, consisting of a few flaps of the rounded wings, followed by a deep swooping glide, before the next series of flaps helps it gain height again.

The wings are boldly barred black and white, with a striking white oval patch on each wing near the body – a feature lacking in the lesser spotted woodpecker. The back is plain black (again, different from the lesser spotted, where the white bars cross the back as well), and the underparts are white save for a bright scarlet patch beneath the tail of both sexes. In addition, the male has a small block of scarlet feathers on the nape of his otherwise black crown.

Woodpeckers perch, or rather cling, to the sides of tree trunks and branches in a characteristic head-up position developed in the course of evolution as the tail feathers have become specially strengthened and inflexible, serving as a third leg, or prop, to use in climbing in much the same way as we balance on a shooting-stick. This adaptation assists a particularly powerful grip. Woodpecker legs are short but muscular, with strong toes tipped with long, sharp claws which give an effective hold even on the smoothest-barked trees such as beech.

Unusually for a bird, the toes are arranged with two pointing forwards and two back, (a condition called zygodactyly), which gives optimum performance on a vertical surface. Thus woodpeckers move vertically or often in a spiral up the trunk, and occasionally laterally. When they have finished searching for food on one tree, they swoop off to the base of another tree or branch and begin to ascend once again.

Woodpecker headaches? The most obvious wood-pecking adaptation is, of course, the beak. In the great spotted woodpecker this is relatively short, stout and sharp, with a squared-off end like a small chisel – an appropriate simile: rather than bludgeoning its way into the wood by sheer power, the woodpecker uses its beak as a combination of hammer and chisel, inserting the tip into the crack it has made and using its powerful neck muscles to twist the beak and prize off flakes of wood.

One obvious question relating to wood-peckers is: why don't they get splitting head-aches? The answer lies partly in the robust

scarlet nape-patch

white shoulder patch

plain black back

Great spotted woodpecker

scarlet under-tail coverts

nest chamber

Below: A female great spotted woodpecker can be distinguished because it does not have a red nape patch like the male. Note the red under-tail covert.

Pied and white wagtails

Pied wagtails are far commoner than the two other species of wagtails in Britain and Ireland. On almost any area of turf, shingle or rock, in towns or in the countryside, they can be seen hunting insects, with quick dashes, swerves and dramatic leaps into the air.

Above: A female pied wagtail at the entrance to her nest in a rock crevice. Unaided by the male, she builds the nest of mosses, grasses and dead leaves, and lines it with feathers or wool. Her clutch normally consists of five or six eggs, which are greyish-white and freckled with black or brown. She also undertakes most of the incubation, which lasts for two weeks; but she hands over responsibility for feeding the young to her mate when the time comes for her to lay again.

The pied wagtail is a familiar, lively and popular neighbour of man. Its bold black and white plumage, conspicuous habits and loud, distinctive 'chis-ick' call are easy to recognise and help to make it so well-known. It is surprisingly widespread, too: as widely distributed as any British bird, it breeds throughout our islands (but only occasionally on the Shetlands) and is thoroughly at home in city centres and on riversides, meadows, farms and seashore – in fact, almost anywhere except the open mountains and in woodland. One of its commonest vernacular names, water wagtail, is not as applicable as it might be, for it is not as closely associated with water as its relative, the grey wagtail. It is predominantly

a bird of moist places, but not necessarily of the very margins of open water.

The pied wagtail is a truly British and Irish species, for its breeding range is virtually confined to these islands. It is replaced on the Continent, and as far north as Iceland, by the grey wagtail race referred to – somewhat confusingly – as the white wagtail. Birds belonging to this Continental race migrate through Britain in spring and autumn to and from their northern breeding areas, which are in northern Scandinavia and Iceland. Some occasionally stay to breed in Scotland and on the northern and western islands. These birds are noticeably whiter than our pied wagtails, and in spring it is easy to distinguish them from the British race. In autumn the task is much more difficult, as the young of both races are very similar.

Chasing after a mate As April arrives each year, the wagtails prepare for another breeding season. Males begin to establish territories, and several of them may pursue a single female in erratic and excited chases, each displaying to her when on the ground by throwing back his head and displaying his bold black gorget (throat patch). The competition of courtship eventually results in a successful pairing; then the newly paired birds spend some days together strengthening the bond between them, and establishing their breeding territory and nesting site.

Pied wagtails nest in a wide variety of sites,

wherever an adequate crevice will conceal the nest. As well as choosing holes in banks, ivy-covered trees or cliffs, they often favour man-made objects: farm machinery, outbuildings or woodstacks are common sites.

A partial migrant All wagtails are insect-eating birds, but only the yellow wagtail migrates completely to warmer latitudes when the British winter reduces the abundance of its food. The pied wagtail demonstrates an interesting half-way stage between migration and year-round residence.

The appearance of increasing numbers of pied wagtails on school playing fields, in town parks and sewage farms in August and September is evidence of the fact that at least part of the population is migratory. In the south of Britain young birds predominate among those that migrate, but from further north there is a greater percentage of adults. All these birds flying south from Britain are bound for south-west France and Iberia, as is shown by the recovery of ringed birds. Birds from the south of England tend to travel further than those of more northerly origin; some of the southern birds fly as far as Morocco.

The other part of the population remains in Britain, one of the few species of insectivorous birds to gamble on finding an adequate supply of insects through the winter months as an alternative to facing the hazards of a long two-way migration. Through the British winter, the pied wagtail's secret lies in the ever-replenishing supply of insects to be found at the edge of water. Individual birds establish themselves in a winter territory along a river bank (sometimes a lake or other stretch of water) and defend it resolutely against others of their kind.

They feed along a fixed route near the water edge, returning each time to the starting point by the time the waters of the river or lake have delivered another supply of tiny insects and other invertebrates. To share the territory with another bird would be self-defeating for

grey back of head

♀ black cap

White wagtail

light grey back

grey back may have an olive tinge

♂

whitish grey flanks

♀

black throat

Pied wagtail

black crown and back

lower breast white

smoky grey flanks

♂

Pied wagtail (*Motacilla alba yarrelli*); the British and Irish subspecies. Some individuals are resident and others are summer visitors. Length 18cm (7in).

White wagtail (*Motacilla alba alba*); the Continental subspecies, seen in Britain occasionally as a passage migrant.

Right: The white wagtail is similar in appearance to the female of the pied wagtail, but its back is a lighter shade of grey.

Below: A female pied wagtail stands on a log in a typical jaunty attitude. Pied wagtails forage energetically, running jerkily on short turf, shingle or rock. With tails flicking non-stop, they make rapid dashes and swerves to catch their insect prey. Sometimes they leap into the air in dancing flight, to catch insects on the wing.

both, and would tip the balance between survival and failure. Defence of the territory is therefore crucially important.

Communal roosts At most times of the year outside the breeding season (except when winter is at its severest), pied wagtails roost communally, normally choosing reedbeds, scrub or bushes. An interesting development of this has been an increasingly common adaptation to the urban environment – roosting on buildings and trees in city centres. Here the winter temperature can be a little higher than in the open countryside.

In a further adaptation to man's presence, they have been recorded as roosting in commercial glasshouses, sometimes in large numbers. Heated glasshouses obviously have enhanced survival value for them in cold winter months, and may also be thought of as giving security from predators. On the other hand, however, little owls and cats have sometimes discovered these roosts, and as there is small chance of escape the results can be disastrous.

Grey wagtail

The grey wagtail is similar to the yellow wagtail, except for its blue-grey upperparts. This difference is 'clinched' by the habitat – the grey wagtail lives beside rocky streams, while the yellow wagtail prefers damp meadows and marshes.

The grey wagtail is somewhat confusingly named: although it is true that the upperparts of the bird are a bluish grey, the feature that most often catches the eye is the brilliant patch of lemon yellow on the under-tail coverts and on the belly. In summer this yellow colouring often extends up on to the breast. It is at all times conspicuous, even in birds seen flying overhead. Thus it would seem sensible to call this the 'yellow wagtail'. However, the true yellow wagtail has yellow upperparts as well as underparts; besides its difference in colour, the yellow wagtail is distinguished from the grey by the habitat in which it is seen, for it is a bird of damp meadows and marshes, only occasionally being seen on arable farmland, while the typical habitat of the grey wagtail is beside fast-flowing water.

Changing with the seasons Unlike yellow wagtails, which are migrants visiting us in summer from Africa, most grey wagtails remain in Britain or Ireland throughout the year. Their plumages, however, change with the seasons. In summer, the male grey wagtail

Above: The grey wagtail's nest is built by the female (shown here). She performs the bulk of the work of incubation, which takes 13 to 14 days. However, both sexes feed the young. In many lowland areas, two broods are raised, and the season usually starts early. Most pairs produce their first eggs in the second half of April. Natural nest sites include cavities between exposed roots, wall crevices (as shown here), and holes in the banks of streams.

Right: A grey wagtail nest with 5 eggs. Apart from this rather unusual nest site, other man-made sites used by grey wagtails include mills, bridges and weirs. Indeed, a good way to find the birds is to seek out old mills, which are favoured haunts.

has a conspicuous white stripe above and below the eye, and a large black 'bib', while the female's throat is whitish. In winter, the sexes are difficult to separate, both having buffish-white throats and pale buff breasts, with the yellow restricted to the vivid patch below the base of the tail. Young birds are grey-green above and dirty white below, with some dark marks round the throat.

Beside rivers and streams The map of the grey wagtail's breeding distribution shows a uniform coverage of Ireland, much of Scotland, Wales and western England. The only 'blank areas' are in East Anglia, the easternmost Midlands and Lincolnshire. In the western part of its range, the grey wagtail is typically a bird of shallow, fast-flowing rivers and streams, preferring to feed along the waterside or where the water is broken up by pebble banks.

Metallic call Often the first indication of the presence of grey wagtails, if they are not seen flying in an undulating path low over the water, is their frequently uttered call. This is considerably higher-pitched and more metallic than that of the pied wagtail. The grey wagtail's 'tzi-tzi', although formed of two distinct syllables, lacks the harsh emphasis of the pied wagtail's 'chiz-zick' call.

In mild winters, the song starts soon after Christmas. It is often said that the bird sings infrequently and even stops singing early in spring, but this may be because the sound is difficult to hear well against the background noise of fast-flowing, tumbling water. The song, in fact, sounds like a squeaky version of the descending trill of a blue tit's song, or perhaps a treecreeper's song without the terminal flourish. This is so different from the song of other wagtails that if the singing bird cannot be seen, the sound can cause moments of uncertainty even for the experienced ear.

Varied diet The grey wagtail's food consists of small animals – insects for example – that the bird gathers as it dashes nimbly among the pebbles and boulders, or runs across floating water plants. Sometimes a grey wagtail seems to tiptoe along the brink of a weir, risking being swept away by the rushing water. At other times (particularly

Grey wagtails in summer

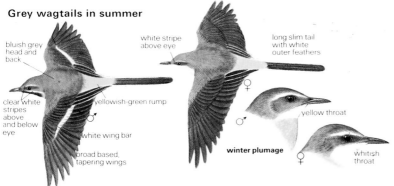

bluish grey head and back

white stripe above eye

long slim tail with white outer feathers

♀

clear white stripes above and below eye

yellowish-green rump

♂

yellow throat

white wing bar

♂

broad based, tapering wings

winter plumage

♀

whitish throat

Grey wagtail distribution

when columns of midges are 'dancing' in their mating flight) grey wagtails fly out over the water and hover, as flycatchers do, to snap insects from the air. Besides aquatic and terrestrial insects, the birds take a wide variety of small animals, including worms, leeches, flatworms and small freshwater shrimps.

Surviving winter Because their habitat is along the waterside, where a cold winter freeze either kills or covers in ice any animals that the birds need for food, grey wagtails tend to suffer considerable losses in winters with extended and severely cold spells. Upland birds can 'migrate' to lower altitudes in winter without difficulty, but once the lowland streams and lakes freeze, only those birds that can reach a suitable stretch of unfrozen coast can survive. This may help to explain the distribution pattern, with more birds in the west, for the slow-moving streams in the generally colder east freeze quicker, and for longer, than the faster running streams of the west. This makes it rather difficult to

estimate the grey wagtail population: numbers are subject to sweeping variations caused by cold-winter mortality every few years. In 1967, following two severe winters, the population was estimated to be below 10,000 pairs, which is probably the lowest level to which it ever falls. Another estimate, of 25,000-30,000 pairs in 1974, reflects healthier circumstances.

Periods of bad weather provoke long-distance winter flights (better called cold weather movements), and ringed birds have been recovered in France, Spain and Portugal. Most flights are shorter, however. Many birds leave their home stretch of water during the period of moult in late summer, and at this time there are records of ringed birds being recovered up to 160km (100 miles) away from their nesting territories. For much of the year, most grey wagtail pairs stay in their territories and defend them: often both sexes defend their territory from a neighbouring pair, with vigorous posturing and mock combat.

Above: Numbers of grey wagtails are considerably lower in eastern England, where the streams are generally more sluggish and offer few suitable habitats.

Above left: The grey wagtail is distinguished by its combination of blue-grey upperparts and yellow underparts. The extent of the yellow is greater in summer than in winter, and in older birds compared to younger ones.

Grey wagtail (*Motacilla cinerea*). Resident bird living beside fast-flowing streams. Moves south in autumn. Length 18cm (7in).

Right: A male grey wagtail lives up to its name—the wagging of the tail neatly recorded by a blurred stripe on the photograph. There has been a considerable amount of debate concerning the reasons for the tail wagging in the wagtail family, with no certain conclusion. However, one theory that is at least plausible is that against the sparkling, ever-changing background of broken water, the continuously moving, white-edged tail helps to break up the silhouette of the bird and give a good camouflage effect.

Starling

In both town and country the starling (above and opposite) is so familiar that birdwatchers all too often ignore it. Yet, if it were as rare today as it used to be, its superb iridescent plumage would rank it as one of the most beautiful of British birds.

Starling (*Sturnus vulgaris*). Resident; numbers swell in winter with the arrival of Continental migrants. Very common in both rural and urban areas, forming large flocks. Length 22cm (8½in).

The starling is one of our most common birds. More than four million pairs breed in Britain every year, and in the winter they are joined by at least 30 million more individuals that migrate here from northern and eastern Europe. Yet, up until the middle of the last century, the starling was relatively uncom-

mon in Britain. The rise in the British population is part of a general pattern throughout Europe in which starlings have increased in numbers and spread westwards.

Omnivorous eaters The reasons for this population increase are not completely understood but an important factor is the bird's ability to live on a wide variety of foods. Fruits, seeds, flying insects, caterpillars, grubs, earthworms and household waste are all eaten, although the amounts taken of these different foods vary with the season. In spring the starling's diet consists mainly of insects and their larvae; in summer fruits become important; by winter these are replaced with seeds. Throughout the year, however, animal foods remain an important source of protein.

Another reason for the starling's success is that, during the last century or so, large areas of Europe's indigenous forests have been cleared to create grassland for farming. Close-cropped grassland is the starling's favourite habitat and you can often see them probing

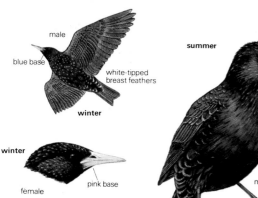

Above: Starlings are so familiar that their beautiful iridescent plumage is too often overlooked. In autumn they develop white-tipped feathers on the breast; these remain until spring when they grow new feathers. Males and females can be distinguished by their eyes—female eyes have a distinctive brown ring—and, during winter and spring, by the colour at the base of their bills.

Right: Juveniles are grey-brown with white chins until summer, when they develop adult white-tipped plumage.

the problem that a flock can grow too big for the food source, with the result that bickering and fighting ensue.

The starlings' omnivorous diet means that, depending on what they are eating, a large flock can either inflict great damage or be of great benefit. The starlings' consumption of large numbers of leatherjackets is an obvious boon to the farmer but, on the other hand, they can devastate cherry orchards that are in fruit.

Roosting by the million As well as feeding in flocks, starlings also roost in flocks. Sometimes more than a million birds gather together in night roosts, attracting large numbers of predators. In places such as Trafalgar Square in London, huge flocks can be seen wheeling around and darkening the sky at dusk.

Quite why starlings roost in such numbers is not yet known, but the advantages must be considerable since they outweigh the attentions of predators. It may be that roosting presents a good opportunity for poorly fed birds to learn from their better-fed neighbours the location of good food supplies.

Nesting in letter boxes The starling's choice of nesting site shows again how well it takes advantage of opportunities presented by man. Its most typical nest site is a natural hole, usually in a tree but also in a cliff. However, any hole of the right size and situation will do

grass roots for invertebrates such as caterpillars, earthworms and leatherjackets (the larva of craneflies and a serious agricultural pest).

During the breeding season starlings spend most of their feeding time in grassland but at other times of the year they spread out into new habitats—a necessity if they are to take full advantage of their omnivorous nature. Bushes, hedgerows and trees are visited by starlings for fruits such as cherries, elderberries and sloes; they also search stubble fields, newly sown cereal fields and farmyards for seeds.

Forming flocks People often ask how starlings gather so quickly and in such numbers when food is put out into a garden. Starlings have an excellent memory, especially when it comes to remembering places where food appears regularly and in abundance. These places are always under observation by at least one bird. When food appears, one starling flies down to investigate. If it begins to peck, then all the other starlings nearby recognise this as a sign of food and fly down to join in. Within a very short time a feeding flock has formed.

The formation of a flock for feeding is advantageous for the flock members in that they can feed much faster than when they are on their own. There are many more eyes on the look-out for predators such as cats and sparrowhawks. Against this, however, is

Right: A flock of starlings searching for food. The starling's remarkable increase in numbers during the last century is, in part, the result of its omnivorous habits. Its diet ranges from seeds and fruits to insects, grubs and earthworms, and includes household waste as well.

Mimicry in birds

The starling's song is not particularly musical but it is remarkable for its mimicry. Sometimes it mimics phrases from the songs of neighbouring starlings, but it can also mimic the calls of other birds, including bullfinches, curlews, tawny owls and green woodpeckers. It can even imitate mammal noises—as well as inanimate sounds, such as telephones ringing.

Ornithologists have discovered that, with some species, if a male possesses a wide repertoire of songs it has a better chance of breeding successfully. This explains why starlings make such a variety of noises but not why they mimic 'foreign' sounds rather than create their own distinct sounds. That remains a mystery.

Starlings are closely related to those master-mimics, the mynah birds. Unlike the mynahs, however, starlings cannot imitate human speech. Mimicry is not confined to the starling family: parrots and jackdaws reproduce words, and many species imitate other birds.

Above: A waxwing in winter.
Note the yellow tail band.

Waxwing (*Bombycilla garrulus*). Irregular winter visitor from Scandinavia and northern Russia, appearing in 'irruptions'. Length 18cm (7in). Sexes alike.

Waxwing

The waxwing does not breed in Britain, for its home lies in Scandinavia and the north of Russia. It visits us only in winter, but even then its appearances are unpredictable.

One morning in early December 1970 a roadside bank in Aberdeen was suddenly transformed from brilliant scarlet to a subtle pinkish-brown. The scarlet had been an almost total cover of cotoneaster berries, upon which had settled a flock of over 400 waxwings, colourful and bizarre immigrants from Scandinavia which had just completed their crossing of the North Sea. They were busily replenishing the energy stores used on the journey by devouring the cotoneaster berries.

A handsome visitor The waxwing is a strikingly handsome bird, about the size and build of a starling. Its flight silhouette is in fact very similar to that of a starling, with long pointed wings and a short square-ended tail. If a waxwing flies low overhead, you can see that its bill is noticeably shorter than that of the commoner bird, while the tip of its tail carries a bright yellow band. Although it does not often call, the waxwing's voice can also betray its identity, for its usual note is a thin, high-pitched trill (its Russian name – 'sviristel' – means 'reedpipe bird').

When seen perched or feeding, the waxwing is unmistakable. The general colour of the head, breast and belly is pinkish-brown, but the back is a darker brown. The rump and tail are grey, the latter shading into black with a conspicuous yellow tip, while the under-tail is a rich, dark chestnut. The chin is black and a black line extends round and behind the eye. The forehead is chestnut, shading into pinkish-brown on the top of the head, where the feathers are elongated into a remarkably long crest.

The flight feathers are mainly black but carry white markings. The bird's name is derived from the red tips to the inner flight feathers (secondaries); the webs of the feather tip are fused to the shaft, resembling bright red sealing-wax.

Britain invaded Despite this conspicuous appearance and the bird's tendency to form flocks (sometimes large, like the one in Aberdeen), the waxwing is unfamiliar to most people because it is an irregular visitor, whose arrival follows irruptions from its breeding areas (Scandinavia and northern Russia) in the manner of crossbills and the much rarer nutcracker and Pallas' sandgrouse. These irruptive species visit our shores infrequently, but when they do arrive, they tend to occur in substantial numbers.

A flock of over 1000 waxwings was seen near Louth in Lincolnshire during the early days of an invasion in the autumn of 1965.

Waxwing irruptions

When Britain plays host to these northern invaders, many other European countries – normally far south of the birds' range – also receive wandering birds. During large irruptions waxwings may range as far south as Italy, Spain and Portugal (shown on our map in a dotted line), but in most years they are able to spend the winter on their northern nesting areas. The solid lines on the map indicate the main advances of the birds in an irruption year.

Irruptive invaders

Waxwing
from N Europe
and Asia

rowan berries

Nutcracker
from Central
European
mountains

Arolla pine
seeds

Crossbill
from
N Scandinavia

spruce
cone
seeds

Pallas' sand grouse
from SE Europe
and Asia

grain

Blue tit

British populations
swollen in winter
by irruptions
from N Europe

beech mast

Great tit

Such large flocks are typical of the early arrivals and therefore tend to occur along the east coast. As the birds move further into the country, these large flocks break up so that later in the winter, and the further west one goes, the smaller the flocks tend to become. Nevertheless, flocks of a hundred or more do occur occasionally in Ireland.

The number of birds that arrive in Britain during an invasion can vary widely from a few tens to several thousands. Equally variable is their time of arrival. In 1965 the earliest birds appeared in September, while in the much smaller invasion of the 1956-7 winter waxwings were not seen until February.

Once an invasion of Britain occurs, they move from their initial landing places on the east coast and spread to other parts of the country, but the extent to which more westerly areas receive visitors depends to a certain extent on the size of the irruption. When numbers are small, the waxwings may remain near the east coast, but after a large immigration, as in the 1965-6 winter, the westward spread during the early part of the invasion is followed in the spring by a return to the east of the country as the birds that have survived our winter prepare to return to their breeding grounds. Most waxwings have left Britain by the end of April.

Population and food supplies This unpredictability over the waxwing's arrival in Britain and southern Europe is ultimately related to the bird's diet. In spring and summer waxwings do in fact eat insects, but at other times of the year they are vegetarians. In fact they are among the relatively few species that can, if necessary, survive on a diet consisting solely of plant material. Within the vegetable realm, however, waxwings prefer berries and it is this specialisation which forces them to vacate their breeding areas

periodically.

Most fruiting trees do not produce large crops every year, rather they crop heavily every second year, but even this heavy crop can be quite variable. In the vicinity of the breeding areas rowan, hawthorn and juniper are the waxwing's main autumn and winter foods. If a series of good breeding seasons coincides with reasonable winter berry crops, the waxwing breeding population increases over successive years and may extend the breeding area southwards. Once a high population level has been attained, a failure of the berry crop will force these birds to emigrate in search of sufficient berries to survive the winter.

Above: Besides the waxwing, other bird species arrive suddenly in Britain from time to time. When their populations have become large—this coinciding with a failure of the fruits or seeds upon which they depend— they leave their normal areas in search of food to keep them alive over winter. This is called an 'irruption'.

Below: Cotoneaster berries, and also those of rowan, hawthorn and juniper, provide the waxwing's main food in the winter.

Jay

Jays are our most handsome and distinctive crows.
They are shy birds, and you never find them far away
from trees. In autumn they are busy collecting acorns
for their larder – in one wood 30 jays stored an
estimated 200,000 acorns in just four weeks!

The jay belongs to the crow family, but it has much brighter plumage than its relatives. At close range it looks quite exotic. Its crest, delicately spotted with white and black on the forehead, is raised when it is displaying to other birds. It has pale blue eyes and a broad black moustachial streak; most of the body is pale pinkish-brown. The flight feathers are black and grey, with a conspicuous patch of white, and the wing coverts are beautifully barred with pale blue and black.

Elusive bird Jays are shy and restless birds, and you may find it hard to get a good view. Most often you just see them flying away, when the large, white patch just above the black tail is very noticeable. They have broad, rounded wings and their flight often looks weak and laboured. At a distance, jays can be mistaken for hoopoes, an unrelated bird found in Europe which is fairly similar in size and shape and also has black, white and pink plumage.

Oak woodland is the jay's preferred habitat and you rarely find them far from trees. Unlike our other crows–magpies, carrion crows, rooks and jackdaws–jays seldom venture out into open fields. When they are searching for food in the trees or on the ground, they tend to hop and leap about, rather than walk or run.

Jays are often quite noisy, so you may hear them before you see them. The main call can be heard from far off. It is a loud, often twice-repeated, rasping shriek of alarm which they make when disturbed. People have also heard jays make a variety of chuckling and chirruping calls, a buzzard-like mew and even a low, warbling song.

Like their relatives, jays are intelligent, opportunist birds, and adapt to various diets. Usually they feed on the woodland floor, eating tree nuts such as beechnuts, sweet chestnuts, hazel nuts, pine seeds and especially acorns. They also eat fruits such as pears, plums, cherries and other soft fruits. In the summer they search for eggs and nestlings of other woodland birds, and they have been seen eating mice, slugs, worms, insects, woodlice, spiders, bread, fish and even bees. In gardens some jays have learnt to eat peanuts by tipping the holder upside down and shaking the nuts to the ground. Unlike crows and rooks, they rarely eat carrion or grain, and they have little effect on agriculture.

Acorn hoarders The jay's favourite food is acorns. In September and October when the acorns ripen you can see jays searching methodically for them in and beneath oak trees. However, instead of eating only what they require and leaving the rest to fall to the ground where all kinds of animals and birds would find them, jays hoard them. By making their own private larder, they can be sure of enough food to last throughout the year.

Jays can hold up to nine acorns at once in their specially large oesophagus, but more usually they take just three or four.

crest · wing coverts · white rump and black tail conspicuous in flight · flight feathers

Opposite: The blue and black wing coverts and pinkish breast make the jay one of the most attractive of woodland birds.

Above and below: The favourite food of jays is acorns. Each jay's larder consists of several thousand acorns collected over about two months. A storing trip takes only a few minutes, and in autumn you may see jays flying back and forth all day.

Crow, rook and jackdaw

The rook, crow and jackdaw all co-exist on farmland without competing for food.

The crow, rook and jackdaw are all outwardly similar members of the crow family – so similar, in fact, that many people refer to them all simply as 'crows'. They are all common species on agricultural land, but they are able to share this habitat because each exploits it in a different way, so that they do not compete with one another for the necessities of life – food, nest sites and living space.

Three black birds Although they are superficially just black birds, these three 'crows' do differ in appearance. The most distinct is the jackdaw, which is the smallest of the three at about 32cm (13in) long. It is mainly black, but its chief distinguishing feature is the colour of the cheeks and nape, which are a silvery grey.

At close range you can see that the black feathers of the crown, wings and tail are glossed with blues and greens, and that the eye is a conspicuous bluish silver. In flight, the fast wing beats and the call of the jackdaw are also characteristic. The most usual call is a short, high-pitched 'chack'.

The rook and crow are similar in size, about 45cm (18in) long, and at a distance both appear uniformly dark. The adult rook, however, is glossy bluish black or purplish black all over, while the crow is generally a duller black with little gloss. The bills of both species are much longer than that of the jackdaw, but while that of the crow is black, with bristly feathers around its base, the bill of

Above: Rooks at a rookery near Selborne in Hampshire. Rooks build their nests in the upper branches of tall trees, while crows nest in the fork of a branch.

Below: For people who live in northern Scotland and the northern half of Ireland, separation of the rook and crow is a much simpler matter than in the south. In these places there is a different variant of the crow called the hooded crow or grey crow. Its back, belly and breast are grey.

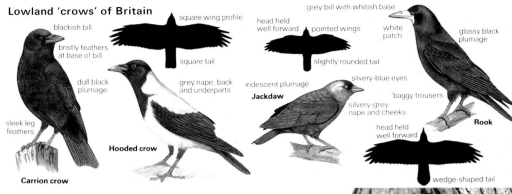

Lowland 'crows' of Britain

blackish bill

bristly feathers at base of bill

dull black plumage

sleek leg feathers

Carrion crow

square wing profile

square tail

grey nape, back and underparts

Hooded crow

head held well forward

pointed wings

slightly rounded tail

iridescent plumage

Jackdaw

silvery-blue eyes

silvery-grey nape and cheeks

head held well forward

grey bill with whitish base

white patch

glossy black plumage

'baggy trousers'

Rook

wedge-shaped tail

the adult rook is grey, tending to white at the unfeathered base.

Social or solitary Differences in the appearance of our three lowland crows are rather subtle, but other aspects of their lives show more marked variation–particularly regarding their degree of sociality. Crows are generally solitary creatures, spending their time alone or in pairs, although family parties can of course be seen for a few weeks after the young leave the nest. Rooks and jackdaws, on the other hand, live in flocks which can number from a dozen or so to several hundred, and sometimes over a thousand birds.

For most of the year rooks and jackdaws live in mixed flocks, and often these flocks are joined by other birds such as starlings, lapwings and gulls. However, the country adage 'one rook is a crow; a flock of crows are rooks' is not absolutely true, for occasionally rooks, especially juveniles, do feed alone and crows, especially youngsters, do form flocks.

Differences in sociality tend to be stricter during the breeding season, when pairs of crows invariably defend the territories in which they feed and build their nests. Rooks and jackdaws are generally colonial, and solitary nests are something of a rarity. The rook's nesting colonies are the familiar rookeries which can number from a few nests to over a thousand, but these really large rookeries occur only in Scotland. Both the rook and crow build their nests in trees, using twigs, earth and grasses. They usually select tall trees, but while the crow builds its nest in a fork, the rook chooses the slender upper branches.

Apart from their noisiness, jackdaw colonies are less obvious than rookeries because the nests are built in holes. The most frequently used holes are those in buildings (especially derelict buildings, but also the chimneys of inhabited premises) cliffs and trees, but other sites, such as rabbit burrows, are sometimes used. In large holes, vast quantities of sticks and grasses are used to construct a base for the nest, which is lined with wool and grass; in smaller holes the nest consists of little more than the lining.

Carrion crow (*Corvus corone corone*). Resident bird of farmland and gardens. Plumage is uniformly dull black. Length 45cm (18in).

Hooded crow (*Corvus corone cornix*). Northern subspecies of carrion crow with grey plumage on back and underparts. 47cm (18½in).

Rook (*Corvus frugilegus*). Resident farmland bird with glossy black plumage. Length 45cm (18in).

Jackdaw (*Corvus monedula*). Resident on farmland. Small crow with grey patch on nape and cheeks. 32cm (13in).

Right: Jackdaws nest in holes, usually in colonies.

Below: The crow is a solitary feeder and nester.

Magpie

The magpie is notorious for its habit of stealing other birds' eggs and chicks. You are most likely to catch it in the act in summer – at other times it eats almost anything.

Magpies are members of the crow family and are easily distinguished from their relatives – indeed from all other British birds – by their distinctive black and white colouring. Whether young or old, male or female, all have the same boldly patterned plumage which, at a distance, is only black and white, without any other colours or even shades of grey. The black head, back, wings and tail contrast with the pure white underparts and shoulder patch. Apart from the coloration, you can identify magpies easily by their long,

wedge-shaped tail – half the bird's total length – and by their short, rounded wings.

Nest predators Like others of the crow family, magpies will often plunder eggs and nestlings of less aggressive neighbours – particularly in farmland. Searching methodically for a suitable nest-worthy habitat, such as a thick, overgrown hedge, a single magpie may find several nests in quick succession. When a small bird sitting on a nest sees a magpie, it may 'freeze' until the last possible moment – hoping to be missed. Once the magpie

Opposite: Typical magpie country.

Above and opposite inset: with their striking black and white plumage, magpies are unmistakable.

Magpie (*Pica pica*), 45cm (18in) from beak to tip of tail. Resident. Distribution – see map below.

Magpie distribution

Magpies are probably capable of living anywhere in the British Isles, but the present breeding distribution is distinctly patchy in northern England and Scotland. Here persecution from gamekeepers – who rear grouse on the moors and pheasants in the valleys and dislike the magpie's habit of stealing eggs – is still common. Built-up areas with less keeping around cities such as Glasgow and Aberdeen act as refuges and support expanding populations. Gaps in eastern England may reflect changing agricultural practices.

discovers it however, the other bird must retreat hastily, and magpies have even been seen catching small birds in flight.

Like birds of prey, magpies are mobbed by smaller birds that must have no difficulty in recognising this particular enemy. Large birds are generally better off against magpies; their nests are only robbed when left unguarded, so the parents sit tight regardless.

When there is plenty of food, the nest of a bird such as the woodpigeon (in which both sexes incubate the eggs) is only uncovered during the changeovers, so the magpie may make several visits before it gets a meal. In some other species where only the female bird incubates the eggs, she must feed and return to the nest as soon as possible, especially if the eggs are not well hidden from view. In only a few seconds a magpie can force its way to a nest and eat or carry off the eggs or nestlings–leaving only a few fragments of eggshell. The magpie's job is relatively easy early in the summer when nesting cover is thin and food shortage forces many birds to spend more time feeding and less time incubating. Fortunately most birds can lay another clutch of eggs.

Wide-ranging diet Apart from this form of plundering–which is really a summer sideline–magpies mainly eat insects and larvae such as ground-dwelling beetles and moth caterpillars. However, magpies are opportunists and take whatever food they find. They eat small mammals such as voles and mice and also carrion. Magpies also feed on the more nutritious parts of plant matter such as fruits, nuts, berries and cereal grains, as well as on some invertebrates–slugs snails and worms–and a range of household scraps. Occasionally you may see magpies perching on the backs of farm animals where they eat fly larvae and parasitic ticks, as well as

Above: The magpie's flight is usually direct and several magpies may follow each other in single file. The inner webs of the main flight feathers are white.

Left: At close range, especially in bright sunlight, iridescent green and purple colours are reflected by the magpie's wing and tail feathers.

Below: Magpies find much of their food on the ground, such as this dead rabbit. They walk or hop along the surface with the tail held a little elevated.

pluck hair or wool to line their nests.

Nests and young The best time to look for magpie nests is in the winter, when the trees have no leaves. Each spring magpies have a strong tendency to return to their old nests–adding to them or building on top of them. The nests may be renovated but still stay empty for two months before the female lays her eggs.

Magpie nest sites range from the top of tall, isolated trees to thick, thorny hedges or thickets at the edge of a wood, and even on sea-cliffs. Though easy to see, the nests are rarely easy to reach.

The nest is constructed of sticks, and is thickly lined with mud and a layer of grass roots. Most magpies also build a dome of thorny twigs above the nest, leaving only a single, inconspicuous entrance at the side. The parents, which are said to pair for life, participate in building.

The female lays her eggs in April and has only one brood per year. The number of eggs varies from five to eight, though up to ten have been recorded. Only the female incubates the eggs, which take about 17 days to hatch. After this both parents feed the nestlings for three to four weeks. You can see family parties of magpies throughout the late summer and autumn; and you may spy the young jumping around using their short tails to help them balance each time they land.

Decline and rise Magpies are more widely distributed in the world than any other crow except the raven. In the British Isles, however, their distribution has been affected by many years of persecution. Shooting, poisoned bait and traps have reduced the magpie population throughout Scotland and parts of England.

Wren

The perky, diminutive wren – the smallest British bird apart from the goldcrest – is ideally suited to its foraging life in the undergrowth of woodland and hedgerow and, with ten million breeding pairs, is our most numerous species.

Opposite: Typical hedgerow habitat of a wren. Inset: A wren at its nest.

Below: The plumages of both sexes are identical.

In legend the familiar brown wren is condemned to live a skulking life of shame for cheating in the great election to find the king of the birds. The story goes that the birds decided to choose as their king the one which could fly the highest. Hoping to win the contest, the cheeky wren concealed himself in the plumage of the mighty eagle and hitched a ride for most of the way, only emerging to outfly the eagle when it finally tired. The strength of this legend, which appears in many countries and cultures, testifies to Man's ancient association with and fondness for the perky little bird.

Tiny troglodyte The wren prefers to frequent holes and corners in cliff overhangs, derelict buildings, outhouses, tree roots and piles of boulders. Its scientific name means 'the cave-dweller' – a name not to be taken too literally, but nevertheless apt since the bird is one of the few able to exploit such recesses and cavities. It is an active little bird, full of verve and familiar in town and country.

The rounded, dumpy body, short whirring wings and cocked tail may look ungainly, but in fact the wren is superbly equipped for its ground-foraging way of life. It creeps about in the undergrowth in a characteristic crouched posture – very much like a small rodent – negotiating its way efficiently through narrow openings and working energetically through tangled vegetation, tree roots and

brambles. On a branch, its tail-cocked perching position is unmistakable.

Year-long songster The sexes are indistinguishable in plumage, but only the cock sings. For the size of the bird's body, the volume and carrying power of the song is remarkable. The male sings consistently throughout the year and song is important in his life. He uses one type of call – a vehement, rattling warble usually lasting a few seconds – for a variety of purposes: territorial warning and defence, courtship, attracting others to roost and communicating with partners. In the excitement of courtship and nesting, he will even sing with his beak crammed full of building materials!

Wren (*Troglodytes troglodytes*); 10cm (3¾in) from beak to tail; distribution widespread; resident.

Above: A male wren singing to proclaim his territory. Apart from a series of loud warbling calls, the wren's repertoire includes cheery trills and a scolding 'tit-tit-tit' sound.

Right: The wren's domed nest, made of moss, dry grass and bracken and lined with feathers, makes a secure, snug home for the young. Some wrens prefer to nest in close proximity to Man and choose odd sites to build – such as in an old cap hung in a shed.

Numerous nests The wren's breeding season starts from the second half of April onwards. It is catholic and often quaint in its choice of nesting sites, frequently ignoring natural recesses in hedge bottom, ivy bank or upturned tree root in favour of man-made places such as outhouses or the corners of gardens.

The cock builds several nests – outsize, domed structures of moss, dry grass, bracken or leaves – to tempt his mate. The hen selects the one of her choice, lines it with feathers, then lays from five to twelve eggs and incubates them by herself for 14 or 15 days. The glossy white eggs are often speckled with minute black or red-brown spots at the large end. When the young hatch, the male leaves the female to do all the feeding. The hen usually rears two broods a season, especially in more vegetated areas where food is plentiful. The male bird – not the most diligent of parents – may install several females in succession in different nests.

Success story The wren is a successful and adaptable bird – something that is particularly noteworthy since it is the only Eurasian representative of an extensive family of otherwise exclusively New World birds. Not only is the wren one of the most widespread of all our birds, it is also extremely numerous. Densities of up to 100 pairs per square kilometre have been recorded. At the same time, the wren is vulnerable in hard winters, when numbers may fall dramatically. However, the rate of recovery can be equally dramatic: after the cold winter of 1962-63, the wren recovered numbers faster than any other common bird.

The wren is almost entirely insectivorous. Its diet is composed mainly of the larvae of small moths, flies, beetles and other insects, as well as spiders, mites and a limited variety of small soft-bodied invertebrates – all probed, extracted or caught with the bird's fine, slender, slightly curved bill. It is little wonder that protracted hard weather – which decimates insects – spells disaster for the wren. Unfortunately, it is our one garden visitor that is not drawn to bird tables, so it is no use putting out extra food in the hope of saving it from starvation. In times of plenty, however, there are probably up to ten million breeding pairs of wrens in existence.

Quite a crowd One oddity of wren behaviour is communal roosting which sometimes occurs in particularly severe weather. Wrens are usually solitary at night, but large numbers are sometimes found roosting in very confined spaces, the birds huddled together in a feathery mass with tails pointing outwards. As many as 30 or 40 individuals have been found in one nest box, in tier on stifling tier. Obviously, the insulation obtained by this crowding has a high survival value in hard weather. It helps the birds retain the precious body heat they have gained from hard-won insect food foraged during the

short winter daytime. After the young have fledged in summer, but before they have become independent, parent birds can sometimes be seen shepherding their families to the safety of a communal roost.

Island races Wrens are not only found in woodland, farmland, river banks and suburban gardens–where we are most familiar with them; they also occur on sea cliffs and mountainsides. They even inhabit some of our furthest–flung islands, particularly Shetland, St Kilda and the Hebrides. On these islands the species has been isolated for 6000 years or more and has produced distinctive, clearly separated local races. The island birds tend to be larger and greyer in colour and have heavier chestnut-coloured barring on the back than their mainland relatives.

The wren hunt The wren frequents the dwellings of Man more than any other bird, and it is not surprising that legends about it abound. One curious and ancient custom– the wren hunt–which originated over 1000 years ago took place (in various forms) in

many parts of England, and was particularly popular in Ireland, parts of Wales and the Isle of Man. The hunt was specially associated with St Stephen's Day (26th December). Wrens were hunted along hedgerows, and through woods with sticks, stones, bows and arrows or birch rods; any found were killed– often ritually. They were then borne through the town on an elaborate bier or specially constructed wren house by grotesquely dressed 'wren boys'–all to the accompaniment of traditional wren-hunt songs. In many ceremonies, money was solicited by the wren boys for 'the burying of the wren'. The hunt persisted until very recent times, and in Ireland is still practised. Its origins go far back into history: it is said that a wren hopping on a drum awakened the Danes and foiled a stealthy Irish attack.

Fortunately for the wren, it has outlived the barbarous hunt; now, though we no longer have the farthing coin which carried the wren emblem and testified to its popularity, the bird is fully protected by the law.

Above: A parent wren bringing a beakful of insects to its young in the nest. Its short wings make the wren's flight rapid and whirring. Note the characteristic white eye stripe.

Polygamy in birds

Most birds have only one mate; the advantage is that both parents help to rear young. Some birds, however, practise polygamy–having more than one mate. Male wrens often do this, especially where food is plentiful and the hen can feed the young on her own.

There are two types of polygamy. Simultaneous pairing can take place with two or more females (as with corn buntings). With successive polygamy, the male initiates consecutive broods with different females. Male wrens do both. The advantage is that the largest possible number of broods can be produced without the male increasing the size of his territory; also the female may have the opportunity to select more vigorous, active males–to the benefit of the species.

Well-adapted for creeping about in the undergrowth, the wren has an unmistakable bobbing, jerky method of feeding on the ground.

Blackcap and garden warbler

These two warblers nest in thickets and open woodland. It is hard to get a good enough view to tell which is which; if you succeed in coming close up to them, you may notice that one has a 'cap' – but the other has no distinctive markings at all!

Above: A garden warbler tidies its nest. The nest is more substantial than that of the blackcap, but both species use similar materials.

Birdwatchers have a habit of referring irreverently to some groups of birds as 'little brown jobs'. On account of their rather drab plumage, the similarity between species, and the consequent difficulty in identifying them, many of the warblers fit nicely into this category of birds. In fact, the garden warbler is so featureless that it has been said that its best field character is its lack of distinguishing marks!

In addition to looking rather alike, warblers also have similar life-styles. All but one (the Dartford warbler) of the British warblers are summer visitors; they all eat insects, and most have fairly melodious songs. When we look closely at the biology of similar-looking and closely-related warblers however, we find that there are important ecological and behavioural differences between them. It is, in fact, these differences that enable such outwardly similar species to live in the same district without severely competing with one another.

The blackcap and garden warbler are two species that illustrate this point well. They are closely related, both being members of the genus *Sylvia*. They are both typical warblers, with fine bills, bristles round the base of the bill and fairly short, rounded wings; and both feed by gleaning insects from foliage and catching other insects in flight. They are about the same size, being 14cm (5½in) long and weighing around 20g (¾oz).

Look-alikes of the thicket

earth-brown
upperparts

Lesser whitethroat
13.5cm (5¼ in)

black eye-patch

white underparts

Garden warbler
14cm (5½ in)

brown back
plain breast

pale buff
underparts

males have black cap
(females reddish brown)

slight eye-stripe

grey-brown
upperparts

Nightingale
16.5cm (6½ in)

pale grey
underparts

Chiffchaff
11cm (4¼ in)

Blackcap
14cm (5½ in)

broad chestnut tail

grey upperparts
with greenish tinge

Above: The female blackcap
does have a 'cap', but it
is an attractive reddish-
brown instead of black.

Right: A blackcap nest with
eggs. The eggs of both
species have white, yellowish
or greenish backgrounds,
blotched and spotted with
brown or grey. Garden
warbler eggs tend to be
slightly larger and glossier,
and often number only four
compared to the blackcap's
usual five.

Even their songs are so similar that most
people are unable to distinguish them. The
experienced ear, however, recognises that the
rich warbling song of the blackcap consists
of more varied notes than does the warbling
of the garden warbler, and that the latter
sings in longer phrases.

Hide and watch them Song is certainly not
a good identification feature, however, and
for most people the only way to decide between the two species is to obtain good views.
Then, the birds are more readily distinguished.

The garden warbler is pale buff below and
earth-brown above. It has no eye stripe or
other head marking, or indeed any other
patterning that can be regarded as a distinguishing feature. Fortunately for the birdwatcher, however, it is the only warbler in
Britain and Ireland to lack such markings.
The blackcap is a greyer bird, being grey-
brown above and a paler ashy grey below,
but its best field character is the colour of the
forehead and crown. In the male, these parts
are glossy black, while in the female this 'cap'
is reddish-brown. Young males in the autumn
can look slightly strange, with both black and
brown feathers in the cap.

Once you have determined that the bird is
either a blackcap or a garden warbler, some
other slight differences between the two
species become apparent. Although the songs
are very similar, the two birds tend to sing in
different places: the garden warbler sings low
down in thick undergrowth, where the songster is well hidden, and the blackcap sings
on favoured perches in bushes or tree-tops,
although again usually hidden by the foliage.

Different habitats This difference in singing
position may seem trivial but it is, of course,
related to the habitats that the two species

Opposite: A garden warbler feeds its young. These fledge when about ten days old. This rapid growth is very important for their survival, keeping to a minimum their time of greatest danger, for nests low down in the bushes are well within the reach of foxes, weasels and other denizens of the thicket. Each year, about half of the nests of both blackcaps and garden warblers are plundered by these predators, which find it easier to locate a nest containing calling chicks than one on which an adult bird is silently incubating. The shorter the time the chicks remain in the nest, the greater their chances of survival.

prefer. Again, there are close similarities, and blackcaps can be found breeding alongside garden warblers. Both species inhabit open woodland and copses with thick undergrowth, often of brambles, in which the birds nest. Large gardens, too, may play host to one or both of the warblers. But while garden warblers often nest in thickets where there are no trees, blackcaps seem to require that tall trees should be a feature of the habitat. Blackcaps are also more likely to nest in areas of evergreens than are garden warblers.

Both species build their nests in dense thickets, especially of brambles, but once again slight differences occur in the actual positioning of the nest. Once you know the bird must be either of these two species, the height can often be a helpful guide. Nests between 30 and 60cm (1 and 2ft) above the ground could belong to either species; but a nest below 30cm (1ft) is likely to belong to a garden warbler, and one above 60cm (2ft) is probably that of a blackcap.

Blackcaps arrive first The general lifestyles of the blackcap and garden warbler are there-

fore very similar, although differences in song, habitat and nest position can be noted. These may appear minor to us, but they are undoubtedly very real to the birds. Much greater differences, however, become apparent between the two species when we look at the timing of events in their life cycles.

Blackcaps make their presence felt by singing from March onwards. Those that sing in early March are probably birds that have spent the winter in Britain—for although the species is overwhelmingly a summer visiting one, small numbers do stay for the winter in Britain and Ireland. In late March, the returning migrants begin to swell the numbers; this arrival continues during April. Males arrive first, and quickly establish territories and start to sing, so that when the females arrive a week or two later, pairing can occur without delay. Nest-building and egg-laying take place in late April and early May. This early breeding, and the rapid development of the young, enable some pairs of blackcaps to rear two broods each year.

Above: A garden warbler surveys its territory. This is the only bird in our countryside to have such an utterly bland appearance: indeed, the absence of any stripes, contrasting colours or white marks is the best way to recognise the species.

Garden warbler (*Sylvia borin*); summer visitor; warbler typical of thickets and large gardens; sings from low down in bushes. Length 14cm (5½in).

Blackcap (*Sylvia atricapilla*); mainly summer visitor, with small numbers overwintering; warbler nesting in thickets with tall trees; sings from tree-tops or bushes. Length 14cm (5½in).

Male garden warblers arrive a week or so in advance of the females and similarly devote their time to establishing territories and singing. Garden warblers, however, do not begin to appear until late April, and their arrival continues through May. They are consequently unable to breed as early as blackcaps, and the peak of nest-building and egg-laying for garden warblers does not occur until the middle of May.

Migration patterns Why should there be this difference in the time of arrival, and hence of breeding? For the answer to this question we have to look beyond our shores. The garden warbler has a far longer migration: its wintering grounds range from tropical western Africa (Guinea and Nigeria) to Kenya, and from there to southern Africa. Blackcaps, too, travel to Africa, but their wintering range generally lies north of that of the garden warbler. Some blackcaps winter around the Mediterranean, and a few even stay in southern England. This species therefore travels a much shorter distance on its migration and this, together with its greater ability to utilise winter foods such as the berries of holly, privet and ivy, means that it can undertake its relatively brief and rapid migration early, permitting an early spring arrival in the breeding area.

Not only do garden warblers arrive later, but they must also depart earlier for their autumn journey to Africa, and they make their preparations for this (by feeding to store fat) well in advance of blackcaps; and so the featureless warbler of our scrubby woodlands has a hectic summer season. Could it be that this hectic life and all the dangers of the long journeys contribute to its scarcity, compared with its close relative? Blackcaps are three times as abundant in Britain.

Dartford warbler

The Dartford warbler is the only British bird that lives exclusively on heathland. This fact alone places it among our most endangered species.

Much has been written in recent years of the disappearance of our southern lowland heathland, its specialist reptile inhabitants—the smooth snake and the sand lizard—and its one specialist bird, the Dartford warbler. The Dartford warbler is a true specialist, entirely dependent on these low heaths dominated by gorse and a mixture of heathers (usually ling and bell heather or sometimes cross-leaved heath). It is the dense cover provided by these plant species, as well as the unique invertebrate fauna of the heaths, that the bird needs for its survival.

Other bird species occur as close neighbours of the Dartford warbler on the heaths, including the stonechat, the grasshopper warbler, the whitethroat, the hobby and the nightjar, but apart from the resident stonechat all these others are annual visitors coming from the south to breed in the warmth and plenty of our temperate summer. These birds thrive on the shrinking heathland but, unlike the Dartford warbler, each can also prosper in other habitats. If the heathlands disappear completely or become too fragmented, the Dartford warbler must inevitably vanish with them.

The first recorded description of the Dartford warbler was based on two individual birds shot in 1733 on Bexley Heath (now known as Bexleyheath, and a far cry from heathland for it is today a populated suburban district) near Dartford in Kent. At that time similar heathlands spread extensively across lowland England, and the warbler had a range extending from Cornwall to Norfolk and from the Isle of Wight as far north as Shropshire and Staffordshire. Today, only a residual population exists on remnant heathland in Hampshire and Dorset, with unsteady outposts in Devon, the Isle of Wight, Surrey and Sussex.

Hard winters It seems clear that the Dartford warbler has always been subject to fluctuations in its fortunes, certainly so far as total numbers are concerned, even in times when its heathland home was far more extensive than it is now. Hard winters, in particular, take a heavy toll on this small insectivorous bird: after the severe and protracted winter of 1962-63 the population crashed from about 460 pairs to a mere 11. Its powers of recovery, however, are shown by the fact that by 1970 the numbers had picked up again to about 70 pairs, and then climbed to 560 pairs by 1974. Then the hard winter of 1981-82 reduced the numbers again, to perhaps half the previous summer's total.

On individual heaths, the density of Dartford warblers is inconsistent and often erratic; frequently the bird is numerous in one area, but scarce in another that was previously favoured and held good numbers. Uncontrolled fire is a serious factor in reducing the population, as in the dry summer of 1976 when severe heath fires destroyed many hundreds of acres of deep, mature gorse and heather; the damage was temporary in some areas, but permanent in others where reclamation of the ground for agriculture followed the burning.

A hidden bird The Dartford warbler is a shy and elusive bird, in many respects the archetypal skulking warbler, moving through thick cover with utmost ease and all too easily avoiding detection. On bright days it may show itself more readily, giving quick glimpses of its distinctive cock-tailed form before diving again into thick cover. Its appearances in the open are fleeting, and any obligatory movement from thicket to thicket involves only low darting crossings of open areas.

When glimpsed in the open there is no con-

Above: The upperparts are grey-brown, more slate-grey on the head, and the underparts a dull pinkish chestnut. Brightest among the bird's features is the reddish-orange eye ring, which gives the eye an unusual impression of size and a quality of penetrating brightness.

Below: In Britain the Dartford warbler is at the northern edge of its world range, which reaches south to the Mediterranean and North Africa.

Dartford warbler distribution

fusing this diminutive bird with any other on the British list. Its small body size is equalled by the exceptionally long tail, which makes up half the total 12.5cm (5in) length. It weighs a mere 9-10 grams (⅜oz). The tail, characteristically cocked and frequently flicked, gives the bird much of its unmistakable outline, the remaining impression being of a dark coloured bird with small, rounded body, fine bill and a high forehead and crown. Its large reddish eye ring is immediately noticeable.

Displaying in April For a short period in early April, the cock birds are briefly conspicuous as they advertise their territory and sing. They have a lively dancing display flight in which the male bird rises above the dense canopy of gorse or heather and flutters down on vibrating wings. This display is reminiscent of that of a whitethroat, although it is neither as elevated nor as abandoned. The short, musical song also is similar to that of the whitethroat, but more mellow and liquid. The song is delivered from deep inside the gorse, or in a brief excursion to the topmost swaying twigs of a bush. Sometimes it is performed as an accompaniment to the dancing song flight.

Dartford warblers, sedentary throughout their range wherever they occur, are thus on site when the breeding season arrives and are among the early breeders. By mid April in a warm spring the first nests are built in the rank heather and gorse. The nest, although built by such a small bird, is remarkably robust, outlined first with twigs of heather and grasses and then shaped with finer grasses, rootlets and hairs, often woven with a little thistledown, wool or spiders' threads and individual feathers.

Three or four eggs are normally laid, dirty white in colour and finely spotted with lavender brown. The cock bird plays a small part in the incubation, which is chiefly carried out by the hen. The eggs hatch within a fortnight of the start of incubation.

Winter's shortage Very few species of wholly insectivorous small birds have evolved a sufficiently sound strategy to survive the vagaries of a British winter with reliability. The Dartford warbler faces no serious hardships in spring and summer, when the heathlands throb with the volume of insect life and the birds find an easy living. They have a ready harvest of small beetles, spiders, midges, small butterflies and moths, caterpillars and other larvae.

In winter, however, the choice narrows dramatically. The critical factor is the depth of cover provided by the heather and gorse. Deep under this canopy, even when it is covered with a thick layer of snow, the tangle of branches still provides a subsistence diet. Here the small warblers forage for heathland spiders, hibernating insects and the depleted stock of other invertebrates. In the hardest winters of all, shortages of these bring heavy losses to the Dartford warbler.

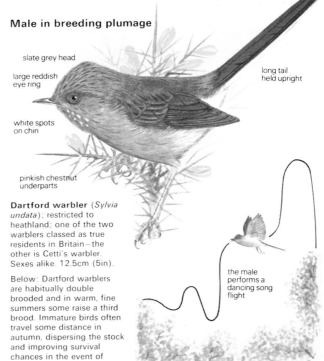

Male in breeding plumage

slate grey head

large reddish eye ring

white spots on chin

pinkish chestnut underparts

long tail held upright

Dartford warbler (*Sylvia undata*); restricted to heathland; one of the two warblers classed as true residents in Britain – the other is Cetti's warbler. Sexes alike. 12.5cm (5in).

Below: Dartford warblers are habitually double brooded and in warm, fine summers some raise a third brood. Immature birds often travel some distance in autumn, dispersing the stock and improving survival chances in the event of locally severe conditions.

the male performs a dancing song flight

Chiffchaff, willow warbler and wood warbler

Our warblers are grouped according to whether they are birds of reed-beds, scrub or leafy treetops. Here we look at the 'leaf explorers'.

Above: A willow warbler sings amid the opening buds. Besides the warbling song, the bird has a faint 'hoo-eet' call. The chiffchaff also has a similar call, sung slightly faster.

Right: Plentiful down surrounds the eggs in a willow warbler's nest. All three leaf warbler species usually lay 6 or 7. Only the females incubate, and this takes 13 days. The young fledge within 2 weeks, so sometimes there is time for a second brood.

Three species of leaf warbler are found in Britain and Ireland: the willow warbler, the chiffchaff and the wood warbler. Many people find warblers of any kind difficult to identify because they are invariably well camouflaged, retiring birds. Leaf warblers provide additional problems because they look so similar to one another. A leaf warbler can generally be described as a small, greenish-brown, lightly built bird with a fine, insect-eating bill, a pale stripe above the eye and yellowish underparts, flitting about in the canopy of a tree. This description applies to virtually all the *Phylloscopus* (leaf warbler) species that occur in the Old World (there are about 30 of them). It certainly applies to

Britain's three species.

The chiffchaff This, the dingiest of the three, has olive-brown upperparts and yellowish-buff underparts, an indistinct eye stripe and, usually, black legs. In keeping with its plumage and its name, its song is the least varied, alternating between two monotonous squeaky notes – 'chiff' and 'chaff'. Sometimes one note predominates as the bird 'misses' the other.

The chiffchaff is the earliest of our summer migrants: the harbinger of spring. The first birds arrive in early March, the last in April or May. However, this pattern is complicated by the tendency of an increasing number of chiffchaffs to overwinter in southern England. Although these hardy individuals may fly north to Scandinavia and beyond to breed, they are usually still here when the British breeders arrive.

The chiffchaff requires both bushy undergrowth for its nest, and tall trees as song-posts and feeding sites. While it can therefore live in well-grown deciduous and coniferous woodland, it is excluded from many areas where tall trees are uncommon, particularly parts of northern England and Scotland.

The willow warbler This bird is greener above, and more yellow below, than the chiffchaff; it has a stronger eye-stripe and, usually, pale legs. The overall impression it gives is of clearer colours and a 'cleaner' appearance.

The first willow warblers to arrive, usually in mid or late March, signal that the spring influx of visiting birds is under way. Their song is one of the most welcome country sounds, especially as it typically rings out from the heart of a colourful pussy willow tree on a bright sunlit morning. Starting quietly, the musical warbling gains volume and pitch and then descends back down the scale to a deliberate final flourish.

In its choice of habitat, the willow warbler is the least fussy of the three leaf warblers. Almost any wooded or open bushy area is suitable, provided the canopy is not too dense. Ideal habitats range from damp areas with willows (as its name suggests) to young conifer plantations and small copses. The

willow warbler is the commonest and most widespread of all our summer visitors, breeding throughout Britain and Ireland, even in sites close to built-up areas.

The wood warbler Of the three leaf warblers, this is the most brightly coloured, having yellowish-green upperparts, a sulphur-yellow throat and breast, a white belly, a noticeable yellow eye stripe and pale yellow eye stripe and pale orange legs. At 12.5cm (5in) long, it is also noticeably larger than the other two leaf warbler species, for they each measure only 11cm (4¼in) in length.

The wood warbler is the last of the three leaf warblers to arrive, mainly between mid-April and mid-May. Full appreciation of its song is certainly only achieved when you can both see and hear the bird in action. Starting with a steady 'stip, stip, stip', it accelerates to a marvellous, far-carrying trill which sets the whole bird quivering with the effort involved. The wood warbler also has a second, less well-known though equally distinctive song: a piping 'piu' repeated several times in quick succession.

The wood warbler is very particular in its choice of habitat: it prefers mature oak, birch, beech and chestnut woodland with little or no undergrowth. The sessile oak-woods of the valleys of western Britain are ideal, but this type of habitat is not common elsewhere. Consequently this species is the least widespread, being scarce or absent from wide tracts of England and Scotland. For every one of our breeding wood warblers, there are about ten chiffchaffs and a hundred willow warblers.

The breeding season Males of all three species typically arrive to set up territories a week or two earlier than their mates, often in the same area in which they were raised. Their beautiful, domed nests, almost spherical with the entrance at the side, are solely the work of the females. Leaves, grass, stalks, moss and perhaps bracken comprise the main structure, but whereas the wood warbler lines its nest with fine grass and hair, the other two use feathers. Each species hides its nest among low-growing plants and bushes. The chiffchaff builds its nest a foot or two above the ground in most cases, while the others make

Willow warbler (*Phylloscopus trochilus*). Summer visitor; length 11cm (4¼in).

pale yellow eye stripe
light yellow breast
white belly
pale orange legs

Willow warbler distribution

Chiffchaff distribution

Chiffchaff (*P. collybita*). Summer visitor; 11cm (4¼in).

white eye stripe
yellowish-buff breast
white belly
blackish legs

Wood warbler (*P. sibilatrix*). Summer visitor; 12.5cm (5in).

yellowish-green upperparts
yellow eye stripe
bright yellow throat and breast
white belly
brown legs

Wood warbler distribution

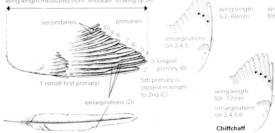

Wing formulae

Wing formulae are a series of measurements made to prove the identity of a bird such as a leaf warbler. In some cases, the first measurement alone is sufficient, but in others as many as four are necessary:
A How long is the wing?
B Which primaries (or primary) are longest?
C Which primaries have the same (or nearly the same) length as the second?
D Which primaries have an emargination?

SAMPLE WING

wing length measured from 'shoulder' to wing tip (A)

secondaries   primaries
10 9 8   7   6   5
3 longest primary (B)
2
1 (small first primary)   5th primary is closest in length to 2nd (C)
emarginations (D)

Willow warbler

wing length 53–68mm
emarginations on 3,4,5

Wood warbler

wing length 69–81mm
emarginations on 3,4

wing length 59–72mm
emarginations on 3,4,5,6

Chiffchaff

● emarginated primaries
Nos 1–10 = primary feathers
── line showing relative length of 2nd primary

Above: The chiffchaff is the least colourful of the three leaf warblers: its upperparts are olive brown.

Left: The wood warbler has brighter plumage than the other two species. Its nest is made at ground level and is domed, with the entrance at the side.

Below: The chiffchaff's nest is normally sited above ground level in the shrub layer; the bird is dependent on bushy undergrowth for nest sites.

theirs at ground level among grass and dead leaves.

Moult strategy One of the most distinct differences between our three leaf warblers, though perhaps the least obvious to the casual observer, is the timing of their feather moults. The only feature they share is that the young birds of all three species undergo a partial moult in autumn before they leave this country. (A partial moult is when the birds replace their body feathers, but not their wing or tail feathers.)

After this stage, chiffchaffs undergo a partial moult each winter and a complete moult each autumn; wood warblers undergo a complete moult each winter and a partial moult each autumn; and willow warblers undergo two complete moults, one in winter and one in autumn. To moult the entire plumage twice in each year is highly unusual, and so the willow warbler is in a class of its own in this particular respect. Curiously, there seems to be no obvious advantage in this behaviour, for all three strategies are demonstrably successful.

End of the season Late summer is the time when each individual bird must find extra food to fatten itself. This facilitates the growth of new feathers after the moult, and then fuels the bird's migration journey south. Leaf warblers are quick and agile birds, hopping to and fro to pick up tiny insects and caterpillars from twigs and leaves, hovering

to catch those out of reach or darting out to intercept them in flight. At this time of year, berries provide additional variety, and those chiffchaffs that stay for the winter occasionally visit bird tables for fat, meat, bread and other household scraps.

It is remarkable that such tiny birds, weighing some 10g ($\frac{1}{3}$oz), are able to fly to winter quarters as far away as Africa. Migration begins as early as the end of July. The first to leave are willow warblers, which migrate to tropical west Africa, some even crossing the equator. Most wood warblers migrate up the Nile valley to southern Sudan. The last to leave are the chiffchaffs, many of which fly no further than the Mediterranean.

Goldcrest and firecrest

Contrary to popular belief, Britain's smallest bird is not the wren; it is just pipped at the post by the goldcrest and its less common relative, the firecrest.

The goldcrest and firecrest are not just the smallest birds in Britain; they are also the smallest in the whole of Europe. At just 9cm (3½in) long, they are 5mm (¼in) shorter than the wren. Both birds are also extremely light, weighing no more than 5g.

By far the more common of the two species, the goldcrest can be seen in most parts of Britain, whereas the firecrest has only recently begun to breed here and is still confined to southern and eastern England.

The goldcrest The most noticeable feature of the goldcrest is the lemon-yellow stripe, bordered by a black line, on its crown—this is the crest after which it is named. During display, or in winter when a competitor for food comes too close, the bird's feathers become erect and the stripe widens. In the male, the raised feathers reveal that the crest has a deep orange centre.

The rest of the goldcrest's plumage is much drabber since it was developed not for display but to provide camouflage in conifer woods. The upperparts of the body and tail are olive-green and the underparts buff. The wings are greenish-black with feather margins tinged yellow, and there are two distinct white wing-bars close to where the wing meets the body. The eye of a goldcrest is large and dark, and is surrounded by a broad

Above: Coniferous forests and woodland are the most common habitats for the goldcrest, though it is becoming a familiar bird in gardens having conifer trees or hedges. Goldcrests also inhabit deciduous woods, but usually in small numbers. Only after a mild winter, when the goldcrest population tends to 'explode', do they become common in deciduous woods.

Goldcrest (*Regulus regulus*). Resident; length 9cm (3½in), which makes it, jointly with the firecrest, Britain's smallest bird. Between 5 and 13 extremely small white eggs flecked with brown are laid between March and August.

Goldcrest

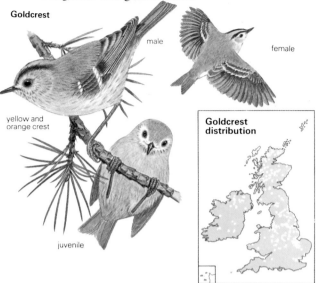

male

female

yellow and orange crest

juvenile

Goldcrest distribution

died. But, in the decade that followed, a run of mild winters allowed the population to increase tenfold from the low point of 1963.

The breeding season Nest-building begins in March. The nest consists of a basket of mosses, held together by woven cobwebs and suspended hammock-like in the fork of two twigs. Most are built in thick foliage towards the end of a branch, though less often in ivy or honeysuckle close to a tree trunk; or a prickly bush such as gorse, may be chosen. Both sexes help in the construction.

A typical clutch of eggs is between seven and ten, though it can range from five to thirteen; the eggs are incubated by the female alone. The young brood is fed by both parents on the typical goldcrest diet of insects, mites, spiders and their eggs and larvae. The young fledge after about 20-23 days. In most seasons the parents can easily manage to rear two broods such a high reproductive capacity helps the population to recover from severe winters.

Once they have fledged, the young goldcrests usually join up with other woodland

pale ring of feathers that give the bird a look of permanent surprise.

Nationwide distribution The goldcrest is widely distributed in the British Isles, being absent only from the fens of East Anglia and the Scottish Highlands, though it is rare in the Hebrides, Orkneys and Shetlands.

Its favourite habitat is coniferous forests and woodlands. As more and more conifer plantations become established, so the goldcrest has spread out and increased in numbers, and it is now also beginning to colonize garden conifers.

Despite being so common in coniferous habitats, the goldcrest can be extremely difficult to observe since it spends much of its time high up in trees. A good way of detecting a goldcrest is to listen for its song: a pulsating series of 'zee-zee-zee' squeaks, breaking into a 'deedly-deedly-deeee' and ending with a flourish. The song is extremely high-pitched; one of the signs of increasing age in a bird-watcher comes when he or she visits a conifer wood in spring and does *not* hear a goldcrest (the frequency range detected by the human ear decreases as people age).

Coniferous woodland is the most important habitat for the goldcrest, but it can also be found in deciduous woods, though usually in far fewer numbers. However, after a succession of mild winters, the goldcrest population can multiply dramatically, the birds inhabiting even lowland oakwoods in large numbers.

Just as mild winters lead to a population explosion, so a severe winter can lead equally dramatically to a population crash; the heat loss from such a tiny body during a long winter's night can be too great for the bird to survive. During the exceptionally severe winter of 1962-3 about 60% of our goldcrests

Above: and right: Male and female adult goldcrests differ most noticeably in the colour of their crests, the male's (see right) being more orange than the female's. The juvenile goldcrest lacks any crest. Goldcrests are found in most parts of Britain.

Below: A goldcrest feeds its young, a task shared by both parents. The chicks fledge after about three weeks which, in most seasons, leaves plenty of time for a second brood.

birds, such as tits, wrens and warblers, to form large foraging parties. As autumn progresses, our resident goldcrest population is joined by often considerable numbers of Continental migrants. Since the Continental winter is so much more severe than ours, this migration obviously has survival value; nevertheless, it is remarkable that so small a bird routinely makes such a hazardous journey—often crossing the North Sea at the height of the autumn gales.

The firecrest In appearance, the firecrest is similar to its commoner relative, but its plumage is much brighter. Its upperparts are greenish-gold with a mantle of delicate bronze over the shoulders. The underparts are paler and more silvery than those of the goldcrest. The most striking difference, however, is on the head. The eye has a black stripe running through it; below this is a short white stripe, and above a bolder, long, white stripe which offsets the black-bordered crest. Both sexes of firecrest have an orange-yellow crest, though on the male it is much deeper and richer in colour.

Once rare migrant Not so many years ago, the firecrest was a rare passing migrant and much sought after by birdwatchers. Each spring, a few arrived at isolated spots along the south and east coasts of England as far north as Norfolk. A few birds were also sighted each autumn on their way southwards. This migration still takes place, but small numbers of firecrest are now beginning to settle in Britain, instead of just passing through. The first sighting was in 1962, when some recently fledged chicks were seen in the New Forest. A small but regularly breeding population has become established at several sites in that area, and other counties in southern and eastern England have also been colonized.

This colonization is paralleled by an increase in the firecrest's Continental range and in the number of firecrests seen in spring and autumn at the regular migration-watching spots. Ornithologists do not yet know why this is happening, though it is possible that, in the past, firecrests were simply overlooked by birdwatchers and so their numbers were thought to be lower than they actually were.

Similarities to goldcrest The firecrest breeds in similar habitats to those of the goldcrest, and its way of life and food are also similar. On the Continent, however, the firecrest tends to be a bird of open, usually deciduous woodland, whereas the goldcrest usually inhabits conifers. So, in Britain, the goldcrest occupies both its own habitat and the firecrest's as well. Yet, when the firecrest started to colonize Britain it chose to settle mainly in dense conifers—the stronghold of the goldcrest. Not surprisingly, there have been reports of territorial fights between the two.

As with the goldcrest, the best way to locate breeding firecrests is by their song. This is very similar to that of the goldcrest but, with practice, the two can be told apart. The firecrest's song consists of a harsh and repetitive 'zit-zit, zit-zit . . .' that accelerates towards the end but lacks a terminal flourish. The best time to hear it is in late May and June; firecrests rarely sing later in the season than that.

Above: Until about 20 years ago, the firecrest was seen only as a passing migrant but it has now settled in the same habitat as the goldcrest. On the Continent, however, it tends to be a bird of deciduous woodland.

Firecrest

orange crest

female

Firecrest distribution

Firecrest (*Regulus ignicapillus*). Resident; length 9cm (3½in). Distinguished from the goldcrest particularly by its black eye-stripe. The eggs are similar but laid in May–July.

Below left: Breeding firecrests are confined to southern and eastern England.

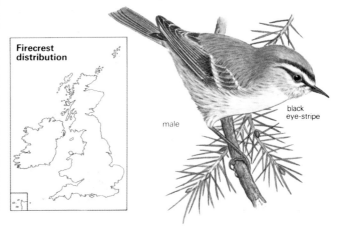

male

black eye-stripe

Whinchat and stonechat

Chats are delightfully extrovert in their behaviour, posing obligingly in full view while they sing from the top of a bush or tuft of grass. Our two species are the stonechat, which is a resident bird, and the whinchat, a summer visitor.

Above: A male stonechat perches on a prominent tuft of grass to sing and survey his territory. This scene is in county Galway in the west of Ireland, where the climate is a little milder than elsewhere. The stonechat's combination of a sedentary existence and demonstrative habits makes it an easy bird to observe.

Opposite right: A male whinchat, with a freshly caught small heath butterfly.

Both the stonechat and the whinchat are plump, colourful, upstanding birds, characteristic of open habitats with few trees. Both species are small, measuring only 13cm (5in) from beak to tail. Their English names are for the most part appropriate, since their alarm calls sound just like two pebbles being knocked together – hence 'chat' in imitation of the sound. Whin is another name for gorse, so you might expect the whinchat to be more common in gorse than the stonechat – but this is not the case.

Easy to recognise Both stonechats and whinchats are easy to identify. The male stonechat is an elegant bird, with a black or dark brown back, head and throat, highlighted by a pure white, though incomplete, collar. His chest is conspicuously reddish, fading to white on the belly, and when he flies, or as he flicks his wings while perched, you see white marks on the wings and a pale rump. Females and young birds are similar but much less striking, being more brown than black and having relatively little white.

The male whinchat is also elegant. He has

older. The wings, too, are black, with a striking white patch in mature birds. Females and young birds are far more difficult to tell from redstarts unless a good view is obtained, but black redstart underparts are always grey, and never buff or orange as in the common redstart.

Across much of Europe and Asia, the natural habitat of black redstarts is rocky mountainsides, where they feed on a wide variety of insects caught on the ground or on the wing, and nest in crevices between boulders. Black redstarts also form an attractive component of the bird life of many European towns and cities, usually associated with large old buildings where crumbling masonry has provided suitable nest-sites. In their association with man they are probably most typical of the whitewashed walls, geraniums in hanging baskets and colourful tiled roofs of Mediterranean cities, towns and villages. Particularly numerous in southern France and Germany, they range as far north as Denmark and Latvia to breed. They are short-haul migrants; the more northerly birds winter in the Mediterranean basin, while some populations rarely migrate at all.

In consequence, it comes as something of a surprise to find that a bird so numerous, homely and widespread on the Continent should be so scarce in Britain. Perhaps one hundred pairs breed in England in an average year, mostly in the south and east. It is also

Above: Redstarts are hole-nesters, and it is often argued that keen competition for the nest holes (from tits, pied flycatchers, nuthatches and others) is the only restriction on the growth of the redstart population.

surprising to discover that only in the middle years of the present century did they become firmly established here as breeding birds.

Wartime arrival The story of their colonization is an intriguing one. Apart from a few isolated records, the first substantial breeding reports were published in the earliest days of World War II. In May 1939 a male was found singing in Bloomsbury—in most illustrious circumstances—from the towers of the University of London and the nearby British Museum. Bombing had begun in real earnest when breeding was proved in the summer of 1940, in Inner London and again illustriously, this time in the shadow of Westminster Abbey. Although breeding was reported in

Above: A young black redstart perches on scrap metal. Besides derelict factories and yards, the birds also favour some active sites—docks, warehouses, gasworks and power stations.

Redstart (*Phoenicurus phoenicurus*); summer visitor to mature, open woodland; 14cm (5½in).

Black redstart (*Phoenicurus ochruros*); small breeding population in towns; 14cm (5½in).

other southern counties, London remained the stronghold of the British breeding population as it increased over the wartime years. Many of the breeding pairs were in the City of London, and took advantage of the devastated buildings and piles of rubble (doubtless reminiscent of mountain screes) in the blitzed areas to feed and to conceal their nests.

The many reports and articles on black redstarts that were published during the war rarely gave any detail of the habitat, probably for reasons of security so that the enemy did not gain too clear a picture of the extent of the damage. By the end of the war, the black redstart population, though still with its stronghold in London, was spread over at least 11 counties and had reached about 50 pairs.

At that stage, startling fresh information was released. In 1944, the journal *British Birds* published retrospective information on breeding, described as 'one of the most remarkable discoveries of recent years in British ornithology'. A caretaker at the Wembley Palace of Engineering (which housed the great Empire Exhibition of 1925) told the authors of the article that during the years 1926-41—since the closing of the exhibition—three pairs of black redstarts (and once four) had nested there every year.

After the war, the breeding black redstart population fluctuated, sometimes reaching 60 recorded pairs, sometimes falling as low as 20. In the early 1970s there was a continuing rise in the number of nests reported, and the present-day level of around 100 pairs was established. About one third of the breeding population is in the London area, the remainder largely in the south-east and East Anglia, with a scattering of records in the Midlands and the most northerly in Yorkshire and Cheshire. In a 1977 survey, 98% of sites described were man-made.

Robin

The robin (below and opposite) is a particular favourite among bird lovers; everyone enjoys the attentions of this familiar redbreast in the garden during winter. But despite all the efforts made to feed this bird in the harsh weather, thousands perish each year.

The robin enjoys a popularity with man unrivalled by any other species. A familiar visitor at the bird-table in winter and constant gardening companion, even nesting in the toolshed, it is a year-round bird. This close association with man is a special feature of the robin's relationship with the British. Robins of exactly the same species nest over most of Europe, but a tendency on the continent to shoot and eat small birds has made robins there generally shy and retiring woodland birds.

The bird's popularity in Britain has built up over the years and legends about the bad luck incurred by anyone harming a robin go back to the 16th century. A Christian link has been

attached to the legend because the robin's red breast was supposedly stained by blood after the bird had been pricked by Christ's crown of thorns. This is why the robin features prominently on the earliest Christmas cards.

Pairing and nesting The adults get together as pairs in early January. As they look exactly alike, the sexes can only recognise each other by display and posture. An unmated male singing loudly in his territory will, at first, behave aggressively to any intruding robin. If the intruder is a male it either retreats or tries to oust the occupier. If the new bird is a female seeking a mate, she persists in approaching the resident male, apparently unimpressed by his threats. Over a period of some hours, sometimes as much as two days, the bond between the two is built up so that they accept each other.

In many species this pair-bonding is directly followed by nest-building and egg-laying. With the robin, pairing is accomplished weeks or even months before any nesting attempt is made. During this time the birds occupy the same territory and recognise each other as mates but do not pay much attention to each other. As the weather improves the hen bird starts to build her nest, using moss and dead leaves and lining it with hair. In the natural state she may choose a rocky crevice or hollow of a tree, most often, a bank or an ivy-covered tree—usually well concealed and difficult to find.

However some robins select the most unlikely sites. One nest was found in a chest of drawers in a toolshed. The drawer was half-closed and the nest at the back was only discovered when the drawer was opened.

When she begins to build the nest the female also starts to receive food from the male. This so-called 'courtship-feeding' was initially thought to be a ritual designed to reinforce the pair-bond between male and female. In fact it is an important source of food for the female—one that she almost completely relies upon during incubation.

The clutch of white eggs with pale reddish freckling is laid, one egg each day, and the complete clutch is generally five or six eggs, although up to nine have been recorded. The

Robin (*Erithacus rubecula*). Also called redbreast; 14cm (5in) from beak to tip of tail; 5-9cm (2-4in) high. Distribution nationwide.

Below: Hungry fledglings wait to be fed in their nest, which is usually made up of twigs, grass and moss. Robins are well known for making their nests in such unlikely places as kettles, old buckets—even the pockets of jackets left in garden sheds.

incubating female loses the feathers from her breast and belly and the blood vessels just under the skin enlarge greatly. The bare skin and increased blood supply allow her to transfer heat more efficiently to the eggs.

Greedy chicks After two weeks the eggs hatch out and the blind chicks, covered in thin dark down, increasingly dominate the parents' lives with their enormous appetites. Both adult and young robins feed on insects, spiders and worms. They do not generally eat seeds or berries. About 15 days after hatching these young robins, now weighing more than their parents, leave the nest.

Two particularly attentive parents were reported by naturalist David Lack. They

built their nest in a cart which had to go on a 200-mile round trip just after the young hatched. Undaunted, the adult birds accompanied their offspring, feeding them on the way.

When the young birds leave the nest they face two or three days of great danger since they cannot yet fly well. At this stage they have a soft speckled brown plumage with no trace of their parents' red breast. By the beginning of June they start to lose their body feathers and to develop their red breasts —growing from the bottom upwards. The wings do not moult but continue to develop until July of the next year when they reach their full size.

Five or six eggs—12mm (½in) long—are laid and incubated for two weeks. Eggs generally have a whitish background and orange/brown freckles.

Nests vary in size. They are made of dead leaves, grass, moss and hairs; very few feathers are used as lining.

Second brood Once the young are fledged the adults build a new nest within the same territory and, unless they are prevented for any reason (disturbance by a cat, flooding of the nest in bad weather or thoughtless hedge-cutting), will raise another brood in May. During the summer for a period of five weeks, the adult robins replace their old feathers with new ones. They stay in the same area, but make themselves less obvious and less active, concealed in shrubberies and thickets. During this moult the adult robins also fall silent—the only time of the year when the robin song is not a feature of the British countryside.

As the second brood of young birds acquires its red plumage and the adult birds their replacement plumage, the autumn song starts up. The rich and fruity spring song of the males gives way to the thinner, more piping song of young and old, cock and hen, as each claims its own territory; this is kept, with a few local alterations, through the winter until pairing takes place. In times of real food shortage, territoriality breaks down as all the birds concentrate on feeding.

Population control Although some British robins migrate each autumn, most stay within a mile or two of their birthplace. So what happens to all these robins? If each pair of adults raises two broods with five or six young in each, there are six times as many robins at the end of the breeding season as at the start. A single pair would become almost ten million pairs at the end of ten years—about twice the total British population of robins. In fact the majority of them die. As many as a million robins may be killed by cats; while owls, cars, plate glass windows and harsh winters also take their toll. Sadly, but naturally, of the original pair and their offspring, on average only one adult and one youngster survive to breed the following year. Harsh winter weather often provides the greatest danger; so millions of people who feed birds leave out all sorts of titbits—even mince meat and grated cheese—to ensure that 'their' robins are the ones to survive. This feeding also encourages the robins to stay in backyards and gardens.

Left: A spotty juvenile robin, speckled brown and with no hint of a red breast which develops later in the summer. In its first year, the robin has a one-in-six chance of survival.

Below: Proudly displaying its red breast and singing its rich spring song, this robin lays claim to its territory and warns off other birds.

Competing for space

Almost all birds are territorial. It is generally during the breeding season that each bird defends a home area, and will not tolerate any bird of the same species apart from its mate within its territory. Robins are no exception, and like other song birds (such as blackbirds and song thrushes) they stake out quite large claims by their presence at strategic songposts. Other birds restrict themselves to much smaller areas—gannets, for instance, only defend the immediate nest area.

The blackbird singing on your television aerial may seem full of the joys of spring but, much more important to itself and other blackbirds, it is saying: 'This is part of my territory—keep off'. If the message is not understood it may still have to chase off the encroaching birds—a sight often seen when disputing birds dart at each other along a lawn or hedgerow without actually making contact. It is both these aggressive flutterings and song patterns that prevent actual fighting—unless large numbers of birds are competing for a very small territory.

Nightingale

The nightingale is justly praised for its tuneful singing, but it cannot excel in all things: despite its wonderfully varied musical performance, it is an unobtrusive, dull brown bird, here for a short breeding season spent hiding in the thickets.

The nightingale combines the extremes of delightfully melodious singing and a generally uniform, unremarkable plumage. It is about half way in size between the robin and the song thrush, two fellow members of the thrush family. In its general posture the nightingale is comparable to these two birds. Its plumage, however, is considerably less colourful than that of other members of the thrush family, being chestnut-brown all over the upperparts and paling to a rufous fawn beneath. The most interesting feature is the tail, which is frequently flicked while the bird is perching, sometimes catching the light and revealing a rich rufous quality.

Like the robin's, the nightingale's eye is large and dark; but the legs are stouter than those of the robin. Young birds, before the autumn moult of their first year, have scaly, pale fawn fringes to many of their feathers, and unless you catch a glimpse of the tail you might easily mistake them for young robins.

Thicket dweller According to one country saying, the distribution of the nightingale, the cowslip and the hop have much in common in England; and this is indeed broadly true. Most nightingales breed to the south of a line between the Severn and the Humber, preferring habitats with a well-developed and dense undergrowth. Thus most are found in woodland areas, usually of deciduous trees and very often of oak, with the mature trees widely spaced. Towards the north-western fringe of this breeding range, the wooded slopes of river valleys are particularly favoured.

Over the last few centuries, the distribution of the nightingale right across Europe has contracted considerably. Possibly this is partly due to wholesale trapping (particularly on the Continent) of nightingales for caging as song birds or, even more unpleasantly, for

Above: The nightingale has three main adaptations to its life in the thickets. The beak is suited for taking large and small invertebrates as well as berries. The legs are strong enough for ground foraging, and the large eye enables it to see well in the dense undergrowth.

Previous page: The rich tone of the plumage is seen on the rump and tail.

Below: The nightingale is restricted to the south and south-east of England.

Nightingale distribution

Right: The nest is either low down in the vegetation – frequently bramble or nettles – or actually on the ground. It is always in an overgrown and inaccessible spot. In many cases nightingale pairs return to exactly the same spot each year.

sale in delicatessens. Though this does still occur, it seems more likely that the major factor in the decline is the loss of the appropriate type of deciduous woodland. This is due both to modern farming, with its demands for full land usage and increased field sizes, and to modern forestry practice, in which broad-leaved woodland is replaced by dense plantations of conifers.

Watching for nightingales Generally, nightingales are shy, rarely venturing into the open, so for many of us this is a bird far more often heard than seen. Considerable patience, and quiet watching from semi-concealment in an area with several nightingale pairs—and preferably with some paths to provide open ground—is required to obtain even fleeting glimpses. If you are lucky, a male nightingale may choose to sing from a perch in your line of sight, head thrown slightly back, throat bulging, giving you a chance to see the performance as well as hear it.

More often, apart from the song, much of what you hear in the undergrowth is the surprisingly varied repertoire of 'chack' and 'churr' noises with which the nightingale deters intruders from approaching its place of concealment. You may also hear the soft 'weet' call that the pair use to keep in contact.

Our best night singer The voice of the nightingale, heard solo at dead of night, comes through the clear, warm early summer air as one of the most delightful bird songs in the world. The song period is, however, short, generally spanning the second half of May and the month of June, but rarely continuing as late as July.

For quality, range and versatility the nightingale's voice cannot be matched, even among British birds with their exceptionally rich songs. Part of the enjoyment stems from

the sheer variety–from throaty chuckles to far-carrying whistles–and part from the quality of the tonal range, from rich, deep phrases to the purest of treble-like trills and flourishes.

Special adaptations In the shelter of its habitat of thick undergrowth, the nightingale spends much of its time concealed from view. It is one of the more terrestrial birds in the thrush family. Strong legs and large eyes are adaptations to this mode of life, as also is the beak. Though not so stout as the conical beaks of the finches, nor so fine as that of insect-eaters such as the pied wagtail, the well pointed but strong beak of the nightingale allows it to tackle most soil and litter-dwelling invertebrates. These range from tiny insects and spiders to caterpillars and worms. The beak is also suited to feeding on berries as they become available later in the month. At this time they are invaluable as a sugar-rich resource to help the nightingale put on fat as a fuel reserve for the long migration south.

The breeding season Nightingales perform a pairing display which is rarely seen because of the dense cover in which it takes place. It involves much ritualised posturing, with wings drooping and fluttering, and with tail fanned. After the display, the nest is built low in the vegetation or, quite commonly, on the ground. It is always well concealed from disturbance by humans and large predatory mammals or birds, although it is not safe from such predators as weasels or mice. The nest is basically constructed of dead leaves, usually those found lying nearby. Those found in England are most often held together by fine twigs or stout grasses. The lining of the cup is of fine grasses and hair, and the normal clutch is four or five (occasionally six). The eggs are brown, so densely speckled as to

broad, rounded wings   'wing-fanning' display

white breast

adult   ♂

fanned tail

large dark eye

mottled head

underparts look 'scaly'

juvenile

appear almost uniformly coloured. Because of their early departure on migration, there is normally time for just a single brood each season.

Long-distance migrants Nightingales desert their breeding woods from late July onwards. Ringing results indicate that most nightingales cross the Mediterranean in autumn and fly over the western margins of the Sahara Desert. Their wintering areas are in tropical West Africa. As with many other migrants, individual breeding birds often return to precisely the same patch of dense cover in successive years, for unless the site has been cleared by man, nightingales keep to their traditional nesting grounds.

Nightingale (*Luscinia megarhynchos*). Summer visitor breeding in thickets. Splendid song audible at night. 16.5cm (6½in).

Below: After an incubation period of about a fortnight, the brood hatches. In their earliest days, nightingale chicks have the same speckled appearance as young robins – a resemblance which continues into the juvenile stage. The season is too short for more than one brood.

Night singing birds

It is interesting to note that nightingales sing a great deal during the day as well as the night, but in the daytime their song tends to be drowned by the richness of other birdsong heard at this time. However, *why* they sing so much at night is intriguing, and by no means well understood. Few other songbirds sing at night, but two that do, the grasshopper and the reed warblers, are both birds of dense cover, like the nightingale. Also like the nightingale, they are summer visitors to this country, migrating by night to and from wintering areas in Africa.

One theory is based on the observation that males usually migrate some days in advance of the females. On arrival, they set up territories and defend them by song, and then it is thought that they sing to the night skies to attract the females as they pass over. Although plausible in this context, the theory leaves unexplained the fact that all these species continue their nocturnal singing until well into the breeding season.

Song and mistle thrushes

The clear, musical, flute-like notes of the thrush
family are justly famous. On most days of the year
from the first light of dawn to late dusk you can hear
the vigorous, repetitive phrases of the song thrush,
and the more leisurely song of the mistle thrush
which continues even in the rain.

Apart from the Shetland Islands, there are few places in the British Isles where you will not find a song thrush; they are a familiar part of our daily lives, and one of the first birds children learn to recognise. The mistle thrush, however, is slightly less widespread and is absent from Shetland and Orkney, and decidedly scarce in the outer Scottish islands.

People sometimes think the two species are difficult to separate. Both are immediately recognisable as thrushes, with medium length, fairly stout bills, speckled underparts, brownish upperparts, long legs and rather large eyes. The mistle thrush is slightly longer than the song thrush but there are other differences as well. The upperparts of the song thrush are a warm brown, and those of the mistle thrush a distinctly greyer brown. You can see these features quite clearly when the birds are in flight. As the birds pass overhead, look at the axillaries (the feathers covering the 'armpits'): they are a flaming orange-yellow in the song thrush and white in the mistle thrush. The tail of the song thrush is a uniform brown but the mistle thrush has whitish tips to the outer tail feathers. The underparts differ as well: both birds have dark brown breast spots on a pale background, but the spots of the mistle thrush are bigger, more rounded, and altogether bolder, on a paler background.

Rich song All members of the thrush family sing loud, clear, musical flute-like notes. The special qualities of the song thrush are its vigour and repetition. The bird sings the same notes two, three, even five or six times – sometimes you could swear that it is practising a choice phrase. The song thrush uses favourite note sequences time and time again, interspersed with numerous other notes and phrases, many of them mimicking other birds. Some species, such as the chaffinch, sing rather poorly at the start of the season and their performance steadily becomes more polished, but the song thrush sings well right from the start, and some people think its performance is enriched with age.

The mistle thrush has a more limited song – a sequence of a few notes in permutation. It is loud, clear, full, rich and leisurely, and could be monotonous if it were not for its fine quality.

Aerial song posts Members of the thrush family like to sing from high song posts, and song thrushes and blackbirds have been quick to commandeer television aerials. The mistle thrush prefers to sing from the topmost branch of a tall tree, and its readiness to do so even in heavy rain has led to its widely used folk name, stormcock. In most

Right: Song thrushes excel in cracking snail shells and extracting the flesh, thus providing themselves with a valuable source of food when drought drives the worms deeper. They beat the victim against a stone or hard surface ('anvil') to break it.

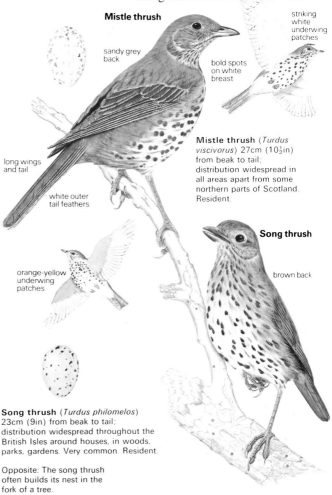

Mistle thrush

striking white underwing patches

sandy grey back

bold spots on white breast

long wings and tail

white outer tail feathers

orange-yellow underwing patches

Mistle thrush (*Turdus viscivorus*) 27cm (10½in) from beak to tail; distribution widespread in all areas apart from some northern parts of Scotland. Resident.

Song thrush

brown back

Song thrush (*Turdus philomelos*) 23cm (9in) from beak to tail; distribution widespread throughout the British Isles around houses, in woods, parks, gardens. Very common. Resident.

Opposite: The song thrush often builds its nest in the fork of a tree.

years song thrushes start to sing in November –even October–and do not stop until July or later. The mistle thrush does not start singing until the turn of the year and usually ends at the beginning of June.

The call notes of the two species are quite different. An alarmed song thrush says 'tchouk tchouk . . .', the notes coming faster and closer together when the bird is particularly anxious. The mistle thrush has a loud, vigorous call which sounds rather like a football rattle.

Habitat preferences Although the two species are frequently found in the same acre of ground, they have different habitat preferences. Song thrushes are at home in gardens and shrubberies, and you will probably see more nesting around houses than in farmland. You might hear eight or nine individuals on a half mile walk on a mild November morning, which suggests a density of one bird every hundred yards or so.

Mistle thrushes are always more thinly distributed and seem to require much larger territories. They too penetrate urban areas, but they tend to favour parks, cemeteries, and playing fields rather than gardens. Large mature gardens and parklands, on the other hand, are typical habitats for them. In the breeding season you may find them in woodlands and even conifer plantations, so long as there are grassy rides or adjacent grasslands for spring feeding.

Song thrushes tend to favour the same type of habitat in winter and summer, although the higher ground is vacated before the cold winter weather sets in, and a proportion of the population migrates. In northern Britain the migration is chiefly to Ireland, but those individuals that migrate from the south make chiefly for Iberia. In harsh

Above: A juvenile song thrush can be distinguished from an adult by its speckled back plumage. Song thrushes nearly always sing from an elevated song perch.

winters, non-migrating song thrushes may suffer so severely that they are obliged to carry out a cold-weather movement–an emergency migration. The small proportion of song thrushes that migrate usually go to France.

Song thrushes are solitary and flock together only on migration. Mistle thrushes, on the other hand, tend to move about in family parties at the end of the breeding season; the parties later amalgamate to form loose flocks of up to 100 birds which roam the countryside together, penetrating even wild upland country in their search for food. During midwinter the flocks split up and the birds occupy their territories for the start of a new breeding season.

Superbly structured nests Mistle thrushes tend to start breeding two or three weeks earlier than song thrushes, work on the nest often starting before February is out. In both species the hen alone builds the nest, which is well-engineered and incorporates grasses and mud for bonding. The nest of the song thrush is especially beautiful– smooth, symmetrical, and rather like the inside of a coconut shell.

The song thrush is versatile and adaptable in its choice of nest sites, hiding–or sometimes failing to hide–its nest in bushes and shrubs. Its willingness to live so close to man enables it to exploit such unlikely sites as the top of the cistern in an outside lavatory, although

Left: An egg and some chicks of a song thrush. This species is unique among European birds for its habit of plastering the inside of its nest. The plaster is made from dung or rotten wood mixed with saliva.

Below: A song thrush removing a faecal sac from its young. The parent does this to keep the nest clean, depositing the sac some distance from the nest.

natural sites greatly predominate.

The mistle thrush normally builds its nest in the fork of a tree, perhaps 7-9m (20-30ft) up, and remarkably well hidden. From this vantage point the incubating female keeps a watchful eye, crouching low if she suspects she is being observed. Mistle thrushes are fearless in the defence of their nests and young, and do not hestitate to tackle birds much larger than themselves. Apart from egg-stealing members of the crow family, their chief avian predator, and the song thrush's as well, is the sparrow-hawk. Peregrines occasionally eat them.

There are four or five song thrush eggs in a clutch, each a beautiful blue thinly speckled with black. They are incubated by the hen alone, and take 13-14 days to hatch and a similar period to fledge. A second brood is often followed by a third. The mistle thrush may lay three to six eggs, though four is normal. Their background colour varies from cream to pale greeny-blue, and they are dramatically blotched and speckled with sepia. The incubation period is the same as for the song thrush, but the young may take a day or two longer to fledge. The juveniles develop speckled back plumage which they lose when they become fully mature by the following spring.

Feeding habits Thrushes feed on fruit for much of the year; the rest of the time they rely on worms, insects and other invertebrates.

You often see them feeding on lawns: a quick hop forward to focus more accurately, using monocular vision, (not to listen); a few vigorous pecks, and the worm is dragged out. Song thrushes crack snails on their 'anvils' (stones), and during snow cover they ferret about for food in hedge bottoms and even among the marram grass along the coast. Mistle thrushes are more reliant on worms and insects, often feeding in the centre of fields. In a sense the feeding habits sum up the temperaments of the two species: the mistle thrush bold but wary, even self assertive; the song thrush more retiring, and often unobtrusive.

Above: A mistle thrush feeding its young. Fruit is an important part of the diet of both species, but particularly of the mistle thrush which favours mistletoe berries — hence its name. In northern Britain rowan provides tasty berries and even isolated trees far up on the fellsides may be visited and stripped bare. Holly, yew, hawthorn and, later in the winter, rose hips and ivy berries are also eaten by both species.

Identifying songbirds

Redwing

Song thrush

Blackbird ♀

Fieldfare

Blackbird

The blackbird – one of the most familiar and best loved of our garden birds – is often regarded as uninteresting because of its very familiarity. In fact, because it is so easy to study, more is known of its life-style than of almost any other bird.

Above: A male blackbird with jet black plumage and bright orange bill. This bird is easily recognisable by its jaunty, hopping gait and also by its habit of standing with head cocked to one side, listening for worms.

Opposite: Although blackbirds are so often seen in our gardens and parks, they are predominantly woodland birds. Beech woods such as these provide food for blackbirds among the leaf litter.

The blackbird, a bird familiar to everyone, is a successful and adaptable species whose natural habitats, before man started to make his mark on the British countryside several thousand years ago, were woodland edges and natural clearings. Now it not only frequents gardens in town and countryside but also most of the hedges over the millions of acres of British farmland.

The blackbird's very numbers allow it to be studied in much greater detail than most species; thousands are ringed each year and nest-recorders are able to find and record nests in great quantities.

Male, female and juvenile The adult male is quite literally a 'black bird', with a wholly black plumage relieved only by a bright orange bill and an orange eye-ring. The younger males, hatched the previous summer, retain their old flight feathers and some wing coverts, giving their wings a peculiar 'patch-work' effect where the old brown juvenile feathers contrast with the newer ones grown during the post-juvenile moult in their first autumn. The females are much browner, with a pale throat and speckling on the breast. Juvenile birds of both sexes have rich brown centres to many of their body feathers, but these are retained only for a month or two.

Territorial song and combat The blackbird's year, in Britain, may be said to start in February when the singing males begin to define their territories for the coming breeding season. This is not only accomplished through the exceptionally melodious medium of their song – used by the birds to announce their presence and continuing occupation of their territories – but also by physical displays.

These displays are particularly visible on a lawn, where two males may posture at each other for periods of ten or twenty minutes at a time. Often they never come to within a metre of each other but, just occasionally, physical warfare breaks out. Later in the season, when the adjacent males are both paired, such posturing (and even fights) may have extra protagonists – three or even four territories may meet on a lawn and the females may join in.

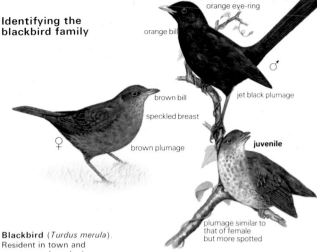

A long breeding season It often seems as if the blackbird breeding season extends from early April through to the end of May. This is indeed the time when they are at their most conspicuous, but many pairs already have a nest with eggs in the middle of March (or even earlier), and may continue with breeding attempts right through to July or even early August, provided the weather is suitable. Early broods are often quite successful for the predators, such as cats, jays, magpies and crows, which take such a toll on nests, are not yet active.

During April, when most species have started to nest, the blackbird's success is at its lowest (although clutch size is then at its highest); success is higher in May and June when there is plenty of cover for the birds to nest in.

The clutch of three to five (sometimes six) eggs is laid in a nest which, although it contains a layer of mud, is lined with grasses. The blackbird's eggs are a dull blue-green with reddish-brown speckling.

Incubation, carried out mainly by the female bird, lasts for about a fortnight from the laying of the penultimate egg, and the young are then fed – on worms and other animal food – at increasingly frequent intervals by both parents for two weeks before they fledge. This is their most vulnerable period for they are still unable to fly for up to 36 hours after fledging and are at the mercy of cats or any other predator able to withstand the brave and noisy attentions of the parent birds. The youngsters may be fed by their parents for a further three weeks – first by both and then later only by the male, as the female will already be sitting on her next clutch.

The annual moult At the end of the breeding season – which may be as early as mid-June in a dry year when the blackbirds are unable to find their food easily, or as late as mid-August in a wet summer – the adults undergo a complete moult to replace all their feathers. At the same time the partial moult of the juveniles takes place and, for a few weeks, the blackbirds, although still present, are not at all easy to see.

However, a little later they become much more conspicuous, particularly to anyone with an orchard and windfall apples or with ornamental shrubs bearing a good crop of berries. Although worms are readily taken at all times of the year, most of their food during the autumn and winter is fruit (where bird-table food is not being exploited).

Urban versus country populations Our own breeding blackbirds are mostly fairly sedentary, although ringing has shown some movement, particularly from northern and upland areas in winter. Indeed, it is certain that the majority of blackbirds hatched in Britain move no more than a kilometre or two from their natal territory throughout the whole of their lives. This has enabled detailed research to unravel the different pressures on different

Identifying the blackbird family

orange eye-ring

orange bill

brown bill

speckled breast

brown plumage

jet black plumage

♂

juvenile

plumage similar to that of female but more spotted

♀

Blackbird (*Turdus merula*). Resident in town and country gardens, hedgerows, woodland edges throughout the British Isles. 25cm (10in).

Right: An albino blackbird. This species seems to be prone to albinism, as many records show. The birds may be partially albino, with just a few white feathers here and there, or pure white, as here.

Below: A female blackbird sunbathing, with wings spread wide. Note the speckling on the breast. Blackbirds are one of the most common bird species of British gardens, on a par with the robin and the acrobatic blue tit.

Above: A juvenile blackbird – the body feathers of the young birds often have rich brown centres.

Left: A blackbird's nest (close to the ground) and the eggs. Unlike the nest of the song thrush (a close relative of the blackbird), which is just made of bare mud, this nest is lined with grasses. A clutch of three to five eggs is usual.

Below: A young blackbird in first-year plumage, with brown primary feathers.

populations of blackbirds.

In urban habitats it appears that adult blackbirds survive very well indeed – the food provided for them on bird-tables keeps them fit and healthy through even the coldest weather, and the experience of their first few years of life teaches them, as it does most urban birds, to avoid cats and cars. Their nests and eggs are, however, much more likely to be preyed upon or fail for other reasons and the few young that they raise have a difficult time surviving all the hazards of city life.

In the country, on the other hand, more young are produced by each breeding pair and they are able to survive better – which is just as well, for the overall adult mortality is higher in the country than it is in urban areas. This seems to be due largely to shortages of food during the winter – urban birds, which have access to more food, put on a greater amount of fat in hard weather to keep them going.

Since they are easy to observe, blackbirds are among the best species to keep notes on. For instance, if the birds in your garden are territorial, or possess distinguishing features, it is possible to list the feeding preferences of particular individuals.

Communal roosts During the winter, in particular, blackbirds spend their nights together in communal roosts. These are often at traditional sites and it has been shown that they chose areas which offer them shelter and safety from predators. The shelter enables them to conserve heat most efficiently, and gathering together in one roost may even serve the birds as an information exchange, so that those with sub-standard feeding sites are able to follow out those who know of the best feeding areas.

These roosting birds are not just the home-grown British population, for vast numbers of blackbirds from Germany, Denmark, Norway, Sweden, Poland and Finland come to Britain for the winter and join our own birds. Many British birds stay in their own home territories but, although some remain territorial, many tolerate visits from the foreign migrants. In the spring, when our own birds are just starting to breed and have already acquired their bright orange beaks, many of the migrants still sport their dull brown winter beak colour.

Albino blackbirds One feature of the blackbird species is that it is prone to albinism. There have been many records of pure white male blackbirds which still show the orange (or yellow) beak and eye-ring (and, in the albino, legs). Often the birds just show a few white feathers flecking the plumage, but this is sometimes neatly symmetrical and progressive – becoming more and more apparent year after year. The whiteness does not seem to put the birds at such a disadvantage that they get caught by cats or other predators, however. In some areas the albinism is transmitted genetically within the population, and pockets of partially albino birds persist for several years.

Blue and great tits

Blue and great tits (a great tit is shown below), delightful to watch as they peck away at food in the most awkward of positions, survive in spite of intense competition for nest sites, devastating predator attacks and near starvation in winter.

Blue and great tits, both colloquially known as tomtits, are popular garden birds which visit bird tables regularly in winter. Both are widespread throughout the British Isles and you'll see them in deciduous woodland, scrubland, hedgerows and farmland everywhere. The blue tit is an agile, aggressive, always excitedly active little bird which specialises in hanging at awkward angles to feed, while the great tit, larger than the blue and twice as heavy, often prefers to feed on the ground like a finch. Male and female blue tits are very similar in appearance. Among great tits a distinguishing feature between male and female is the black line which runs down the centre of their primrose-yellow breasts. This is faint in the female but very bold and wide in the male.

Seasonal foraging In summer blue tits feed mainly on insects, searching for them at the tips of twigs and shoots. In winter this diet is supplemented with occasional nuts and seeds. Since insects are neither active nor easily visible in winter, blue tits have to spend considerable time peering and probing round buds and under flakes of bark to find hibernating adults and larvae. If you observe the apparently aimless acrobatics of a blue tit through binoculars, you'll see that it is in fact purposefully searching every potentially rewarding nook and cranny.

In the garden the boldness and agility of blue tits as they attack peanuts hung in a plastic mesh sock is a delight to watch. They feed on almost everything put out on a bird table except bird seed, but above all they prefer nuts and fat.

Great tits eat much the same food as the blue, but take more vegetable food in winter – particularly seeds and nuts which have fallen to the ground. In fact, great tits are so fond of nuts that 'intelligence tests' have been devised where they demonstrate their inquisitiveness and learning ability by pulling up threads with a nut on the end, or prising open matchboxes to get at the nuts concealed inside.

Attacking milk bottles Sporadic outbreaks of tits pecking open the cardboard tops of milk bottles to drink the cream were first reported in the early 1930s. The habit rapidly spread to become nationwide – an excellent example of how quickly newly learnt skills can spread throughout a population. The post-war transition from cardboard to aluminium foil presented the tits with no problems, and in many rural areas milk bottles now have to be protected as a matter of routine.

Feeding for breeding The breeding season for great tits begins in late March and for blue tits in early April. To get into peak condition for egg laying as early as possible – earlier broods tend to be larger and healthier than later ones – the female must eat prodigiously. In the three weeks before laying begins, she puts on weight at an extraordinary rate, increasing her normal weight by at least a half and sometimes more. Then, over 10 or 12 days, she produces almost her own weight in eggs, laying one each day. This remarkable feat cannot be achieved by the female unaided; the male must feed her. You may well see a pair of tits side by side on a branch, the male offering his mate a beakful of caterpillars which she accepts with rapidly fluttering wings. This behaviour – called courtship feeding – may be essential if breeding is to be successful.

The female tit does all the nest-building, choosing a hole or crevice in a wall, tree or garden nestbox. The nest – a cup of moss, grass, wool, leaves, roots and spiders' webs – is lined with hair or feathers.

All eggs in one basket In summer, in deciduous woodland, both great and blue tits often rely heavily on just one species of insect as food for themselves and their young. In oak woods this is the winter moth which frequently produces huge numbers of caterpillars. The parent birds need to synchronise the maximum food demands of their young with the single, short-lived peak in the caterpillar food supply. They therefore produce a single large brood each year. This is unlike most other small birds which rear two or even three broods a year and thus have two or three chances if anything goes wrong. It is almost literally a case of the tits putting all their eggs in one basket!

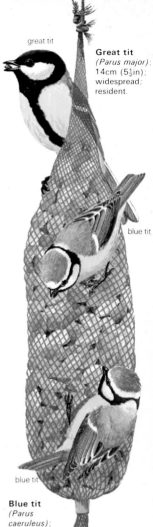

Great tit
(Parus major);
14cm (5½in);
widespread;
resident.

great tit

blue tit

blue tit

Blue tit
(Parus caeruleus);
11cm (4½in);
widespread;
resident.

Left: A blue tit in flight carrying food for its chicks.

Left: Tit attacks on milk bottles, first reported as isolated incidents in the 1930s, are now common all over the British Isles.

Above: Peanuts, which have high nutrional value, are a favourite food of garden-visiting tits.

Left: The aggressive little blue tit raises its cobalt blue crest and droops its wings in characteristic gestures that are both courtship and threat display.

One in ten survive In spring each breeding pair of tits is generally composed of one adult bird which bred the year before and is at least 21 months old, and one young bird which is about nine months old and breeding for the first time. One half of each breeding pair dies each year. For the population to remain steady, only one youngster would need to be reared per pair to replace the dead adult. On average, however, ten youngsters leave each nest in summer. This means that nine die by the following spring – a staggering 90% mortality rate. Gruesome though it sounds, this is an insurance against catastrophe and is quite usual in the bird world. Indeed, if one extra youngster per brood were to survive each year, the whole countryside would soon be overrun by hordes of tits eating up all available resources and precipitating a disastrous drop in the population.

Plenty of predators The high mortality rate is largely the result of natural causes, especially starvation, since inexperienced young birds have difficulty finding enough food in winter. Also, at the start of the season, competition for nesting holes is fierce. Larger birds such as the starling may oust tits from the bigger holes, and tit may oust tit from smaller ones. The larger great tit does not always succeed in evicting the smaller but more aggressive blue. Tree sparrows can squeeze through an entrance apparently only

Above: A parent blue tit bringing a caterpillar to its young. The nest is only relatively secure from predators. Weasels and woodpeckers take a large toll of eggs and young chicks every year.

Left: A clutch of great tit eggs. The blue tit's eggs are slightly smaller but very similar in colour. In both species the female incubates the eggs by herself for 12-16 days, often fed by the male while she is sitting on the nest.

Right: A brood of blue tit chicks in their down and feather-lined nest. The youngsters are fed by both parents and fledge in about 15-23 days.

just large enough for a blue tit, and often build their untidy nest on top of a clutch of tit eggs or, as tree sparrows are late nesters, even on top of a flourishing brood of chicks.

Predators also play a significant part in the high mortality rate, and may account for a third or more of the deaths. Great spotted woodpeckers have a taste for tit eggs and young and can easily open up a nest hole with their strong beak. Woodpeckers capitalize on the fact that well-grown tit chicks are alerted by a shadow falling across their nest hole and jump up to the entrance to grab the expected food from a returning parent. As soon as the unfortunate chicks appear, the woodpecker catches them. In the early days after fledging, the inexperienced youngsters may fall easy victims to hunting sparrow-hawks.

Strangely enough, wood mice and some-times voles climb trees readily and enjoy any eggs they happen to find. The prime predatory mammal, however, is the weasel, which can squeeze through the nest hole without much difficulty. Often the weasel will gorge on young birds to such an extent that it has to sleep off the meal until it slims down enough to squeeze out again. Weasel predation is particularly high in summers when the weather is poor and the young tits are underfed. The hungry chicks squeak noisily for more food and are heard by patrolling weasels on the look-out for prey.

Irruptions The general trend in tit numbers is more or less steady, but there are some fluctuations from year to year. Often, after a series of good summers and mild winters (especially on the Continent), mortality is lower than usual and consequently tit numbers far higher than average. In this situation, the sudden onset of a severe winter, or a shortage of natural food, produces a massive westward movement—called an irruption—as hungry birds move about in search of food. When these hordes cross the Channel, autumn numbers in the eastern counties of England reach spectacular levels. Strange reports sometimes appear of tits eating the putty round window frames and even entering houses and tearing strips of wallpaper off

Mixed flocking

Anyone walking in deciduous woods between August and March is likely to encounter a tit flock. These roving bands of birds operate from ground level to the top of the tree canopy, probing for food and flying from perch to perch. In late summer young willow warblers and chiffchaffs, fattening up before migration, may join the tits. Later goldcrests, nuthatches and chaffinches also turn up, as well as wrens and treecreepers. Wrens tend to search the ground for food, while treecreepers probe the tree trunk for concealed insects. The small coal and blue tits favour the ends of twigs high in the canopy, as do the even smaller warblers which hover in front of the twigs, picking off insects. Lower, on branches and trunk, you'll see great tits and nuthatches whose greater weight excludes them from the canopy. Great tits often feed with chaffinches on the woodland floor, picking up seeds and nuts. One advantage of mixed flocking is that a large group of birds has many eyes to watch for predators and give the alarm quickly. Another is that the trees are exploited for food on every level.

the walls. Irruptions occur irregularly, per-haps only once a decade.

Ringing results show that most of the birds in an irruption are of Continental origin, coming from as far away as eastern Poland. Winters in mainland Europe are generally more severe than in much of Britain and Ireland, so Continental blue and great tits migrate south and west in autumn to escape climatic hardship and to find easier feeding. British birds, on the other hand, tend to stay close to home, and, although they may roam around several parishes, rarely make journeys of more than 30 miles. Many establish a circuit of known good feeding spots and visit each in turn.

Nuthatch

Nuthatches look like small woodpeckers but, unlike
them, can walk down trees head first, and instead of
chiselling out grubs, they split open nuts,
or hunt for insects.

Although superficially similar to our wood-peckers in its choice of habitat and in its behaviour, the nuthatch is generally thought to be more closely related to the tits and tree-creepers. True, it climbs with great ease even on the trunk of the smoothest-barked beech tree, but the nuthatch's toes are arranged three forward, one back, as in the other families of birds within the passerine order, not two forward, two back as in the wood-peckers. It is also true that the nuthatch has a large, dagger-shaped beak just like a wood-pecker's, but this is the result of 'parallel evolution' (in other words it has evolved over the ages to do the same sort of work, but in a totally different bird), and the nuthatch lacks the extremely long tongue that the wood-peckers use to extract their insect food.

There are other, subtler differences. Wood-peckers always move head-up on a tree-trunk, leaning back on their stout tail feathers as if these were a shooting stick. But nuthatches can move with similar ease head-up, head-down, or horizontally across a trunk. Their tails are short, and the tail feathers are of normal shape, flexibility and toughness: only rarely do they come into contact with the bark at all, and nuthatches are able to rely on their strong claws alone to maintain their position on the trunk.

Nuthatches are attractive woodland birds, slightly more than sparrow-sized, neat but not gaudy. They are dove-grey above, white on the throat and the sides of the face, and a rich, cinnamon-tinged fawn on the belly. On each flank, and extending up under the wing, is a rich chestnut patch, considerably more extensive in area and darker in colour in the male than in the female, so with a little practice it is possible to separate the two sexes. The effective-looking beak leads to a striking long narrow black patch, running through the eye and backwards on to the nape.

Wing display When a nuthatch flies directly overhead, its underwing pattern becomes visible: the underwing is silvery white and grey, with a black blob beneath the carpal joint (equivalent to the wrist). In much the same way as kingfishers, nuthatches flick their wings open and shut while perched during display. The other feature of display is the song: a loud, clear and ringing trill in rapid tempo. Most other nuthatch calls are loud and clear, too, particularly the often-used metallic 'chwit-chwit' and piping 'twee'. They are at their noisiest in late winter and early spring, but once breeding gets under way they are much quieter, so much so that you might suspect that they had left the area.

Nuthatch distribution This is rarely the case, for nuthatches are among the most sedentary of our birds, rarely moving more than a mile or two from the area of their birth. Their distribution is an interesting one: over an area roughly south of a line from the Wirral to the Wash they are widespread—except in a few lowland areas, principally in Cambridge-

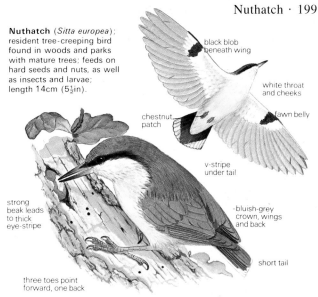

Nuthatch (*Sitta europea*); resident tree-creeping bird found in woods and parks with mature trees; feeds on hard seeds and nuts, as well as insects and larvae; length 14cm (5½in).

black blob beneath wing

white throat and cheeks

chestnut patch

fawn belly

v-stripe under tail

bluish-grey crown, wings and back

short tail

strong beak leads to thick eye-stripe

three toes point forward, one back

Above: The larger and harder nuts, such as acorns, beechmast, hazel cobs and chestnuts, are often carried in the nuthatch's beak and wedged in a crevice in the bark of a tree, or perhaps in a wall. The nut is then hammered and split open with the beak (right).

Opposite: At nest hole.

Below: The nuthatch's toes are arranged three forward, one back, unlike those of a woodpecker, two of which face forward, and two back

shire, which is probably because there are few suitable woodlands. North of this line, there is an outlying area, mostly in Yorkshire, where they occur, but very few other breeding records.

Their range seems to have contracted southwards, as the birds left their northern English haunts, during the 19th century, and at the same time it was noted that they had deserted the parks of central London and some other large urban areas. One suggestion is that this might have been due to increasing atmospheric pollution in industrial areas, reducing the insect food supply. This is borne out by the gap between the present-day Yorkshire outpost and the main area of distribution, this gap corresponding with the location of much of south Yorkshire's heavy industry. Other species sensitive to industrial pollution – such as the kingfisher – are also missing from this area.

Though well-distributed in Wales, the nuthatch is another of those birds (such as the tawny owl and the woodpeckers) whose complete absence from Ireland seems so puzzling. One possible explanation is that being sedentary birds, and having poor powers of long-distance flight, nuthatches were unable to reach Ireland during the recolonization period that followed the last Ice Age, before the rising seas formed what is now the Irish Sea and created an insuperable barrier.

Nuthatches are birds of mature, or even old, deciduous woodland; they sometimes occur in mixed deciduous and coniferous areas, but rarely in woodland that is predominantly coniferous. They particularly favour areas where beech, oak, sweet chestnut, hazel and hornbeam occur, for these provide winter food. Open parkland and, in many parts of England and Wales, large gardens with very old trees, also appear to be attractive to them.

Although the species is widespread within its area of distribution, the nuthatch is not a numerous bird in Britain. There are many sites that seem highly suitable, but where there are no nuthatches at all. Recent estimates put the number of pairs between

Above: Nuthatch eggs, resting on a bed of yew bark flakes. The usual clutch is of six to nine white eggs, heavily spotted with dark reddish brown. Occasional clutches of as many as 13 eggs may well be the product of more than one female.

Below: Both parents share in feeding the young, which fledge after about three weeks or rather longer if the weather at the time is poor. Like the tits, nuthatches produce only one brood.

10,000 and 20,000, which compares unfavourably with ten times that number of coal tits, but is roughly equal to the breeding population of the lesser spotted woodpecker and the long-eared owl.

Patient plasterwork The nest is built in a natural cavity, usually in a decaying broadleaved tree but sometimes in a little-used or deserted building. Most are within a few metres of the ground, but nests at least 20m (60ft) high are on record. Nuthatches take readily to nestboxes, but other, more extraordinary sites include disused woodpecker and sand martin holes, an old magpie nest and even a series (reported from Sussex) in haystacks. Neither the size of the cavity nor that of the entrance hole seem to influence their choice, and nuthatches have a habit – unique among British birds – of cementing up the entrance with mud until the hole is of the right size. When using nestboxes, they also plaster round the lid, from the inside.

Inside the cavity, the nest itself is also of a unique type. The eggs are laid on the floor of the cavity, on top of a layer of flakes of bark (especially of yew or larch if this is available), or of oak or other leaves. When the incubating bird (always the female) departs to feed or drink, she covers the eggs with similar debris, so on a superficial inspection the occupied nest looks like the long-deserted winter lodging of a field-mouse or dormouse.

Bullfinch

The bullfinch, one of our most beautiful garden birds, has a darker side, having earned a reputation as a wanton destroyer of buds on a variety of fruit trees.

The bullfinch is one of our most colourful garden birds, the male's rose-red breast contrasting strikingly with its blue-black chin, cap, wings and tail. In spite of all this colour, however, it is easy to miss a group of feeding bullfinches. Usually all you'll see is a brief glimpse of a white rump flitting along a hedgerow or darting off into the thick cover of scrub or woodland.

Efficient foragers Woodland, especially coniferous forest, is the bullfinch's preferred habitat, but it is a versatile bird both in choice of habitat and in the food it eats. Only the most open land, lacking in bushes and hedgerows, seems to be too bare. A bullfinch rarely moves more than a few miles from

Below: Both male and female birds feed the young. The nest—a platform of interwoven twigs—is easily recognisable, but take care not to visit it too often as you may alert eager predators.

home territory and is expert at seeking out the best food available in its local patch – even to the extent of choosing between different varieties of fruit trees. In gardens and orchards it eats the buds of numerous bushes and trees, especially those of forsythia, apple, pear and plum. The short, stubby bill is ideally suited to this food; it can strip the hard outer husks off seeds and buds with very little trouble.

Adult bullfinches are vegetarians, though they feed their nestlings on large quantities of insects and spiders, which are predigested and then regurgitated for the chicks. As the young grow, the parents start to include seeds in their diet, increasing the amount gradually,

Half-a-tree-a-bird-a-day

Bullfinches eat buds at a horrifying rate. Calculations on fruit farms show that one bird can eat half the buds of a pear tree in a single day. In fact, this only takes about $1\frac{1}{2}$ hours' feeding at a comfortable pace. Rates of 10 to 30 buds per minute are common, depending on the size and type of bud. Fortunately, most bullfinches depend on the seeds and buds of wild plants and only turn to fruit buds as the best alternative when wild supplies have failed.

At present there is no effective bullfinch deterrent which is economically viable. Assessing the cost of bullfinch damage is difficult, even when it is confined to single trees. Damage to plums and damsons is long-term, affecting the growth of the tree and, in subsequent years, the crop. Other fruit trees, notably pears and apples, can withstand substantial bud loss without loss of crop and, though damaged, often produce larger fruit.

The male offers his mate a beakful of twigs as part of the courtship display; bill caressing is another part of their ritual.

until by the time the young leave the nest they are fed almost entirely on seeds. Throughout the summer and until late autumn bullfinches eat a huge variety of seeds – anything from minute grass seeds to the ash keys which hang in inviting bunches and are one of the bullfinch's favourite food.

From December onwards bullfinches eat tree and shrub buds; these contain next year's leaf and flower growth and are very nutritious. Unlike other finches, bullfinches don't have to search ground covered by leaves or snow to find fallen seeds or berries. They husk buds on the tree, leaving a scattering of litter which leads some people to think that they are vandals – destroying but not eating the buds. Many garden plants and commercially grown trees and bushes, cultivated for their early flowering or fruiting capacity, produce large flower buds that swell early in the year when the wild equivalents – hawthorn and blackthorn – are much smaller. Because of the damage done to orchards in southern England, the bullfinch has been removed from the protected bird list in some counties and many are now trapped or shot.

Busy breeding season The bullfinch is one of the many birds which overproduce young each summer to ensure that some survive winter to breed the following year. This is perhaps one of the main reasons why trapping and shooting, even on a large scale, does not seem to have affected the British population.

Above: The juvenile bird does not have the glossy black cap of the adult, nor the rose-red breast. By the end of the year, however, this bird's pale bill will have darkened and it will have a thick, waterproof coat of feathers to protect it through the winter.

Left: Male bullfinch in all the glory of full spring breeding plumage.

Bullfinch (*Pyrrhula pyrrhula*); length from beak to tail 15cm (5¾in); distribution widespread in woodland, plantations, hedgerows and gardens; absent from Isle of Man. Resident.

Most pairs of bullfinches rear two broods of about four nestlings a season; some pairs even manage to fit three broods into a nesting season lasting from late April to August or even September, despite the fact that over half the broods started do not survive. Efficient predators such as jays, magpies, stoats, weasels and cats often find even the best concealed nests and eat the eggs or nestlings. For this reason the bullfinch builds its nest—a distinctive platform of twigs bearing a cup of fine roots lined with hair—in a thick, prickly, inaccessible bush or hedge. The pale blue eggs, dotted with reddish spots at the blunt end, are conspicuous. However, the hen bullfinch with body feathers in a combination of pink, grey, buff and brown, is well camouflaged for sitting on the nest.

Only the hen builds the nest and incubates the eggs. Incubation starts in earnest when the last egg is laid so that they all hatch together—usually on the thirteenth day. Both parents feed the young. While the nestlings are being fed, visits to the nest are kept to a minimum. The parents develop special cheek pouches in the summer and cram them with food to bring back to the young. They sneak silently into the bush together so predators don't follow them to the hidden nest. Because the cheek pouches hold so much food, the youngsters need feeding only every half-hour or so. The young spend 12-18 days in the nest. After this the adults abandon them

and start a new nest.

At this stage you can identify the young bullfinches by the absence of black on the head but from July onwards each bird moults, replacing all its fluffy juvenile body feathers.

Serenades and songs Bullfinches sing most often during the breeding season. Not many people have heard the song because it is very quiet—a soft, pleasant mixture of short, clear piping notes and hoarse wheezes which the cock seems to reserve for his mate. With feathers fluffed, head bobbing up and down and tail cocked to one side, he serenades her to secure the firm pair-bond necessary for successful breeding. More frequently you can hear the short, plaintive, carrying whistle which is used to contact others of the same species. This happens particularly in winter, when several birds—possibly a family party—may flock together where food is to be found. The call has many variations and is sometimes repeated three or four times as a second type of song. The finely tuned ear of the bullfinch can almost certainly recognise individuals by their particular accent—something which must be particularly useful when recently fledged young are still being cared for by their parents. From March onwards, except when the hens are incubating their clutch of eggs, you can often see bullfinches in pairs. It seems from the evidence of ringing that some pairs may well mate for life.

Chaffinch and brambling

The chaffinch, our commonest finch, has a breeding population in the millions. Its close relative, the brambling, visits our woodlands for the winter.

The chaffinch is the most widespread and numerous British finch, and one of the most numerous of all British and Irish birds, especially in winter when our resident chaffinches are augmented by extra millions of European birds. Estimates of our breeding population made during the last 40 years have

ranged between four and seven million pairs. The species is ubiquitous throughout the British and Irish mainlands, but uncommon in the Hebridean Islands, the Orkneys and Shetland.

White wing bars The summer plumage of the male chaffinch is unmistakable: a deep wine-pink breast contrasts with a dove-grey crown and nape and a black forehead, a russet mantle and dark blackish-brown wings and tail. White feathers are visible at each side of the tail, even when it is tightly closed; but perhaps the most conspicuous recognition feature of all is the double white wing bar. The two bars are as clearly visible on the perched bird as in flight. The foremost white bar covers the 'shoulder' (the wrist in human terms) of the closed wing in a broad white patch; behind this, the greater coverts carry a more slender stripe.

These striking wing markings are also seen on the female, which is otherwise clad in a mixture of browns and beiges for camouflage. In winter, the male too is more sombre in

Above: Chaffinches usually raise only one brood each year, and begin their nesting activities in late April or early May. The nest is one of the most neatly constructed, and well concealed, of all our birds' nests. The basic structure is of moss, with a framework of grass and rootlets. The outside of the nest is usually ornamented with lichen or flakes of white bark taken from birch trees, if the nest happens to be in or near one of these

Right: The cup is lined with soft hair or feathers, and usually contains 4 or 5 eggs, but occasionally nests with as many as 8 are found. The eggs are whitish blue, marked with dark purplish-brown spots and squiggles.

plumage, when subtle camouflage among the stubble is more important than the bright colours of display. At all times of year, both sexes have a grass-green rump patch, which is particularly noticeable when you see the birds taking off.

Chaffinch song Chaffinches start to sing early in the year: from February onwards in the south (later in the north) their boisterous song can be heard in almost any part of the countryside. It consists of a long descending trill with a final swashbuckling flourish. One of the most intriguing questions of bird song is how such complicated and often beautifully melodious phrases are passed on from one generation to the next.

Recent research at Cambridge University has gone some way towards unravelling this mystery in the case of the chaffinch. The Cambridge experiments suggest that the basic framework of the song is inherited, for it is produced 'automatically' even by a young male chaffinch reared in total isolation. In the wild a young male, possessing these instinctive foundations of song, listens to his elders and gradually develops the quality, and the trills and flourishes, of his full song. In such a way, local 'dialects' develop: West Country chaffinches, for example, sound as different as their human counterparts do to a visitor from, say, London.

Woodland bird Chaffinches are essentially woodland birds, but they inhabit a wide range of different types of woodland. The densest populations are normally found in mature broadleaved woodland, especially oak with wide glades, but most other types of woodland (including the darkest and densest Norway spruce) support chaffinches, as do scrubland, farmland, parks and gardens. In remote areas in the north and west, it seems that even a clump of weatherbeaten trees or

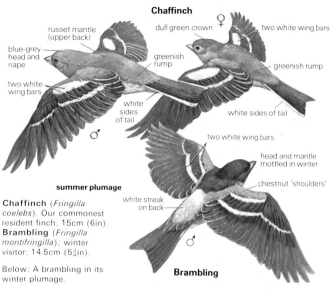

Chaffinch (*Fringilla coelebs*). Our commonest resident finch; 15cm (6in).
Brambling (*Fringilla montifringilla*); winter visitor; 14.5cm (5¾in).

Below: A brambling in its winter plumage.

bushes is sufficient to encourage a chaffinch pair to take up residence. In winter, many forsake woodland and join other finches, sparrows and buntings on farmland, especially where plenty of cereal or weed seeds are available.

Varied diet In summer the diet is very varied, not having such a high seed content as that of most finches. It includes small snails and worms, various fruits and seeds, and often aphids gathered high in the woodland canopy. For the first few days after the young have hatched, chaffinches feed their brood mostly on insects, and their beaks, relatively long-pointed and slender for finches, are suitable both for this and for the small seeds that they also tend to select. In winter, foraging is done more often on the ground than in the treetops, and seeds tend to predominate.

The brambling Bramblings breed from northern Scandinavia eastwards into Siberia. Their chief breeding habitats are birch woodland and the mixed woodland fringes of large expanses of coniferous forest. In winter they

migrate south to the Mediterranean and west to Britain and Ireland.

Like the chaffinch, the brambling has white wing bars: these are much less bold than those of the chaffinch, and are not always visible when the bird is on the ground, though they can be seen clearly when it is in flight. When flying, the brambling shows a more mottled upper surface than the chaffinch, with a conspicuous white patch on the rump, which is its best identification feature. It contrasts strongly with the green rump of the chaffinch.

On the ground in winter, the mottled plumage is good for camouflage, but a close view reveals the orange breast of both male and female, the all-brown or blackish-brown heads, and the orange-buff shoulder patch of the male, all of which help to separate the brambling from the chaffinch. As winter progresses into spring, the mottled blackish

Above: A female chaffinch. At all times of year, in flight or on the ground, the common chaffinch call is 'pink, pink' – the basis of the Dutch name for the species, 'fink', and indeed the English word finch. This same call, more stridently produced, is used as an alarm, to warn, for example, of the approach of a jay or the presence of a roosting owl.

Left: A male chaffinch in the snow, towards the end of winter. In winter, his plumage is less vivid than in summer. After the autumn moult, most of the newly grown body feathers have broad buff fringes. As winter proceeds into spring, the fringes wear off, revealing the beauty of his plumage beneath – in time for the spring display. In this bird, the fringes are almost worn away, but still dull the full brilliance of the plumage.

brown head and mantle of the male brambling become glossy black as the paler feather fringes wear away, and he comes into his breeding plumage, which we are only rarely lucky enough to see.

The male's plumage is much more striking than his song, which is a metallic, poorly formed jumble of 'dwee' calls and chirrups. Bramblings have several flight calls – a low-pitched 'chuck-chuck-chuck' and, more characteristically, a hoarse 'zweek' and a metallic 'dwee' which rises in inflection as it ends.

An irregular visitor As a winter visitor, the brambling is irregular in the extreme. In most years there are a few bramblings scattered throughout Britain, but occasionally (and normally in years when there has been a very heavy crop of beech mast) numbers are much higher. The erratic nature of brambling migration is largely responsible for this. Instead of adopting a routine pattern of autumn and spring migrations to and from regularly used wintering areas, bramblings move to wherever their food is easily found.

This means that birds wintering in Britain one year may be found (say) in northern Italy or Yugoslavia the next. Most arriving migrants reach our east coast – often in company with Continental chaffinches – in October and early November; in years of low numbers they may not even reach the West Country. The return journey usually starts during March.

Beech mast is an important component of the winter diet, which also includes a few late berries and many seeds. Bramblings are usually seen foraging on the ground under a large area of mature, widely spaced and heavily cropping beeches; otherwise they can be found with other finches and buntings in weed-grown fields, stubbles, and around feeding places for farm livestock, where seeds have dropped from hay and straw.

The only positive British breeding record of bramblings was in 1920 in northern Scotland, but recently there have been several instances indicative of breeding elsewhere in Britain. These suggest that the brambling may follow two other Scandinavian birds, the fieldfare and the redwing, and establish regular breeding colonies.

Which are our commonest breeding birds?

The most reliable guide at the moment is the B.T.O.'s survey of 1968-72. Although this is now over a decade old, the populations of the birds referred to here happen to be generally stable ones, which means that the overall picture still applies today. Another point to remember is that populations of some of the species mentioned here rise in winter. The highest breeding population of all is that of the wren, estimated at 10 million pairs or more. After this the picture is a little confusing, for estimates can only be rough and include guesswork, however well informed. The blackbird probably takes second place, with a firm estimate of seven million pairs. However, the chaffinch population is estimated at between four and seven million pairs, as is that of the starling. Coming in the middle of this range are the less vague figures of around five million pairs each of robins, dunnocks and blue tits. The house sparrow's possible range of three and a half to seven million pairs may place it among the highest populations.

Goldfinch

With a broad yellow band stretching across its wings, the goldfinch lives up to its name. Parents and young birds feed in family groups attractively called 'charms'.

It is not just the yellowy gold patch along the wings that makes the goldfinch instantly recognisable. The red, white and black striped head pattern is also unmistakable. The tail and rest of the wings are black, with delicate white markings. In spring look for the white tips to each wing feather – by the end of the summer when the feathers are nearly a year old they have often worn away. In flight

you can see the goldfinch's whitish rump, similar to that of a bullfinch or brambling. A warm buff-coloured back and flank feathers complete the bird's neat and tidy appearance.

Seed-eaters Thistles are the goldfinch's most important food plant. It eats the seeds from mid-summer through to autumn, and even in winter if they are still available. Often the goldfinch prefers the easy pickings of seed heads that have fallen to the ground, and leaves the seeds that remain on the plants. These then provide a useful reserve of food when snow covers the ground.

During the summer months, the goldfinch's diet includes a variety of other seeds as they ripen, though it prefers those from plants in the daisy family, for example groundsel, dandelion, ragwort and sowthistle early in the summer, hardheads in August, and later still burdock which is an important winter food. The goldfinch is the only bird able to reach the seeds buried in the depths of teasel flower heads; in fact, these seeds are eaten mainly by the male goldfinch which has a slightly longer beak than the female.

Above: Most finches have wing bars, but none are as large and striking as those of the goldfinch. The bright yellow patch is obvious even on perched birds. The goldfinch's scientific name comes from *carduelis* the latin for thistle. The seeds of this plant are the bird's favourite food.

Goldfinch *(Carduelis carduelis)*, 18cm (7in) from beak to tip of tail. The two sexes are almost identical in colour and size, and there is no distinct winter or summer plumage. Although not thought of as migratory, about three-quarters of British goldfinches leave here usually in October.

There is, however, a risk factor: sadly, goldfinches occasionally get trapped by the powerful hooked seed heads of these plants, and die.

Versatile feet The goldfinch uses its feet to hold food while it eats – something that few other birds can do. From a firm perch, the feeding bird pulls a thin seed-bearing stem with its beak and places it under its feet to hold the stem steady while eating the seeds.

A trick commonly taught to goldfinches in the sixteenth century – caught and caged for their colourful plumage and song – involved a repetition of this pull and hold procedure. The birds could only get food and water by pulling the strings of a cart, without letting go, and drawing the cart up a slope.

Song-flights The goldfinch has a pleasant, canary-like, twittering song. You can hear the song throughout the year, but the bird sings most regularly from March to July, either from a perch or in flight. In a display above his territory, the male has a rather hesitant song-flight with deep, slow wing-beats and spread tail. Like other finches, the normal flight is undulating; during this flight the goldfinch often repeats a characteristic 'stickelitt' call.

Building a nest Goldfinch territories are usually small, and several pairs may nest together in a loose colony. The swaying outer branches of large trees, bushes and tall

Above: Goldfinches have long, narrow tweezer-like beaks that can prise open prickly seed heads to extract seeds that other birds cannot reach. Equipped with relatively short, stout legs, goldfinches are acrobatic birds, clinging to swaying plants like tits.

Left: Both parents feed the nestlings on regurgitated seeds and a few insects, often collected some distance away. The mother normally produces two broods a season. The earliest chicks leave the nest in June. In years when the summer is warm and dry and food is abundant, breeding continues into August or even September, enabling a third brood to be raised.

hedges might seem precarious for a nest, but the goldfinches favours such sites. In a garden the bird often chooses a fruit tree for a nest site, but there are no hard and fast rules—anything from a full-grown horse chestnut to ivy on a wall will do.

The nest, immaculately neat and compact, and deep enough to retain the eggs and chicks in windy conditions, is bound firmly to branches with spiders' webs. Rootlets, dead grass, hair and wool are the usual nesting materials, while wool and fluff from ripe seeds, especially sallow catkins, are used to make a soft, warm lining. The goldfinch may attach moss and lichen to the outside of the nest. Occasionally these birds make use of unusual nesting materials. A few years ago, at East Malling Research Station in Kent, one pair of goldfinches carefully untied plastic labels from trees, and used them to decorate their nest.

Both adults fly to and fro together during construction of the nest, but only the female builds—the male watches her. The female lays about five or six eggs and does all the incubating. The male has the task of collecting food for himself and his mate at this time so the female need leave the nest only to stretch her legs, to drink or to preen. The eggs take nearly two weeks to hatch, and the young can fly in two to three weeks.

Safety in numbers Like other finches, goldfinches are gregarious; breeding pairs and family parties flock together in places where food is plentiful, in groups given the attractive name 'charms'. This enables young birds to learn where to find food, and offers some protection by virtue of the group's large numbers—many pairs of eyes spot danger more easily than one.

Many parents and young birds leave Britain, migrating to their wintering grounds in Holland, Belgium, western France, Spain and Portugal. Until the end of the nineteenth century, many were trapped on the south coast of England as they migrated. Trappers used a cage with an automatic trap door called a *chardonneret*—from the French for goldfinch.

World-wide distribution The absence of goldfinches from much of Scotland and their scarcity in northern England, despite the presence of suitable habitats, suggests that the climate in these areas is unfavourable to the birds. Their natural range extends throughout much of Europe, to western Asia and North Africa, but not much further north than southern Sweden.

Attempts to introduce the species to several states in North America have failed, perhaps because of competition from the native American goldfinch. Nevertheless, it was successfully introduced to Bermuda, Australia, Tasmania and New Zealand—perhaps too successfully in the latter case, where it has become something of a pest on strawberry farms, nipping seeds from the ripe fruits.

Above: Until they moult in the autumn, the young goldfinches have pale heads without the red and white pattern of their parents. The young birds also have streaks on their back and flanks, and have the same wing-bars as the adults.

Right: The smooth, finely spotted eggs are laid in nests usually 4-15m (13-50ft) above ground. Despite these often dangerous heights, the deep nest provides ample security.

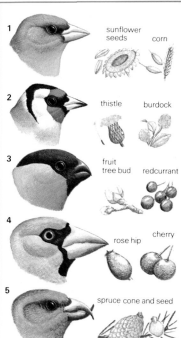

Fitting the bill

The **greenfinch (1)** with its 'general purpose' seed-eating bill tackles small seeds like those of chickweed and groundsel, or larger seeds such as bramble, sunflower and corn.

A long, thin tweezer-like bill enables the **goldfinch (2)** to delve into the prickly seed heads of thistles and teasels.

The short, round bill of the **bullfinch (3)** is sharp at the edges—ideal for nipping off and then peeling buds. Only the **hawfinch (4)** with its strong skull and jaw muscles can crack open the large hard seeds of cherries and damsons. These are held between special pads in the massive bill, and crushed slowly—the beak exerts over 45kg (100lb) of pressure. The upper and lower parts of the **crossbill's (5)** beak twist and cross. This is effective for prising open the scales of spruce and pine cones—the bird then uses its long tongue to scoop out the seeds.

1 sunflower seeds · corn

2 thistle · burdock

3 fruit tree bud · redcurrant

4 rose hip · cherry

5 spruce cone and seed

Hawfinch

The hawfinch–a large species of finch–is equipped with a disproportionately large bill which can exert as much power as can a man with a pair of pliers. Cautiously concealing its movements in the foliage of tall trees, it presents a unique challenge to the most patient of birdwatchers.

Below left: A female hawfinch–less colourful than the male–on a low garden wall. The habitat of this species ranges from mature deciduous woodland, which is its commonest haunt, to mixed woodland, large parks, and gardens with trees. Hawfinches can even occupy scrubland areas that have a few trees. In winter and spring they frequent cherry, plum and damson orchards.

Hawfinch distribution

Above: Our hawfinch population is estimated at about 10,000 pairs. Most of them are in central and south-east England, where woods with hornbeam trees are plentiful.

Below: The normal hawfinch clutch is of 4-6 eggs, buff or blue in ground colour with various darker blobs and squiggles adorning them. Most clutches are laid in May, and incubated by the female alone for 11-13 days. Both parents feed the youngsters after hatching, and they fledge a fortnight later.

To see the hawfinch, our largest and most spectacular species of finch, is regarded by ornithologists as a considerable achievement. Despite its size, this bird is extremely secretive and normally very quiet, betraying its presence in the neighbourhood only by a series of 'tick' calls–sounding a little like those of the robin.

It feeds both on the ground (where you are most likely to get a chance to see it) and in the trees, but if disturbed on the ground it flies up into dense cover, often being so wary that half an hour may pass before the first individuals drop down from the branches and cautiously begin to feed again.

Stocky outline Slightly smaller than a song thrush, the hawfinch is a stocky bird. In flight it has a characteristic heavy-headed, short-tailed appearance. Its flight path is steeply undulating, with a brief burst of wing-flaps followed by a glide rather like the flight of a woodpecker. Also reminiscent of a woodpecker are the conspicuous broad white wing-bars, clearly visible from above or below. The white flashes on either side of the stumpy tail

are very noticeable in flight.

On the ground, the first feature that catches the eye is the enormous head and beak, which seem out of proportion to the rest of the bird. The head is pale chestnut in the male, drab brown in the female–in both cases set off from the rich rufous-brown back by a grey or fawn collar. Both sexes have a black

'mask' round the base of the beak and a large black bib. The massive beak, slightly larger in the male than the female, is silver-grey with black edges and a black tip. Shaped like a triangular pyramid, it may be as much as 18mm ($\frac{3}{4}$in) long, wide and deep.

The belly and flanks are rich buff, and against them the wings appear dark, almost black. A close view reveals that the outer flight feathers are grey-brown, but they are largely concealed by the inner feathers that overlie them. These have a rich purplish sheen and peculiar splayed ends, almost like old-fashioned curled moustaches. They are thought to play a part during courtship display. The white wingbar is clearly visible on the folded wing, shaded with brown or chestnut. The legs are pale yellowish-brown, and the eyes have a most unusual marbled pink iris surrounding the dark pupil, particularly in the male.

Young birds are altogether drabber, with a yellow-washed appearance and speckled slightly on the belly and flanks. After they moult in August and September of their first year, they become difficult to distinguish from the adults.

Calls and songs By far the best way to spot hawfinches regularly is to become familiar with their call. This is the sound the birds make at all times of year for such purposes as maintaining contact or warning of approaching danger.

The hawfinch makes its call both in flight and when perched, so it is advisable to look both up *and* around. Although the call has much in common with that of a robin or song thrush, the 'tick' or 'tchick' is rather more abrupt and clicking than in either of the other two species. A good way of learning to make the distinction without error is to gain access to a recording. Several of these are available through specialist shops or the main ornithological societies such as the RSPB or the British Trust for Ornithology.

The song, however, is an entirely different matter. This sound, usually more musical or attractive than the call, is made at a specific time of year—the breeding season—and its purpose is to advertise territory and attract a mate. There are few, if any, good recordings of the hawfinch song, partly because the birds are so shy and difficult to approach, and partly because it is so quietly uttered. Produced from March to May, it is a hesitant but tuneful jangle, perhaps most reminiscent of the song of the goldfinch.

A widespread bird Despite these difficulties in seeing hawfinches, recent surveys on a county and national scale have shown them to be quite widespread across England and southern Scotland. The major concentrations, perhaps associated with the distribution of one of their favourite foods—hornbeam seeds—are in central and south-east England, while the records fall off rapidly in Wales and the West Country. There are few records from

chestnut head

rufous brown back

white tail flashes

Juvenile

short tail

two wing bars

crescent markings on belly

black mask

grey collar

head and beak are unusually large

young birds have a yellower appearance

Ireland and none breed there today, though one pair did nest in County Kildare in 1902.

Recent estimates suggest that the population may amount to about 10,000 pairs. From such historical records as there are–mostly associated with hawfinch attacks on cherry crops–it appears that they were restricted to the south-east until the middle of the 19th century, when an expansion phase began to give hawfinches their present-day distribution pattern.

Feeding hawfinches The presence of feeding hawfinches in an orchard is given away in winter by large numbers of neatly split fruit stones on the ground. During the summer, look for shredded pea pods, another favourite food. As with several other finches, insects feature considerably in the diet of the nestlings, but at other times they eat a wide variety of seeds, ripe and unripe, from herbaceous plants, shrubs and trees. Like bullfinches, hawfinches also turn to buds of both wild and orchard trees.

Among the seeds they eat are the kernels of wild and orchard cherries, sloes, damsons and other plums, and beech and hornbeam

A hawfinch secondary or inner-wing flight feather. At the tip, one corner protrudes in a triangle and the other is cut away in a neat curve. The feather has a blue-green sheen.

Hawfinch (*Coccothraustes coccothraustes*). Our largest finch species. Resident in woodland, especially in fruit-growing areas. Length 16.5cm (6$\frac{1}{2}$in).

Below: Hawfinches often visit puddles to bathe and drink.

Greenfinch

The greenfinch is the largest of a trio of British finches with partly green plumage (the others are the siskin and the rare serin). It is one of our more numerous birds, being well suited to our lowland countryside with its mosaic-like pattern of woods, farmland, hedgerows, thickets and gardens.

Above: A pair of greenfinches (the male is on the right) with four young. In the past, these birds were often caught and caged—such birds used to be called 'green linnets'.

Below: A male greenfinch (right) with a juvenile (left) at water. The juveniles are much less highly coloured than the adults. Many have brown streaks on their plumage, like sparrows.

The greenfinch is one of the most widespread and abundant visitors to bird-tables in Britain and Ireland. It is sometimes disparaged by birdwatchers who are captivated by the acrobatic feats of the blue and great tits as they hang on to strings of nuts. The greenfinch, being a relatively large finch, is not a particularly acrobatic feeder although, in many areas, it has learned to feed on hanging nuts. Some people actually overlook its presence since it is similar in size to the ubiquitous house sparrow, and many greenfinches have rather little yellow or green on their plumage, which strengthens the resemblance.

The adult male greenfinch is a handsome bird, with brilliant yellow flashes on the wings and tail—most obvious when in flight—and washes of green and greenish yellow over the rest of the plumage. The females, and the young of either sex, are less highly coloured, with much brown streaked plumage—like a sparrow's. (In recent years another much smaller finch, the siskin, has also taken to

feeding in gardens, mostly at the end of winter, but there is little chance of the two being confused.)

Habitat and range As with many of our garden and farmland bird species, greenfinches are naturally birds of the woodland edge, finding hedges in arable land, and shrubberies in parks and gardens, ideal places for breeding. They can be found over most of Europe, spreading into Asia in the east and to north Africa in the south, but they are absent from the far northern parts of Europe and Asia, which lack trees or shrubs. Many areas in Britain have reported recent spreads in the breeding range and local increases in numbers.

Seed eaters Greenfinches feed on seeds for almost all their lives. In the autumn the flocks of young birds, which are soon joined by the adults, may become very numerous, with some numbering in the thousands. These large flocks are sometimes seen feeding on ripening corn, gleaning the stubbles or feasting on weed seeds in root crops or on waste ground. Their weight generally precludes feeding from seeds still held on the plants, but they are adept at finding seeds on the ground. They can live well on open ploughed land, finding dormant seeds which may, in some cases, be several years old.

The weeds particularly favoured include charlock, persicaria, groundsel, chickweed and fat hen. When a large flock has found a good feeding site, it is quite possible to hear the birds from thirty or forty yards away – not from their calls but from the cracking of seeds in their bills. All the food is first manoeuvred in the bird's beak to remove the husk, for greenfinches only eat the central nutritious part.

Autumn and winter The autumn flocks frequently contain other finch species, but during the evening the greenfinches tend to roost on their own. The roosting site is often a clump of rhododendrons, laurels or an old hedge with plenty of holly or ivy. The birds prefer roosting sites which are not particularly high, but have plenty of thick cover. Ringing results have shown that the birds move regularly from roost to roost and that, in general, they are a mobile and 'nomadic' species. There are not many indications of movements over 200 or 300km (120-180 miles) within the British population, but many birds from the northern part of the European range travel 1000km (600 miles) or more each autumn and spring.

Cold winter weather is not a serious threat to survival – provided that the feeding grounds are clear of snow. If the weather is very cold and the day-length is very short, they may find it difficult to take in sufficient food to see them through the night. In such circumstance, and during snowy weather, many more may join the flocks feeding in gardens.

Human help Greenfinches visiting gardens take almost any sort of seed. Hemp, peanuts (loose on the ground or hanging) and par-

olive green head and back

yellow tail flashes

yellow edges of primaries

summer plumage

brownish green head and back

wing and tail markings are less vivid than in male

♀

♂

grey wings with yellow flashes

yellow underparts

♂

ticularly sunflower seeds are favourites. As with many species observed at feeding stations, the numbers seen at any instant in a garden are a tiny proportion of all the individual birds using the site through the whole winter.

As many garden bird feeders know, the number of greenfinches seen in gardens reaches a peak in March and April, and many are still present in early May. Ringing returns show that this is the period when more greenfinches die in the wild than at any other time of year. This is easily explained, for the birds have been exploiting a stock of seeds which has not been replenished naturally since the autumn. The food supply has thus

The song flight

conspicuously beating wings

The spring display of the greenfinch includes an interesting song flight. The male performs a circular flight over his territory, flapping his wings in an exaggerated and noticeable manner.

Greenfinch distribution

Greenfinch (*Carduelis chloris*). Resident in Britain and Ireland; partial migrant on the Continent. Habitats include woodland edges, gardens, shrubberies and farmland. 14.5cm (5¾in).

Left: Nesting begins in late April or early May. With six eggs, this is a good clutch for greenfinches; many have only four.

Above: A male greenfinch in flight. The two flight (and contact) calls are 'chup, chup, chup' and 'chit-chit-chit-chit-chit'. When the bird is seen in flight the yellow wing patches and tail edges are conspicuous.

Below: A greenfinch bathing in a stream. Note the stout body (even allowing for the fluffed-out feathers) and the clear pink beak.

six eggs are generally laid in each clutch and incubated for two weeks. The chicks are fed on insects for the first few days, but soon the diet is changed to regurgitated seeds. Two or three broods are often raised by a single pair, and young may sometimes be found in the nest as late as September.

Countless hazards In ideal conditions, the two or three broods raised by a single pair of greenfinches could be expected to produce a total of about 20 birds where there had been only two at the beginning. Nature is not in fact so profligate, for although a highly successful pair may be able to produce three large broods, the great majority of breeding attempts actually fail.

Failure arises in many ways—lack of food may cause starvation, one of the adults may die or be killed, or a predator may find the nest and eat the eggs or young. Apart from these dangers, the eggs might be infertile, the nest may be blown out of its bush or the bush may be destroyed during agricultural or gardening work.

In any case, the production of eggs and the successful fledging of young is not the end of the parents' responsibility, for they also have to look after the young birds, out of the nest, for a period of ten days or more, while they learn about the world and how to find food for themselves.

Resilient population Besides all the difficulties that they have to face at breeding time, greenfinches are affected by wide variations in winter weather conditions from year to year. Despite this, the British breeding population, as shown by the Common Birds Census index, has remained constant over the last 20 years. The two cold winters in 1961-62 and 1962-63 probably halved the population, but it had returned to an average level by 1966.

Since then it has varied by less than 10%, either way, except in 1975 when it was rather higher than normal. These figures are based on observations made on farmland—probably the habitat holding the most stable populations. The figures relating to woodland are based on a smaller sample and show a rather greater fluctuation. The highest woodland population they indicated was in 1966.

The prospects for this attractive bird look excellent, with range expansions being reported during the present century. These have occurred in western areas, where the birds were formerly absent, and also in city centre areas. The most serious problem which they are likely to face arises from the increasing use of herbicides in cereal growing and other farming. If the trend continues, the range of species of weeds which are able to seed and thus produce natural winter feeding for the birds may be reduced. On current evidence, it seems likely that human bird-lovers will more than make up for the deficiency, with the plentiful supplies of seeds and peanuts that they put out for the birds in their gardens.

run out, and continued feeding—by people who put out food for birds in their gardens—is particularly important.

The breeding season During the spring, the males start to give their 'dreeeez' summer call. When displaying, they precede this by a rather weak, chattering song. Displaying males may sing and call from the top of a tree or bush, or may advertise their presence in a characteristic song-flight. In most cases several pairs take up territories close together, each male defending only a small area round the chosen nest site.

The nest is built of twigs, roots and moss in late April or early May, and is lined with fine grass, roots, hair, wool or feathers. Four to

Skylark and woodlark

The skylark is recognisable for its sustained song as it flies in a broad sweep high over open ground. The rarer woodlark sings as it spirals upwards, its distinctive song a rich and beautiful melody.

The woodlark and skylark have very different distributions within the British Isles. To see a woodlark on any but a few lowland heaths in southern England is enough to turn an ordinary day's bird-watching into a red-letter day. On the other hand, the skylark is the characteristic bird of open country and, according to the BTO's field-work completed in 1972, it is undoubtedly the most widespread breeding bird in Britain and Ireland.

The skylark's brown plumage serves as a good camouflage for the bird when it is in the open ground it prefers. Unlike most birds, it sings on the wing, marking out its territory on the ground by circling and singing above it. Its song, which includes mimicry of the notes

Woodlarks are rare birds and the total British population may now number only 150-200 pairs. They are specially protected under the first schedule of the Bird Protection Acts; they only breed in dry areas of heathlands or downlands.

Woodlark (*Lullula arborea*), 15cm (6in) long from beak to tail. Migrant.

Bird song

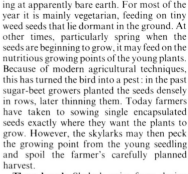

skylark

woodlark

The skylark (right) is famed for its habit of soaring high in the sky, rising and descending repeatedly, all the time pouring out a torrent of song. The woodlark (far right) has a circular song-flight and its song is mellow-toned. Both birds also sing from song-posts. A singing bird is advertising itself. It is proclaiming that it owns a territory and warning its neighbours that it is around. Birds also sing to find a mate. Females may be attracted to a particular type of songster and, with many species, the unpaired male sings a different song from the male with a mate. Winter song is rare in most birds as there are few species that defend their territories or pair up then.

Below: The eggs of the skylark hatch after 11 days incubation, and the young remain in the nest for 8-10 days. Then, although they are not yet able to fly, they leave it and move around in the grass. At this stage their bodies are well feathered, but their wings are not yet grown and they still retain some down.

of other birds, is a familiar and attractive feature of the countryside for much of the year. It is very loud, and a bird which seems to be singing overhead often turns out to be a mere speck in the sky. One singing bird stimulates another: as dawn breaks over an area of downland where there are no larks singing, all the birds start to sing within the space of one minute, producing a complete wall of sound. This habit of singing in flight is crucial to the skylark's ability to colonize truly open areas: other species of open ground are often unable to breed if there are no song-posts from which to sing and mark their territories.

The skylark can often be seen busily peck-ing at apparently bare earth. For most of the year it is mainly vegetarian, feeding on tiny weed seeds that lie dormant in the ground. At other times, particularly spring when the seeds are beginning to grow, it may feed on the nutritious growing points of the young plants. Because of modern agricultural techniques, this has turned the bird into a pest: in the past sugar-beet growers planted the seeds densely in rows, later thinning them. Today farmers have taken to sowing single encapsulated seeds exactly where they want the plants to grow. However, the skylarks may then peck the growing point from the young seedling and spoil the farmer's carefully planned harvest.

Three broods Skylark pairs form during early spring. You often see a singing bird at the end of its song-flight drop to the ground and display to another bird already standing there. The nest is always on the ground, often built into an existing depression such as the hoof-print of a cow. Indeed, some bird-watchers have encouraged skylarks to nest by forming hollows with their heels in firmly rolled grounds.

The nest cup is built of coarse grass and roots lined with fine grass and sometimes hair. The eggs, generally three or four to the clutch, are whitish and thickly speckled all over with olive or brownish markings. The young, which hatch after 11 days incubation, are able to fly at about three weeks old and start to behave more like their parents. They are still easily distinguishable from their parents because of their more blotched and softer brown plumage. A single pair may raise three broods during the breeding season from April to July.

New plumage The only period when skylark song is absent is during the moult in August and early September when young and old alike renew their plumage completely. The young birds lose their soft blotchy plumage and the adults the old, bleached and tattered feathers they have worn for the whole of the preceding year. When the moult is complete, juveniles and adults are indistinguishable. The sexes always look alike, at least to human eyes, but the males average about 6% bigger than the females.

During autumn and winter skylarks often join together in flocks which include young birds and immigrants from further afield. For much of the winter, territorial males can be heard singing in all but the bleakest areas. Only during the period of least daylight does song almost cease–presumably since the full hours of daylight are needed to find food.

Woodlark There is a marked contrast between the widely distributed and familiar skylark and the rare and local woodlark which is limited to southern Britain. Although the woodlark is now a rare bird it was common at the beginning of the 19th century. It suffered particularly during two cold winters in the early 1960s. During the 1970s there were many years when none was recorded but there may now be one or two territories occupied each year. Indeed, since the BTO's 1972 study the distribution of the species has contracted, with the outlying populations in parts of Wales and Lincolnshire in particular diminishing still further.

Woodlarks breed only in dry areas of heathland and downland. They need short grass areas for feeding, longer vegetation for nesting and some vantage points such as trees, bushes or even fence posts for song-posts. The woodlark's song is its most distinguished attribute–few birds have such a melodious and distinctive series of flowing notes which may continue, uninterrupted, for 15 or 20 minutes at a time.

The woodlark looks fairly similar to the skylark but it has a very short tail, (don't confuse it with the tailless, moulting skylark of late summer), a conspicuous dark brown and white mark on the leading edge of the closed wing, and a rather finer bill than the skylark.

One problem with such a rare species is that many inexperienced bird-watchers report tree pipits as woodlarks. Tree pipits inhabit a similar habitat and have a fairly pleasing song, although it is boring and repetitive when compared with a genuine woodlark. Their song flights are also quite similar for although the woodlark commonly sings from a song-post, it also sings during its looping display flight.

Breeding woodlarks are often found in traditional sites after intervals of several years. This may mean that breeding birds had been overlooked in the meantime, but it is much more likely to indicate that woodlarks look for a particular sort of area in which to breed.

The first clutch of eggs, usually three or four, is laid at the end of March or early April and there may be three broods a year. The young birds leave the nest before they can fly and hide singly in the vegetation whilst being cared for by their parents for a further 10-14 days. Both young and old birds moult in late summer and, in European areas where they are more common than in the British Isles,

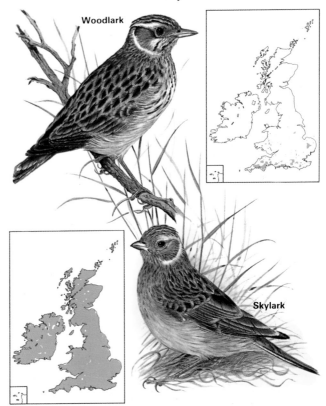

they can often be found in quite large loosely associated flocks on stubble. The song has ceased by this time, but their distinctive liquid call-note of three syllables–'ti-loo-whit'–and their short tails identify them.

Skylark pie? With the great interest in bird-watching and bird protection in the 1980s it is amazing to record that less than 100 years ago there was a thriving export trade with France in dead skylarks. They were netted on the south downs and shipped across the Channel to be sold in French markets.

Skylark (*Alauda arvensis*), 18cm (7in) long from beak to tail. Distribution map opposite. Resident, winter migrants from northern Europe.

Below: Skylarks always make their nests on the ground. These nestlings are about two weeks old and are well camouflaged with their soft brown plumage.

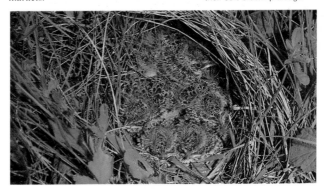

House and tree sparrows

The house sparrow is a species closely associated with man, sharing his environment and sometimes even becoming a pest. Another less numerous species – the tree sparrow – leads a relatively hidden life in our woods and orchards.

The house sparrow is always seen in close association with man, his buildings and his livestock. It might be possible to describe such an association as 'commensal', except that this would imply some form of mutual benefit, or at least no detriment to either partner in the association. Short of enjoying its presence, we derive little benefit from the house sparrow. The bird, on the other hand, while gaining access to plenty of good nest sites (at no cost to us), oversteps the bounds of commensalism in its attacks on our garden plants. This becomes more serious when it attacks our cereal crops: the sparrow ceases to be commensal and becomes a competitor or, in plain terms, an agricultural pest.

House sparrows are not normally birds of open environments such as hillsides or moors. In the vicinity of farm buildings, however, especially those with livestock, a colony of house sparrows is likely to be present. The birds are also common bird-table visitors, eating almost everything that is put out for them. They even feed on scraps of meat, if it is ever available to them.

Above: The house sparrow's nest, made of coarse grass or straw, is roughly domed.

Below: The male house sparrow (right) can be distinguished from the female (left) by its black bib and grey crown.

Variations in plumage In spring, the male house sparrow is an attractive bird, with a grey crown bordered in rich chestnut brown. His back is a mixture of rich browns fringed with golden buff, his breast is greyish fawn and beneath the chin is a fan-shaped black bib. In winter he is drabber, since many of his body feathers have broad buff fringes which gradually wear away to expose the colours beneath in early spring. The upper plumage of the female (both in summer and winter) is a mixture of sandy or greyish fawns and pale browns, and she is greyish beneath. Until they moult in their first autumn, young birds of both sexes resemble the females.

If you travel about in Britain and Ireland, you may notice that house sparrows living far from towns have much brighter plumage than those living in the industrial conurbations, where the sparrows seem particularly dark. In such circumstances, some species of animals have adapted by changing colour to improve their camouflage. Best known is the peppered moth, normally white with a black peppering of spots. By the process of natural

Tree sparrow distribution

Distinguishing 'sparrows' in flight

narrow white wing bar

white collar

black cheek spot

brown shoulder patch

Tree sparrow

brown shoulder patch

grey crown

broad white wing bar

House sparrow

grey head

sharp bill

dull mottled plumage

Dunnock or Hedge sparrow

selection, this moth has gradually evolved darker and darker colours, which improve its camouflage on the grimy trunks of city trees. Recently there was some debate as to whether house sparrows, too, were exhibiting this change (which is called 'industrial melanism'). Samples of sparrows of various shades were examined by experts. A strong superficial correlation was indeed found between darker plumages and more industrialised areas. Washing the feathers of all colour types with strong detergent, however, revealed that the darker ones had been contaminated with soot and other industrial grime, and thus their sombre shades were only 'skin deep'.

Feeding habits The house sparrow is an opportunist feeder, taking what food is easily available in greatest abundance at the time. The diet includes seeds, buds, leaves, shoots, flowers and a huge variety of human food waste and leftovers. Our sparrows are representatives of the largely African weaver-bird family, some members of which are as devastating to crops as plagues of locusts. It is not surprising, then, that our house sparrows flock into the corn at harvest time. Although each bird eats only a few grams of grain in a day, the house sparrow has an extremely wide distribution, and flocks often contain some hundreds of individual birds. The nationwide total of house sparrows is so high that the species is a serious pest, causing many millions of pounds worth of damage each year.

Many gardeners are incensed by house sparrow attacks on their flowering plants. We put out food for them, which they take greedily, only to start to tear apart the crocus and primula flowers when they appear. Although it may be of little comfort to the gardener, there is at least an explanation for this. Notice how often it is the yellow flowers that are attacked. Yellow coloration is associated with flowers that have a particularly strong attraction for pollinating insects, and tends to occur together with a rich supply of nectar. Yellow crocuses, for example, have far more nectar than purple ones. It is this nectar at the base of the flowers that the sparrows are seeking.

Formation of flocks Flocks are very much a part of sparrow life. They are an effective means of exploiting local abundance of food (as in cereal fields) and offer considerable protection from predators. They start to form in late summer, and are often composed largely of juvenile birds. These flocks roam over a distance of several miles. In winter, they join with other species, particularly finches and buntings, on stubble or weedy ground, or around places where livestock are fed.

From late summer onwards, roosting, too, is often communal. Sometimes the roosts are within buildings, and sometimes in the dense shelter provided by rhododendron, hawthorn

House sparrow (*Passer domesticus*). Resident near human habitations. Length 14.5cm (5¾in).

Tree sparrow (*Passer montanus*). Resident in many lowland rural areas. Length 14cm (5½in).

Below: A tree sparrow at its nest site on a cliff. Eggs are laid all through spring and summer, starting in March and continuing into August. Some pairs raise as many as three broods in a season.

two thirds the weight of its larger relative. The sexes are similar in plumage; the all-brown cap, the small black bib and the characteristic black spot in the centre of a white cheek distinguish them from the house sparrow. Their call, a rich, fruity chirrup, once heard and learned is an excellent way of separating the two species at a distance or in flight.

Tree sparrows are just as catholic in their food choice as house sparrows, but tend to shun the presence of man, usually feeding and nesting at a distance from human habitation.

The display pattern and the breeding season are closely similar to those of the house sparrow. The tree sparrow lays from two to eight eggs, usually about six, densely flecked with grey-brown. The nest is often in a hole in a building or a tree. In the latter case, the hole may be a natural one, or else the disused nest of a woodpecker. Tree sparrows readily occupy nestboxes, and are pugnacious in their tenancy of them, even evicting other birds such as blue or great tits, and building their own nests on top of those of the first occupiers. Incubation lasts 12 days, sometimes less, and the brood fledges after 10 days, or sometimes more.

Tree sparrows are nowhere as numerous as house sparrows, and have a much less widespread distribution in Ireland, northern and western Scotland, the Shetlands, Orkney and the Hebrides.

or blackthorn thickets, or ivy-clad trees or buildings.

Nesting sparrows House sparrows can be seen around their nest sites in almost any month of the year, though attendance is at its lowest in late summer and early autumn. Attendance remains low through the winter, increasing as days lengthen and the temperature rises. Most nests are under the eaves of houses, or in some other cavity in a building. Some are in haystacks and more natural sites such as crevices in cliffs or in thorny or dense shrubs like hawthorn. Usually, several pairs build nests in a loose colony.

The song of a territorial male house sparrow is a monotonous, repetitive 'chirrup', a familiar noise to us all as he sits close to his chosen site, often adopting a squat, fluffed-up posture. Just as familiar is the sight of the female, perched on roof or guttering, wings drooped and shivering, soliciting the male's attentions. Sometimes there is a communal display, which becomes more and more excited, sometimes even out of hand, developing into a rough-and-tumble chase. Often a single female is the centre of attraction for several males.

Eggs are laid from March through to August, with each pair attempting two or three, sometimes four broods in a season. Their colours vary from off-white to dull brown, and all are flecked with rich brown. Four or five is the usual number, but clutch sizes range from two to seven. Incubation takes about 12 days, but the time is more variable than in most birds. The young fly after 11 to 18 days, depending on weather conditions and food supply.

The tree sparrow In many ways, the tree sparrow can be considered as the house sparrow's 'country cousin'. It is a slightly smaller, more muscular looking bird, about

Above: A male house sparrow in full breeding plumage.

Below: A tree sparrow in full summer plumage (the sexes are alike). It differs from the male house sparrow in having a brown cap and nape, and a black cheek spot.

Yellowhammer and cirl bunting

Two of our smartest buntings
are the yellowhammer and the
cirl bunting. The yellowhammer
is well suited to our climate,
but the cirl bunting is really
a Mediterranean species.

Buntings are slender songbirds that look similar to finches, with the same stocky seed-eating bills. However, they generally prefer more open country, feed mainly on the ground and have less musical or varied songs than finches. In all except the corn bunting, the male is brightly coloured – male yellowhammers and cirl buntings are particularly attractive – but females and young birds are drab and inconspicuous.

Vivid yellow The male yellowhammer is yellower than all other British birds except the yellow wagtail, and in summer his head is almost totally bright lemon yellow. His underside is also yellow, but with a brownish breast-band and a few brown streaks on the

Above: Yellowhammers are widely distributed in Britain and Ireland, while cirl buntings are limited to southern England. Most birds of both species rarely travel more than a few miles in their lifetime.

Right: A male yellowhammer sits on a typical songpost. You can often hear the yellowhammer's jingling territorial song from late February to August or even September. Traditionally this familiar sound is verbalised as 'a-little-bit-of-bread-and-no-cheese'. A more accurate version might be 'chi-chi-chi-chi-chi-chi-chi-chi-chee'. At breeding time, his song warns other males where his territory is.

Right: Yellowhammers make their nests out of grass and a little moss, and line them with hair, fine grass and roots. Most choose a site within a couple of feet of the ground. Many actually nest on the ground, hidden among grass and other low plants. Some lay eggs as early as mid-April, but most start in May.

flanks. His upperparts are chestnut, and attractively marked with black and brown except for the rump, which is plain. The outer tail feathers are mostly white.

All yellowhammers, whatever their age or sex, have a chestnut-coloured rump – an important distinguishing mark. Young birds and females are much less yellow than males, particularly on the head. They are more heavily streaked and, apart from the rump, are easily confused with cirl buntings.

Active farmland life Yellowhammers are familiar farmland birds; in winter you find them feeding on stubble fields and ploughed land, mingling freely with larks and finches. Often the male's yellow head is the first thing

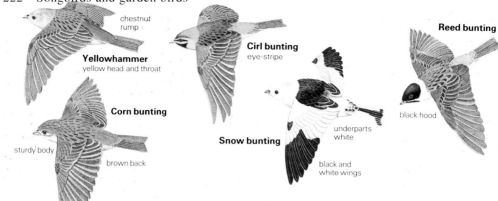

chestnut rump

Yellowhammer
yellow head and throat

Corn bunting

sturdy body

brown back

Cirl bunting
eye-stripe

Snow bunting

underparts white

black and white wings

Reed bunting

black hood

you see as he hops along in a low, crouched position. They often flock together at feeding places, and if disturbed fly into nearby trees for safety. In flight, yellowhammers have noticeably long, white-edged tails and a slightly bounding action. Often they call as they pass over a sharp 'chip' or 'chillip'. Another characteristic call is a low 'dzee'.

They eat mainly seeds, especially leftover corn and the seeds of grass and weeds. They also eat wild fruits such as blackberries and, in summer, insect larvae, beetles, spiders, millipedes, and even slugs and earthworms.

Mixed habitat Yellowhammers nest in almost any country area. Ideally they need open ground for feeding, low scrub for nesting and taller bushes or trees as song-posts. Their favourite habitat is the edge of a young conifer plantation where brambles and other plants are still common; here they reach densities of up to 58 pairs in a square kilometre (150 per square mile). Most of our farmland has an excess of open ground and a

shortage of scrub and song-posts, but fields bordered by hedges with some tall trees are nevertheless quite suitable. Heaths and commons with clumps of hawthorn bushes have always been good yellowhammer sites, but in recent years the birds have spread into woodland.

During the cold winter of 1962-63, the whole yellowhammer population was severely reduced, but since then it has recovered well and there are signs that it was relatively unharmed by the cold snap in January 1982. Each year, the best breeding sites are occupied very early in spring, and late arrivals occupy whatever sites they can. However, now that the population is large again, farmland has become overcrowded, leading to an overspill into woodland rides and edges. Normally yellowhammers ignore these far-from-ideal sites, but since the only alternative is a tiny patch of farmland already filled to capacity, they have little choice.

Bird of many names In the past, the yellowhammer has been known by over 20 different names. Its bright plumage is mentioned in many of these. In Scotland, its local names

Above: left: There are five buntings that nest in Britain and Ireland, the most common and colourful being the yellowhammer. The cirl (pronounced serl) bunting has a very similar plumage but is quite rare. Two of the other species are common: the corn bunting – most frequent around cornfields – and the reed bunting, which favours wetlands. The snow bunting is a very rare British breeder; only a handful of pairs nest on mountains in Scotland, though many more visit us in winter.

Yellowhammer (*Emberiza citrina*); resident farmland bird, with yellow plumage, especially on head of male; 17cm (6½in).

Right: A female yellowhammer at her nest. The usual clutch is three or four eggs, but clutches tend to be smaller in conditions of overcrowding, in poor habitats, in northerly areas or very early or late in the breeding season; this is likely to be because there is not sufficient food for the parents to cope with large broods in these circumstances. As laying can continue until August, each pair has time for three successive broods, but egg-stealing magpies limit some to only two. Incubation takes 12-14 days and is largely the responsibility of the female, who is far better camouflaged than the male. The young fly at 12-13 days.

Above: The easiest way to find a cirl bunting is to listen for the male's rather simple, monotonous song. It sounds like a hurried yellowhammer's song (without the 'cheese'), but it can be hard to judge because yellowhammers themselves sometimes do not complete their song. The song is also often compared to the final rattle of the song of the lesser whitethroat – a warbler which sometimes nests close by. The cirl bunting's usual call is a weak, squeaky 'seep'.

Cirl bunting (*Emberiza cirlus*): resident in farmland in southern England; not unlike the yellowhammer but with black chin and eye-stripe, and olive colour on rump. 17cm (6½in).

include yellow bunting, yellow yorling, yellow yite and yellow yoit; and in some English counties it is known as the yellow amber, yellow yowlie and yellow ring. The lines on its eggs give rise to names such as writing master, scribbling or writing lark, scribblie and scribbler.

Cirl buntings These birds are stockier and slightly shorter-tailed than yellowhammers, but have very similar habits. Their food seems to be similar and you may see both species feeding together. Pairs are usually widely scattered, so that although family groups stay together in autumn and winter, they do not form large flocks.

An adult male cirl bunting is a handsome bird with very distinctive head pattern (although, as with the yellowhammer, breeding colours are subdued in winter). He has a black chin, a yellow-bordered black eye-stripe and a greyish streaked crown. Across the breast is a greyish-green band, and the flanks are chestnut coloured. The rest of the underparts, the tail and the back are similar to those of the yellowhammer except

for the rump, which is an inconspicuous olive colour and not chestnut.

As with yellowhammers, female and young cirl buntings are less distinctive, browner and more heavily streaked, but they still have the tell-tale olive-coloured rump. They lack the male's head markings, although the female has faint yellow stripes above and below the eye.

The song period, breeding season and choice of nest site are similar to those of the yellowhammer. Sometimes the cirl bunting nests in a large garden on the edge of a village, in which case the male may sing from a roof top or television aerial. The female both builds the nest and incubates the eggs, but is fed by her mate at this time. Even when she is feeding nestlings, he gives the food to her and she distributes it.

A more southern species England is currently the most northerly outpost of the cirl bunting; they were first discovered breeding in Devon in 1800. A century later they were common throughout England and Wales, and some bred as far north as Cumberland and Yorkshire. However, since then their range has contracted dramatically, and none now nest north of Worcestershire. At their peak, cirl buntings were more common than yellowhammers, but now you are lucky to find any – only 500 pairs are thought to survive here, compared with one million pairs of yellowhammers.

The cirl bunting is mainly a Mediterranean species, living in vineyards and orange groves, and on warm, bushy slopes. In these places they are still common, and yellowhammers have to nest in mountainous regions to avoid competition. As you might expect, in England cirl buntings only remain in the south and south-west – areas with relatively warm summers and mild winters.

Left: Female cirl bunting at her nest. Cirl buntings choose sheltered farmland habitats with tall hedges and trees, woodland edges, parkland and heaths, especially on south-facing slopes on chalk downland and in coastal valleys. The decline of the cirl bunting may be partly due to destruction of habitat, and also to disturbance; but the underlying factor is probably a change in the climate. The bird is a sedentary species and cannot escape bad weather; our cooler, wetter summers and occasional hard winters since the mid-century have not been to its liking. Outside this country, the cirl bunting is resident in south and west Europe and north-west Africa.

A gallery of beaks and bills

The blackbird has a general-purpose beak but other birds have beaks which are specialised for eating different types of food. This chart illustrates the diversity of beak types possessed by various British species. They are arranged in random order because no really comprehensive categories exist.
Note: The terms beak and bill are interchangeable.

Hawfinch: A unique and powerfull bill for a bird that is a nut and seed-eating specialist.

Robin: A generalised insectivore, hunting on the ground, in trees and also in the air.

Great spotted woodpecker: A strong hammer-and-chisel bill for cutting into both hard and soft wood.

Merganser: A fish-eating duck which is equipped with a saw-toothed bill for holding prey.

Peregrine: Like all the raptors, its bill is specially shaped for tearing prey.

Blackbird: General-purpose beak for eating worms, fruit, seeds, bread, spiders, insects and larvae.

Black-headed gull: A bill like a pair of shears, useful for scavenging almost anywhere.

Heron: Strikes suddenly to stab through the body of a fish, frog, large insect or even a dabchick.

Swift: Its bill is used in the manner of a sweep-net to collect insects while flying.

Partridge: General-purpose bill for various foods from leaves and buds to insects and seeds, including grain.

Treecreeper: Like a pair of tweezers, its fine beak is used to pick up insects from fissures in bark.

Shoveler: An unusual shape of bill, containing a sieve for filtering plankton from the water.

Wigeon: With the tip of its bill it cuts blades of grass, its main form of food, throughout the year.

Snipe: It probes under the turf with its long bill, which is able to feel for worms.

Puffin: This bird is our best example of the use of a colourful bill for courtship display.